Daytrips™
FLORIDA

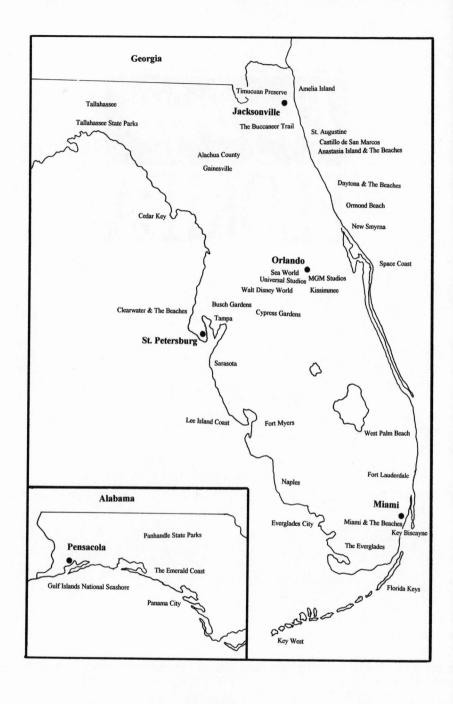

Daytrips™
FLORIDA

50 one day adventures from Miami, Orlando, St. Petersburg, Jacksonville, and Pensacola

BLAIR HOWARD

HASTINGS HOUSE
Book Publishers
Norwalk, Connecticut

While every effort has been made to insure accuracy, neither the author nor the publisher assume legal responsibility for any consequences arising from the use of this book or the information it contains.

We are always grateful for comments from readers, which are extremely useful in preparing future editions. Please write directly to the author, Blair Howard, c/o Hastings House, 50 Washington St., Norwalk, CT 06854; or FAX (203) 838-4084. Thank you.

Distributed to the trade by Publishers Group West, Emeryville, CA.

Edited by Earl Steinbicker, creator of the DAYTRIPS™ series.

ISBN: 0-8038-9380-9

Library of Congress Catalog Card Number 96-077680

Printed in the United States of America

10   9   8   7   6   5   4   3   2   1

Contents

6   CONTENTS

Introduction

The snows and storms of winter in the Northeastern United States and the eastern provinces of Canada usually mean but one thing for the people who live there: escape. And escape they do, southward to the friendlier climes of Florida. The balmy breezes that blow across the state from one emerald ocean to the other, the ever-present sunshine, and the wide sandy beaches have a magnetic attraction for the snowbirds of Canada, the American Midwest, and New England. Each year, more than 41 million visitors from the icy regions of the north follow in the footsteps of Juan Ponce de León and head for Florida.

From Perdido Key in the northwest to Fort Zachary Taylor on Key West, Florida's resorts, theme parks, beaches, and cities offer a veritable cornucopia of vacation and recreational opportunities. From the distinctly southern flavor of the plantation country in the north, to the sub-tropical environment of the south, all surrounded by more than 1,000 miles of sun-drenched sandy beaches and deep green ocean, Florida has something for everyone: environmental treasures, historic sites, high profile tourist and recreation areas, natural wonders and a profusion of wildlife in diverse natural habitats that include lush, sub-tropical forests to glittering coral reefs, to the crystal waters of a thousand inland lakes and windswept salt marshes of a lonely coastline.

And, yes, it's still possible to find romantic, out-of-the-way places where you can take a quiet walk along a moonlit beach, or a gentle boat ride beneath shady tropical foliage, or an isolated barrier island where you can enjoy a private picnic. By day the sun almost always shines, and the sand is soft and sugar-white.

This book is not intended to be a comprehensive guide to the entire state of Florida. Instead, it focuses on five areas of maximum tourist interest— Miami, Orlando, St. Petersburg, Jacksonville, and Pensacola—and takes a close look at 50 of their most appealing destinations, describing in step-by-step detail the simplest way to explore them on your own. Walking is, of course, by far the best way to probe most places. It allows you to see the sights up-close and personal, spending just as much time as you please. The carefully tested walking tours take you to all of the interesting attractions without wasting time, money, or effort. Where you choose to stop along the way is up to you, and you won't have any trouble finding your way with the large clear maps provided.

The destinations should appeal to almost everyone. You'll find not only the usual churches, art galleries, theme parks, historic sites and homes, but also some of the nation's best beaches and outdoor recreation areas.

Dining well is a vital part of any travel experience, and especially so in Florida; you'll discover lots of opportunities listed here. Each daytrip offers a selection of cafés and restaurants; some might be rest stops on the walking tours where you can enjoy a cup of coffee or a snack along the way. They are all price-keyed, with emphasis on the medium-to-low range.

Time and weather are also important considerations, and you'll find all the information you need included in the "Practicalities" section for each daytrip. You'll know when the attractions are closed, which places to avoid, or visit, the time of year when the weather's bad, and you'll find the telephone number of the local tourist information office, just in case you have questions.

One last thought: don't try to do and see everything at any given destination; it isn't necessary. Relax. Be selective. Your daytrip should be fun, not an endurance test. If it starts to become one, slow down, or take time out for a soda. Above all, enjoy yourself. There will always be another day.

Happy Daytripping!

Section I

Romantic destinations are just a daytrip away

DAYTRIP STRATEGIES

Perhaps it was the English who perfected the concept of the daytrip. Certainly they've been enjoying them ever since the advent of the automobile. During the early 1900s, fashionable daytrippers made seaside resorts such as Brighton famous. The establishment of the cross-channel car ferries and hovercraft extended the daytrip to include Dunkirk and Calais.

Today the Chunnel has made it possible for the English daytrippers to travel even farther into the European heartland. Now they can leave home at first light, hop on a train, spend six or seven hours in Paris, and return home again before the bell tolls midnight.

The concept of the daytrip has come only recently to us here in the United States. Those already familiar with the idea agree that it's the best way to get the most out of a vacation buck. Not only do tourists find a daytrip the ideal way to explore the sights and sounds of a given region, but people who've lived there all their lives will discover that it's a great way to explore the regional wonders right in their own back yard.

So what is a daytrip? It's the easy, least expensive way to explore many of the world's most interesting places. You set up a base in a central city, explore it, then plan trips to the surrounding territory by way of one-day excursions.

ADVANTAGES:

While it may not be the answer to every travel situation, the daytrip does offer significant advantages:

1. The freedom to travel light by leaving your luggage in the hotel room while you tour your destination with a map, a guidebook, and a camera in hand.
2. There is no fixed schedule, so you are free to go where and when you like.
3. There's never a worry about reservations, and no moving on from one hotel to the next. Once you've arrived at your base, just unpack your bags and you're ready to go.
4. Flexibility. If the weather's bad, change your plan accordingly. Discover something new or unexpected and you're free to stay a while and explore.
5. You can quit whenever you like and do something else without upsetting a planned itinerary. Want to sleep in? No problem!
6. Get to know your base destination and its surrounding area. Become familiar with the local restaurants, shops, theaters, night clubs, beaches, and other attractions, and you'll enjoy them all the more for it.
7. You'll have the opportunity to try a variety of travel experiences without ever being required to commit more than a day to any one of them.
8. Your clothes will benefit from a single unpacking. You'll even have time to send them out for a cleaning.
9. Your "fixed" address offers a new sense of convenience and security. Family and friends will be able stay in touch while you're away.
10. Economy is always a consideration when making a vacation hotel booking. Search for and take advantage of any long-stay discounts. You can make advance reservations—always more reasonable—without having to sacrifice flexibility.

Best of all, daytrips ease the transition from tourist to accomplished traveler. Soon, you'll be able to tackle complex destinations on your own, free from the limitations of organized tour groups so you can delve and explore out-of-the-way treasures rarely seen by most of the vacationing public.

CHOOSING DESTINATIONS

With 50 daytrips to choose from, and several attractions for each trip, deciding which are the most enjoyable for you and yours might be a problem. You could, of course, settle down and read the book from cover to cover, marking the most appealing spots; a bit time consuming, but at least you'll end up with a broad picture of what's available. An easier way to get started is to just turn to the index and scan it, looking out for the special-interest categories set in **BOLD FACE** type. These will lead you to choices under such headings as Museums, Beaches, Historic Sites, Boat Trips, Airboat Tours, Theme Parks, and lots more.

You can combine elements of one or more trips to create an itinerary all your own. Use the book maps along with a good road map for general routing.

While some of Florida's rural areas can be a bit ordinary, much of its countryside, especially in the coastal areas, is very beautiful, often wild and dramatic. Some of the trips listed in the index as **SCENIC DRIVES** are just that—designed for the pure pleasure of driving, with enough attractions along the way to keep things lively; maybe you'd like to take time out for a picnic. So, let the top down, let the wind blow through your hair, leave all the anxieties of the busy world far behind and enjoy several hours of fun in the sun.

GETTING AROUND

The driving directions for each trip assume that you're leaving either from Miami, Orlando, St. Petersburg, Jacksonville, or Pensacola. Chances are, however, that you might be staying (or living) elsewhere in the particular geographic area, so you'll need to modify the routes a bit.

Route maps scattered throughout the book show you approximately where the sites are, and which main roads provide the most direct route to them. In many cases you'll still need a good, up-to-date road map. The Official Florida Road Map you can get at any in-bound welcome center is adequate, and will provide main road information, along with the locations of some of the more popular sites, parks, and attractions. If you want to get down and dirty however, really get off the beaten path, you won't do better than **Delorme's Florida Atlas and Gazetteer,** a highly detailed, topographical atlas of 127 pages, size 15½ × 11 inches. Many hiking trails, most of the smallest forest roads, the canoe trails, and some fishing locations are shown along with the locations of state parks, national parks, historic sites, and areas of great natural beauty. If you can't get it at your local bookstore, contact Delorme Mapping direct at PO Box 298, Freeport, ME 04032, ☎ (207) 865-4171. They will take your order and you can charge it to your Visa or Mastercard. At the time of writing, the cost was $16.95, plus shipping.

The majority of daytrips in this book are designed to be made by car, and do not lend themselves to public transportation. If you've arrived at your base destination without wheels, you may rent a car at the airport, or at any of the downtown rental company offices; if not, you'll have to limit yourself to those trips that can be done easily by Metrobus or cab, or on foot. True, there are plenty of excursions organized by local companies and, in some cases, you can get where you want to go via Amtrak or Greyhound, but schedules are a bit iffy, and often inconvenient.

Some trips to outlying areas, especially the beaches, can be done by **bicycle**; rentals are available almost everywhere; ask at your hotel lobby.

FOOD AND DRINK

Always the high spot of any vacation, dining must be an important consideration when choosing a destination or daytrip. Several choice restaurants where the atmosphere is inviting, service consistently good, and the food even better, are listed for each base city and daytrip. Many are the long-time favorites of experienced travelers, some are not quite so well known but offer a culinary experience that's decidedly different; most are open for lunch and are located on or near the suggested tour route. Seafood is the ultimate experience in Florida, and you'll find that many of the restaurants listed here offer interesting and tasty variations on the theme, many featuring regional specialties not generally found elsewhere. Others offer ethnic menus; the listings give you an idea of exactly what's available. The approximate price range is shown as:

> $ —Inexpensive.
> $$ —Reasonable.
> $$$—Luxurious and expensive.

Fast-food outlets are, of course, scattered around almost everywhere, and don't take up much of your sightseeing time. An even better alternative is to picnic. Florida must be the picnic capital of the world, and many of the daytrips in this book have picnic areas, some in wild and scenic spots, where you can take time out to enjoy a quiet lunch in the sunshine. Aaaah.

PRACTICALITIES

You'll find a "Practicalities" section for each base city and each daytrip. Those for the base cities provide practical information to the area, while those for the daytrips provide more specific and localized information.

WEATHER:
In Florida, this ranges from almost temperate in the north to subtropical in the south. Rainfall can sometimes be a problem, but on the whole, sunshine is what the state is famous for; you can almost always be sure of some good weather whatever the time of year. So that you'll know exactly what to expect at your chosen destination, you'll find the local climate in the "Practicalities" section for each base city.

OPENING TIMES AND FEES:
When planning a daytrip, be sure to note the opening times of the various sites—these can often be a bit erratic, especially on weekends. Anything unusual that you should know before starting out, such as "don't make this trip on a Monday," is summarized in the "Practicalities" section for each trip.

Entrance Fees listed in the text are, naturally, subject to change—and they rarely go down. On the whole, considering the cost of maintaining the sites, admissions are quite reasonable.

Facilities available at each site are listed in the *italicized* information for that site, along with the address and phone number. These often include restaurants or cafeterias, cafés, information counters, gift shops, tours, shows, picnic facilities, and so on. **Telephone numbers** are indicated as ☎ ; relevant area codes are given in the practicalities section of each trip.

HANDICAPPED TRAVELERS:
Access varies with each individual's needs and abilities, so no firm statement can be made about any site. Those that are generally accessible are indicated with the symbol ♿ but when in doubt it's best to phone ahead.

GROUP TRAVEL:
If you're planning a group outing, *always* call ahead. Most sites require advance reservations and offer special discounts for groups, often at a

substantial saving over the regular admission fee. Some closed sites will open on request or remain open beyond their scheduled hours to accommodate groups.

SUGGESTED TOURS

Two different methods of organizing daytrips are used in this book, depending upon local circumstances. Some are based on **structured itineraries** such as walking tours and scenic drives that follow a suggested route, while others just describe the **local attractions** for you to choose from. In either case, a town or area map in the book always shows where things are, so you're not likely to get lost. Numbers (in parentheses) in the text refer to the circled numbers on the appropriate map.

Major attractions are described, some in fairly extensive detail, some in only one or more paragraphs, complete with practical information in italics. Additional sites are worked into the text. All are arranged in a logical geographic sequence, although you may want to make adjustments to suit your preferences.

Walking tours follow routes as indicated on the accompanying map. In most cases, the number of stops and the estimated time needed to complete the tour are given at the beginning of the text. Estimated times are, however, only a general indication. Sightseeing is a subjective pastime, and one individual might spend much more time on a given tour than another.

*OUTSTANDING ATTRACTIONS:

An * (asterisk) before any attraction, be it a daytrip or just one exhibit in a museum, denotes something special that in the author's opinion should not be missed.

TOURIST INFORMATION

The addresses and phone numbers of local and regional tourist offices as well as major sites are given in the text whenever appropriate. These are usually your best source for specific information and current brochures. You can also contact the following offices for additional help:

VISITOR INFORMATION:
Florida Department of Commerce
Division of Tourism, Visitor Inquiry
126 W. Van Buren Street, Tallahassee, FL 32399
☎ (904) 487-1462

ATTRACTIONS:
Florida Attractions Association
PO Box 10295, Tallahassee, FL 32302
☎ (904) 222-2885

HOTELS AND MOTELS:
Florida Hotel/Motel Association
200 W. College Avenue, Tallahassee, FL 32301
☎ (904) 224-2888

HISTORICAL SITES:
Department of State, Bureau of Historic Preservation
R.A. Gray Building, 500 S. Bronough Street
Tallahassee, FL 32399
☎ (904) 487-2333

NATIONAL AND STATE PARKS:
National Forests:
U.S. Forest Service
227 N. Bronough Street, Tallahassee, FL 32301
☎ (904) 681-7265

State Forests:
Department of Agriculture and Consumer Services
Division of Forestry
3125 Conner Boulevard, Tallahassee, FL 32399
☎ (904) 488-6611

State Parks:
Department of Environmental Protection
Office of Recreation & Parks
Mail Station 535, 3900 Commonwealth Boulevard
Tallahassee, FL 32399
☎ (904) 488-9872

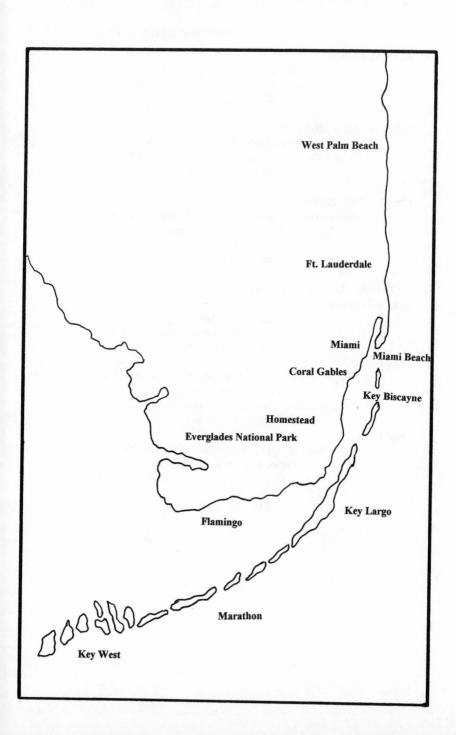

Section II

The Miami skyline

MIAMI AND THE SOUTH

This is the area that first comes to mind when people think of Florida. That's only natural, as four of the state's legendary resorts lie within its boundaries.

The Florida Keys are a magical chain of islands that stretch for more than 100 miles south from Miami into the Gulf of Mexico. From Key Largo to Key West, where it's still "anything goes," the islands glitter in the sunshine like a string of pearls.

Florida's south Atlantic coast, from Jupiter through Palm Beach County to

Miami, is one long beach after another; one magnificent resort community borders the next; and there's little to choose between any of them. Each is a delight unto itself, and each has something unique to offer.

Jupiter, Palm Beach, West Palm Beach, Delray, and Boca Raton offer not only some of the finest beaches in Florida, but the best of the performing arts, golf, deep-sea fishing, spectator sports from tennis to polo, and diving; there are literally hundreds of places where you can strap on air tanks and explore the wonders of the ocean.

Just to the south of Palm Beach County, the Greater Fort Lauderdale District stretches from Deerfield Beach, through Pompano, Lauderdale-By-The-Sea, and a host of suburbs that make up an eclectic collection of resort areas, ranging from Hollywood, where a two-mile boardwalk hugs the beach, to the Wild West town of Davie. Gone are the days when it seemed as if every student from every university in the nation descended on the beaches during holidays. Today, Fort Lauderdale is one of southern Florida's most popular family vacation spots.

And then, of course, there's the Everglades, where you can visit, explore, and enjoy the wonders of a vast natural wilderness; more than 750,000 acres of swamps, marshes, and wetlands that make up the most famous wildlife refuge in the world.

Right next door, Greater Miami is an international destination for tourists and the jet-set. Ever-changing, ever-growing, this section of southern Florida offers a fascinating mixture of cultures, sophistication, and tradition unlike any other. South Miami beach is famous for its Art Deco, and Greater Miami for its museums, art galleries, theaters, nightlife, restaurants, and a zoo that's recognized as one of the finest in the United States.

GETTING THERE:

By Air: Miami International Airport, just seven miles from downtown Miami on the Airport Expressway, is served by every major domestic air carrier and more than 70 international airlines. Most domestic carriers offer several flights into the city each day. Airport transfers are handled by **Supershuttle** (☎ 871-2000), by **Metrobus** (☎ 638-6700) or by cabs that you'll find waiting in large numbers just beyond the baggage claim areas.

By Road: From the north, Miami is easily accessible by five major routes: Interstate 95, and Highways 1, A1A, 27, and 441. From the west, Interstate 75 connects with Interstate 595 which, in turn, joins with Highway 27 and Interstate 95 just to the west and north of Fort Lauderdale.

By Rail: The Amtrak station is at 8303 NW 37th Avenue, ☎ 835-1221 or 800-USA-RAIL.

By Bus: There are Greyhound/Trailways terminals located at 4111 NW 27th Street and 700 Biscayne Boulevard in Miami; in Miami beach at 7101 Harding Avenue; in North Miami Beach at 16250 Biscayne Boulevard. ☎ 800-231-2222.

GETTING AROUND:

Considering the size of Miami, it's a very accessible city. Beyond the convenience of your own vehicle, there are many modes of transport available:

Metrobus (☎ 638-6700) offers 63 Dade County routes, 19 of which serve Greater Miami and the Beaches every day, as well as the Miami Seaquarium, Orange Bowl Stadium, Cultural Center, and Metrozoo. Fares are $1.25 each way, exact change only. Seniors, persons with disabilities, and students pay 60¢ with a bus permit. Metrobuses operate Monday through Friday from 4:30 a.m. until 2:15 a.m. Limited service is available over the weekend. Call for specific routes and times.

Metromover (☎ 638-6700). Individual motorized cars run atop a 4.4-mile elevated loop track that circles downtown Miami, serves the Bricknell and Omni business districts, and connects with Metrorail at the Government Center. Stops include Bayside Marketplace, Miami Arena, the Cultural Center, some hotels, and the Miami Convention Center. The fare is 25¢; 10¢ for seniors, persons with disabilities, and students with a rail permit. Metromover operates every 90 seconds, daily 6 a.m. until midnight.

Metrorail (☎ 638-6700). This 12-mile elevated rail system serves downtown Miami and extends westward to Hialeah and south to Kendall. Destinations include the Miami Arena, Vizcaya, and the Cultural Center. Metrorail connects with Metromover, Metrobus, and Tri-Rail. The fare is $1.25 each way, exact change only. Seniors, persons with disabilities, and students pay 60¢ with a bus permit. Riders can transfer free of charge at the Government Center station. Trains operate daily approximately every 20 minutes—every eight minutes during peak hours—6 a.m. until midnight.

Tri-Rail (☎ 800-TRI-RAIL). This commuter system operates around 15 stations in Dade, Broward, and Palm Beach counties, and services the area between Greater Miami and the Beaches and West Palm Beach. Tri-Rail connects directly to Metrorail for convenient access to or from the downtown area and south Miami at no additional cost. The fare is $3 each way; $5 daily, or $18.50 for the week. A 50% discount applies to seniors, students, and persons with disabilities. Trains operate daily except Christmas and Thanksgiving.

Water Taxis (☎ 545-5051) are perhaps the most convenient way to get around the city. They offer transportation throughout Greater Miami and the Beaches. They can carry from 19 to 49 persons each and are available for one-way or all-day service. Taxis depart from hotels, attractions, restaurants, marinas, convention centers, and parks. Fares vary. Operates daily from 10 a.m.

Taxi Service Rates are $1.75 per mile. A ride from the airport to downtown Miami, approximately eight miles, takes 20 minutes and costs between $15 and $18; Miami Beach is about 14 miles and takes 25 minutes at a cost of about $25; the fare from downtown Miami to North Miami Beach ranges between $26 and $29. **Flamingo Taxi,** ☎ 885-7000; **Metro Taxi,** ☎ 888-8888.

Wheelchair Accessible Van Rentals: Wheelchair Getaways (West Palm Beach) offers full-size mini-vans equipped with lifts and tie-downs. Free airport delivery and pickup. Services in Miami, Fort Lauderdale, and West Palm Beach. ☎ 800-637-7577, local 407-976-9488.

If you arrive by air, you'll probably want to **rent a car.** Almost every rental company has a desk in the baggage claim area of the International Airport. A few helpful ☎ numbers are: Alamo, 633-6076; Avis, 637-4800; Budget, 871-3053; Dollar, 887-6000; Enterprise, 447-0308; Hertz, 871-0300.

If you decide to brave the heavy traffic in the city and drive yourself, you'll find plenty of parking available. Meters are most convenient, but be sure to take note of the time available. The fine for parking on an expired meter is $10; $33 if not paid with 30 calendar days. There are also plenty of parking garages, all strategically placed, and all open 8–5. Contact the **Miami Parking System** (☎ 373-6789) for specific locations, rates and hours. There are also tow-away zones indicated by signs posted at the curbs. Don't ignore a tow-away zone; it's very expensive and the costs will include a fine, storage, and towing charges.

Before you embark on your sightseeing tours, you should study the maps and familiarize yourself with Miami's roadways, then plot your course. The most convenient way to move around the city is the expressway system:

North-South: Interstate 95 is the major expressway. It passes through downtown Miami and Bricknell, and ends at its junction with US-1. A1A (Collins Avenue) is the major thoroughfare in Miami Beach extending all the way to the Art Deco District. Florida's Turnpike and SR-826 (the Palmetto Expressway) are expressway bypasses in the western section of the county.

East-West: SR-836 (the Dolphin Expressway) is the major route connecting Florida's Turnpike to SR-826, I-95 and Miami Beach on I-395. SR-112 is a short expressway leading from Miami International Airport to I-95 and on to Miami Beach via I-195.

Seven causeways link Miami and Miami Beach. Two of them are easily reached by expressways from I-95. They are I-195 (Julia Tuttle) and I-395 (MacArthur). The Rickenbacker Causeway extends to Key Biscayne from I-95 and US-1.

Understanding Directions:

Dade County is divided into four sections: Flagler Street, running east-west, divides the city into north and south. Miami Avenue, running north and south, divides it into east and west. The designations NW, NE, SW, and SE are very important parts of an address. Courts, Places, and Avenues are aligned north-south; Streets and Terraces, east-west. Hialeah, Coconut Grove, Coral Gables, Key Biscayne, and Miami Beach each have their own unique systems of street names and numbers.

ACCOMMODATIONS:

With more than 100,000 hotel rooms available in the Greater Miami area, and as many more in Fort Lauderdale and West Palm Beach, not to mention the Florida Keys, accommodations should not be a problem, right? Wrong. Miami is fast becoming one of the most popular vacation spots **in the world**. Prices are for the most part high, especially at the Beaches and, if you don't have a long-standing reservation, you won't be able to find much of a room. If you intend to visit, be sure to plan ahead and book as far in advance as possible.

PRACTICALITIES:

The **Area Code** for Miami and Florida Keys is 305.

Climate: The weather in the Greater Miami is almost always good. The climate is subtropical, and thus ensures sunshine the year-round. Just enough rain falls during the summer and early fall to ripen the local vegetation and add a little color to the gardens and parks. Miami is a land where the air-conditioner is king. So much so, that you would be well advised to take at least a lightweight jacket to guard against the inevitable chills indoors. The sun is powerful, so be sure to take along adequate protection against the harmful rays and, even then, if you plan to spend long hours outdoors, you'll need to cover up with lightweight clothing.

Most of the major attractions, parks, and museums are open every day except Christmas. Admission run the gamut from free to expensive. Carry your cash in a safe place such as a money belt.

TOURIST INFORMATION:

Greater Miami Convention & Visitors Bureau, 701 Brickell Avenue, Suite 2700, Miami, FL 33131. ☎ 539-3000 or 800-283-2707, Fax 539-3113.

Greater Miami/Homestead/Florida City Visitor Information Center, 160 Highway 1, Florida City. ☎ 245-9180 or 800-388-9669, Fax 247-4335.

Miami Beach Information Center 1920 Meridian Avenue, in the Art Deco District of Miami Beach. ☎ 672-1270, Fax 538-4336.

FOOD AND DRINK:

Miami dining is as diverse as its population. You'll find every style of cuisine available from the traditional fast foods associated with such giants as Burger King and Wendy's to the finest of gourmet delights prepared by the best chefs from France and Europe. Seafood is a staple in many restaurants in Miami and, because of the large Spanish-speaking population from Cuba, Mexico, and South America, so is hot and spicy cuisine. There are thousands of restaurants and cafés scattered all the way from West Palm Beach, through the Greater Miami area, to Key West. Many are excellent but, as always, standards vary. Those suggested restaurants and cafés listed below are recommended, but don't stop there, half the fun is in the exploring and finding out for yourself.

In Coconut Grove:

Café Europa (3159 Grand Avenue) is a Parisian café offering decidedly French cuisine, including *duck á l'orange* and rack of lamb. Open for dinner from 4 p.m. until midnight. Reservations accepted. ☎ 448-5723. $$.

Café Med (3015 Grand Avenue) is a place great for lunch. The menu includes such goodies as brick-oven pizza and Mediterranean salads. Open for lunch and dinner from 9 a.m. until midnight. ☎ 443-1770. $.

Grand Café (at the Grand Bay Hotel 2669 S. Bayshore Drive) is, as its location in one of Miami's five-star hotels would indicate, a restaurant of international standing. The menu is continental, the atmosphere elegant, and the view from the windows outstanding. Open for lunch and dinner from 11 a.m. until 2 a.m., it's a little on the pricey side, but worth it. ☎ 858- 9600. $$$.

Downtown:

Fish Peddler (Biscayne Boulevard just north of downtown) is a good place to eat lunch. Lots of seafood on the menu, including fresh dolphin (the fish, not Flipper), grouper, and lobster. Open for lunch and dinner 11–10. ☎ 757-0648. $–$$.

Las Tapas (401 Biscayne Boulevard) is a Spanish restaurant, open for lunch and dinner from 11 a.m., with all the trimmings, including strolling minstrels. The menu includes fresh seafood, paella, and tapas. ☎ 372-2737. $–$$.

Snappers (Biscayne Boulevard at Pier 5, downtown) specializes in fresh seafood and pasta. Outdoor dining on the bay. Open from 7:30 a.m. until midnight. ☎ 379-0605. $.

DAYTRIPS IN THE GREATER MIAMI AREA:

Miami is truly an international city. With a heritage that spans many centuries of coming and going, it has finally emerged as a melting pot where people from around the world have converged in one great sprawling community. Of these, there's no doubt that the Hispanic, African American, Native American, Jewish, and Caribbean peoples have had the greatest effect on the city's cultural heritage, each adding its own special accent to its ethnic flavor.

Miami's well-documented Hispanic influence began not, as many believe, with Castro's takeover of Cuba, but more than 200 years ago during the second Spanish period of occupation of Florida, following the defeat of the British in the American Revolution. Architectural structures and place names of this early Spanish influence are as much a part of Miami's Hispanic flavor as are the dozens of Cuban coffee bars of Calle Ocho, or SW Eighth Street as it's more universally known. Greater Miami celebrates its Latin roots in the streets all the year long, with festivals and events such as Carnival Miami/ Calle Ocho, held each March; Paseo, nine days of festivities in Little Havana; and Calle Ocho/Open House, the worlds largest block party, which attracts more than a million people each year.

African-American and Caribbean influences have had almost as much effect on the city as its Latin population. From 1896, when Henry Flagler contracted John Sewell and his "Black Artillery," seventeen hand-picked laborers—12 black men and five white—to begin work on the Royal Palm Hotel, African-Americans have had an ever-increasing influence on Miami's metamorphosis. By the 1940s, Overtown was renowned for the major black performers who played its jazz clubs, so much so that NW Second Avenue became known as "Little Broadway." Today, as do the Hispanics, Miami's black population celebrates its heritage through a year-long series of festivals and events: Black Heritage Month in February, and the Liberty City Sunstreet Festival in November and December.

Little Haiti, originally called Lemon City, is one of Miami's oldest communities, and an established cultural center full of exotic sights, sounds, and cuisine; it's the heart of the city's Haitian community.

For convenience, and because Miami is spread out, we've organized sightseeing into tours by specific districts; there are five of them, plus Miami Beach, which is covered separately. Some are far apart, others overlap, but all have attractions you shouldn't miss. And, while none of the tours have a large number of stops, each will take at least a day to complete. You can select one tour and finish it, or you can mix and match. Either way, it's best if you take the time to read what's on offer, study the maps, and then decide what suits you best.

Brickell Avenue in downtown Miami

Downtown Miami

The heart of the city lies, for the purposes of this book, between the Airport Expressway/Interstate 195 and the Rickenbacker Causeway.

GETTING THERE:

GETTING AROUND:

PRACTICALITIES:

FOOD AND DRINK:
See pages 18–22.

LOCAL ATTRACTIONS:
A good place to begin is at the **American Police Hall of Fame and Museum** (1), 3801 Biscayne Boulevard, just north of downtown Miami. You don't have to be in law enforcement to enjoy this museum that's a little out of the ordinary. Exhibits include some 10,000 law enforcement-related items that range from weapons to vehicles, and uniforms to lie detectors. Feel a little ghoulish? You'll want to see the electric chair, view the collection of murder weapons, and take a peek inside an authentic jail cell. Finally, there's a 400-ton marble memorial dedicated to the memory of more than 5,000 police officers killed in Greater Miami in the line of duty since 1960; it's quite impressive and thought provoking. *Open daily 10–5:30.* ☎ *573-0070.* ♿. *Adults $6, seniors $4, children 6–11 $3, police officers $1.*

The **Ichimura Japanese Garden** (2), on the north side of Watson Island, off MacArthur Causeway, was donated to the city of Miami in 1961 by Kiyoshi Ichimura, the founder of Ricoh. The focal point of this large, formal Japanese garden is the Hakkaku-do, an octagonal pavilion of a design typical of the traditional Buddhist shrine. There are also a number of sculptured pieces sent as gifts from Japan, including an 8-ton granite statue of Hotei, the smiling god of prosperity, and a 300-year-old stone pagoda. A flowering rock garden, a lagoon, waterfall and a pond full of golden koi carp complete the illusion of a quiet garden in a far-away land. *Open 8–3, Mon.–Fri.; Saturday 10–4; Sunday noon–4.* ☎ *575-5240.* &. *Free.*

The **New World Center—Bicentennial Park** (3), off Biscayne Boulevard at MacArthur Parkway and NE 9th Street, is in the heart of downtown Miami on the shores of Biscayne Bay. Here you can take time out to sit and watch the world go by, fish a little if you feel so inclined, and enjoy a picnic or a stroll along one of the park trails. If you have kids with you, they're sure to enjoy the playground. *Open daily.* &. *Free.*

*The Bayside Marketplace (4), 401 Biscayne Boulevard, just south of the Bicentennial Park, is a retail, dining, and entertainment center on more than 16 acres of waterfront in the heart of the city's downtown area. It's noisy, bustling, and colorful with an infectious atmosphere that seems a little superficial. No matter, it is, after all, a business district and Bayside really is one of those places you should try to visit while you're in town, if only for its great restaurants. But there's more to the Marketplace than good food. Aside from its 150 shops, stalls, restaurants, and bars, the open plazas create a stage for musicians and street performers who entertain nightly, many of them for free, some for a small donation. Be sure to visit the Hard Rock Café, the International Food Court, and Pier 5 Market. *Open 10–10 Mon.–Thurs., 10–11 Fri.–Sat., 11–8 Sun.; restaurants stay open later.* ☎ *577-3344.*

The **Center for the Fine Arts** (5), just west of the Bayside Market at 101 West Flagler Street, is one of three show pieces at the **Metro-Dade Cultural Center**. More than just a regional art gallery, this is a true center for the fine arts, with a permanent collection and traveling collections on loan from museums and galleries around the world. *Open Tues.–Sat. 10–5 (9 p.m. on Thurs.), and noon–5 on Sun.* ☎ *375-3000.* &. Adults $5, seniors and students with ID $2.50, children 6–12, $2.

The **Historical Museum of Southern Florida** (6) 101 West Flagler Street, is also a part of the Metro-Dade Cultural Center. Here, through a number of special exhibits, hands-on displays, artifacts and memorabilia, you can take a peek into South Florida's turbulent past. Tour the museum on your own or, for a small charge, take a guided tour, which is real value for the money. *Open 10–5 Mon.–Sat. (9 p.m. on Thurs.), noon–5 Sun.* ☎ *375-1492.* &. Adults $4, seniors $3, children 6–12 $2, under 6 free. Call for tour rates.

Finally, **Lummus Park** (7), at 404 NW North River and NW 3rd Street on the Miami River, is where you'll find the old stone barracks that were once a part of Fort Dallas. The fort was built in 1835 at the mouth of the Miami River, and was at one point commanded by General William Tecumseh Sherman; it was eventually abandoned and the post moved to its present site in the park, which is also the location of one of the oldest surviving pioneer structures in Dade County, the Wagoner House. *Open daily.* ☎ *579-6935. Free.*

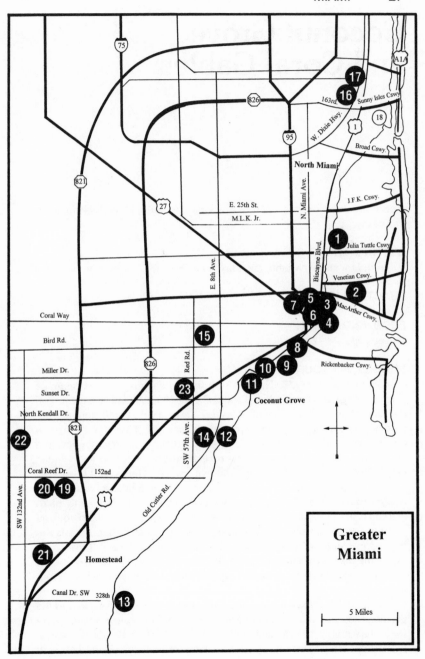

Trip 2

Coconut Grove
and Coral Gables

This is an area along the coast of Biscayne Bay, south of the Rickenbacker Causeway.

GETTING THERE:
From Downtown Miami, take Bayshore Drive to Coconut Grove.

PRACTICALITIES:

FOOD AND DRINK:
See pages 18–22.

SUGGESTED TOUR:
See map on page 27. The first stop on this daytrip is the **Museum of Science and Space Transit Planetarium** (8), at 3280 S. Miami Avenue just off the Rickenbacker Causeway off Bayshore Drive. Here, you'll step into another world. Explore the natural wonders of our small planet through hands-on exhibits that include optics, light, sound, biology, energy, physics, and more. This is South Florida's largest natural history collection and wildlife center, and is home to more than 150 live animals. Here you'll be able to visit the Falcon Bachelor Bird-of-Prey Center, a rehabilitation hospital for injured hawks, eagles, owls, ospreys, and falcons. The museum's planetarium is first class, and if you've never been inside one, it will provide you with an awesome experience: a journey around the Solar System, to galaxies beyond the Milky Way, and into the blackness of outer space. *Open daily 10–6; the box office closes at 5.* ☎ *845-4247.* ♿. *Adults $6, seniors and children 3–12 $4. Extra charge for planetarium, combination ticket available.*

Next, the ***Vizcaya Museum and Gardens** (9), is almost next door to the Science Museum at 3251 South Miami Avenue. This Italian Renaissance-style villa with lovely formal gardens was built in 1916 as the winter home of industrialist James Deering. Its 34 rooms are magnificently furnished with

Vizcaya

antique furniture and decorative arts dating from the 15th through 19th centuries. The grounds encompass more than 10 acres of landscaped gardens with several antique European fountains, all lovingly restored and strategically placed for the best effect. *Open daily the year round. Ticket booth opens 9:30–4:30, but the house remains open until 5, the gardens until 5:30.* ☎ *250-9133.* ♿. *Adults $10, children 6–12 $5.*

Coco Walk (10) is a colorful outdoor retail, dining, and entertainment center located just to the west of Bayshore Drive right in the heart of the Grove. Here you can sample all sorts of traditional and exotic cuisine at any one of more than a dozen restaurants, bistros, and cafés. Like to shop? You can do that too; Coco Walk is a kaleidoscopic collection of neat little shops, stores, and outlets where you can spend hours browsing for goodies, or just wandering around window shopping. *Shops and stores open daily 11–10, from 10–midnight Fri. and Sat. Restaurants and nightclubs open until 3 a.m.*

To the south of Vizcaya via Bayshore Drive, the **Barnacle State Historic Site** (11), 3485 Main Highway, was the home of Commodore Ralph Munroe. Coconut Grove is the product of a friendship between Charles and Isabella Peacock and Munroe. It was here, in 1882, under the encouragement of Commodore Munroe, that the Peacocks established the first hotel on the southern Florida mainland. The hotel flourished, and the community that grew up around it soon became one of the most active and diversified in south Florida.

Today, the spirit of the lifestyles of the Peacocks and Commodore Munroe has been preserved in the Munroe's home, The Barnacle. Enter the park by way of a footpath to Coconut Grove and be transported back to the 1880s; quite an interesting experience. *Open Thurs.–Mon. with tours of the house at 10, 11, 1, and 2:30.* ☎ *448-9445.* ♿. *Adults $3.25, children $2.*

*The Fairchild Tropical Garden (12) is at 10901 Old Cutler Road. Take Douglas Road south to 72nd Street and then go west to Old Cutler Road and turn south again. If you love gardens and flowers this is one you shouldn't miss. The Fairchild encompasses more than 83 acres of tropical botanical gardens, lakes, walks and shaded areas where exotic plants and trees from around the world grow in organized profusion. Opened in 1938, it is now the largest garden of its type in the continental United States. The collection includes rare bromeliads, orchids, and other tropical wonders. The best way to see it is to take the narrated tram tour, the price of which is included in the admission fee. Weekends are often highlighted by special events. So, if you happen to visit on a Saturday or Sunday, you could be in for quite a treat. *Open daily 9:30–4:30.* ☎ *667-1651.* ♿. *Adults $6, children under 13 free.*

*Biscayne National Underwater Park (13) is at the end of SW 328th Street. Continue south on Old Cutler Road, bearing west on SW 220th Street, until you reach the junction with SW 137th Avenue. Turn south again there and proceed to SW 328th Street and turn east. From there drive all the way to the end. This is one of the very special attractions in the Miami area. At the dock, you'll board either a 53-foot glass-bottom boat or a 45-foot diving and snorkeling catamaran. As you make your way out through the wilderness, you'll pass mangrove creeks and islands, and then cross southern Biscayne Bay to the great tropical coral reefs teaming with multi-colored sea life. Drifting over the reef, sometimes only a few feet above the coral, you can see it all through the glass bottom of the boat: angel fish, triggers, sergeant majors, flags, rays, and perhaps even a barracuda or shark.

If you're a swimmer, you can take a snorkeling trip, if you're a scuba diver, you can do that too. For those who don't want to plunge into the ocean, there are canoe rentals and a picnic area. *The park is open 9–5:30 Mon.–Fri., 8–5:30 weekends. Reservations are required for the trips,* ☎ *247-2400. The glass bottom boat leaves the dock at 10 a.m., the family snorkel trip leaves at 1:30 p.m., and the scuba trip at 8:30 a.m.* ♿. *Glass Bottom Boat Tour: Adults $16.50, children under 13 $8.50. Family Snorkeling Tour $27.95 per person. Scuba Diving $34.50 per person.*

Parrot Jungle and Gardens (14), at 11000 SW 57th Avenue, is Miami's signature attraction. From the Biscayne National Park, return the way you came to Old Cutler Road and follow it north to its junction with Red Road (SW 57th Avenue). Turn north there; the Jungle is at the corner of Killian Drive. The park is a unique bird sanctuary and wildlife habitat where more than 1,200 rare and exotic birds can be seen close up and personal. Parrots fly around freely, feed from your hand, and pose for pictures. You can stroll the walkways and see macaws, flamingos, cockatoos, and other brilliantly feathered creatures, along with apes, monkeys, alligators, and giant tortoises in a setting that closely resembles a natural tropical jungle; the eerie sounds of the birds and monkeys calling from the trees are an experience you may never forget. If you have kids, they'll enjoy the petting zoo and, if you decide to stay for lunch, or even have breakfast, the Parrot Café opens at 8 a.m. *The gardens open daily 9:30–6.* ☎ *666-7834.* ♿. *Adults $11.95, seniors $10.95, children 3–10 $7.95, under 3 free.*

From Parrot Jungle, continue traveling north on Red Road (SW 57th Avenue). The **Venetian Pool** (15) is at 2701 DeSoto Boulevard in Coral Gables. This Venetian-style lagoon is carved out of the solid coral bedrock. It's become something of an historic landmark with its fancy swimming pool, caves, stone bridges, and waterfalls. The water is crystal clear, warm and relaxing, and the patios are decorated in pastel shades with palm trees waving overhead; a nice diversion on a hot Miami day. *Open 10–4:30 Tues.–Sun., closed Mon.* ☎ *460-5356.* ♿. *Adults $4, teenagers $3.50, children 3–12 $1.60.*

Trip 3

North Miami

This tour includes attractions north of the Airport Expressway/Interstate 195.

GETTING THERE:
Take Highway 1 north to its junction with NE 163rd Street. Turn west there and drive a short distance to West Dixie Highway and turn north again.

PRACTICALITIES:

FOOD AND DRINK:
See pages 18–22.

SUGGESTED TOUR:
See map on page 27. The **Cloisters of the Monastery of St. Bernard de Clairvaux** (16), 16711 W Dixie Highway, were originally built in Segovia, Spain, in 1141. The ancient building was purchased by newspaper baron William Randolph Hearst. According to Hearst's mother, every time things were going badly for the tycoon he would go out and buy something. The Cloister was the result of one such episode. He bought the building, sight unseen, for $40,000. To move it from Spain to Florida was a monumental undertaking. Stone by stone it was disassembled, the pieces numbered, mapped and packed in more than 10,700 specially made wooden crates.

Twenty-one miles of rail had to be laid to connect the site with nearest line, and then the Cloister was transported wholesale to the United States. By the time it arrived, Hearst had lost interest in the project and the building lay in storage for more 25 years; it wasn't reassembled until 1954, after Hearst's death. Now owned by the Episcopal Church, it is the oldest reconstructed building in the Western Hemisphere, and houses many works of art and antiques. The tour takes about an hour. *Open 10–4 Mon.–Sat., and noon–4 on Sun.* ☎ *945-1462.* ♿. *Adults $4, seniors $2.50, children under 12 $1.*

Greynolds Park (17), 17530 Dixie Highway, is just north of the Cloisters. It's a nice diversion, a great place to have a picnic, and there's lots to see and do for the whole family: an observation tower, New England-style wooden bridge, paddleboat rentals, a playground, walking trails, even a golf course. *Open daily.* ☎ *945-3425.* ♿. *Parking fee.*

From Greynolds Park, go south again, past the Cloisters to NE 163rd Street, turn east and drive to the **Oleta River State Recreation Area** (18) on the banks of the scenic Oleta River and the Intracoastal Waterway. There you'll find some of the finest recreational opportunities in the entire Greater Miami area. It's a remote world of mangrove forests, tidal backwaters, and hermetic marine environments where you see a variety of bird life and mammals, including porpoises and the endangered Florida Manatee.

This park will appeal to outdoorsmen, women, and those who enjoy bicycling, hiking, boating, fishing, and swimming. If you're trailing a small boat, you can launch at the boat ramp; if you've brought a packed lunch with you, the picnic area is delightful. Best of all is the 1,200-foot-long sandy beach where you can swim, sunbathe, and fish. When you're done, there are freshwater showers where you can get rid of the salt and sand. There's also a 1½-mile hiking trail that meanders through the mangroves and woodland. *Open daily 8 a.m.–sunset.* ☎ *947-6357.* ♿. *$3.25 per vehicle.*

Trip 4

The South

This tour includes attractions to the south and west of Coconut Grove.

GETTING THERE:
Take Highway 1 south and then SW 152nd Street west to Metrozoo, just west of the Florida Turnpike exit.

PRACTICALITIES:

FOOD AND DRINK:
See pages 18–22.

SUGGESTED TOUR:
See map on page 27. ***Metrozoo** (19) encompasses more than 290 acres of parkland with 50 cageless exhibits. Here you can see, in near-natural environments, more than 900 animals belonging to 240 species. Several of the exhibits are spectacular. The sight of rare, white Bengal tigers in a moated compound complete with a replica of an ancient Cambodian temple captures the imagination. Other exhibits include gorillas, chimps, rhinos, bears, elephants, orangutans, and koalas, all in areas closely resembling their native habitats.

Wings of Asia is another unique exhibit. Here, in a 1½-acre free flight aviary, some 300 tropical birds flit and fly through the trees and tropical growth of a rain forest. Aside from the exhibits, there's plenty more to see and do: a monorail system, ecology theater, children's petting zoo, three animal shows daily, elephant rides, three food courts, and an observation deck overlooking the African area. *Open daily 9:30–5:50, ticket office closes at 4:30.* ☎ *251-0400.* ♿. *Adults $6, children 3–12 $3.*

Gold Coast Railroad and Museum (20) is not far from Metrozoo at 12450 SW 152nd Street. As you might imagine, this museum is dedicated the golden age of the railroad. Exhibits include some of the great old steam locomotives and the presidential Pullman car *Ferdinand Magellan*, which was used by presidents Roosevelt, Truman, Eisenhower, Reagan, and Bush. Truly a part of American history, the old Pullman is a treat not to be missed. Want to ride the rails? You can, but only on weekends, and then it's "all aboard" a train pulled by a vintage steam or diesel locomotive for a trip on the time machine back to an era we shall probably never see again. *Open daily 10–3.* ☎ *253-0063.* ♿. *Adults $4, children under 12 free.*

Monkey Jungle (21) is a little farther south at 14805 SW 216th Street in the Homestead area. From the Railroad Museum, go west on 152nd to 137th Avenue and turn south. From there drive to 216th street and turn west again; Monkey Jungle will be to your right. This popular attraction celebrated its 60th anniversary in 1996. It's a little expensive if you're traveling with a large family, but it's a rare experience and well worth the price of admission, for here the animals have turned the tables on the visitors. You will be in the cages, while the primates roam free. And they really do seem to enjoy the turn-about, the monkeys that is, for they will perform for you as only they can: their antics are often hilarious. *Open daily 9:30–5.* ☎ *235-1611.* ♿. *Adults $11.95, seniors $9.50, children 4–12 $6, under 4, free.*

From Monkey Jungle, return to SW 137th Avenue and turn north. The **Weeks Air Museum** (22) is at 14710 SW 128th Street. If you are fascinated by old airplanes and the romance of the early days of aviation, or would like to relive military days gone by, a visit to the Weeks is a must. This non-profit organization is dedicated to the preservation and restoration of aircraft from the days when the first pilot adventurers took their first faltering leaps into the air until the end of the World War II era. Here you'll see some of the canvas-and-string airplanes that took to the skies over Germany during World War I, and the sleek fighters and bombers of World War II, carefully restored to full flying condition. You can watch the museum's video collection or visit the gift shop where you'll find a complete selection of books and souvenirs. *Open daily 10–5.* ☎ *233-5197.* ♿. *Adults $6.95, seniors $5.95, children under 13 $4.95.*

Continue north on SW 137th to Sunset Drive, turn east and drive almost to Red Road (SW 57th Avenue) where you'll The **Miami Youth Museum** (23) on your right at SW 72nd Street (Sunset Drive). Although it's classed as a children's museum, there's something for everyone. Here your kids—and you—can stimulate your imaginations, explore and learn in a fun-filled environment with hands-on exhibits. It's a cultural, sensory, and creative experience. The museum features year-round special events, and you can be sure there's always something unusual going on whenever you choose to visit. *Open daily 10–5.* ☎ *661-3046.* ♿. *Adults and children $3, children under the age of 1 free, seniors $2.*

Trip 5

Key Biscayne

The Key is the tiny island just to the south of Miami Beach. For the most part, except when the world of tennis arrives, it's a very quiet place where you can play a round of golf, say hello to TV's Flipper, have a picnic at the Cape Florida State Recreation Area, or enjoy an afternoon of exploration at the Biscayne Nature Center. There are only four stops on this tour, if you don't count the golf course, but you can have a full day on the island if you visit them all.

GETTING THERE:

Take Interstate 95 or US-1 south to SR-913, the Rickenbacker Causeway, and head east onto Key Biscayne.

PRACTICALITIES:

FOOD AND DRINK:

See pages 18–22.

SUGGESTED TOUR:

*The Miami Seaquarium (24) is at 4400 Rickenbacker Causeway, just as you arrive on the island. As sea aquariums go, this one can hold its own with the best. Not quite as large as Sea World farther north, its star attractions are Flipper, the TV superstar, Salty the Sea Lion, and Lolita the Killer Whale. All put on spectacular shows. In addition, you can watch the sharks at feeding time—always a scary experience—handle a starfish, see the endangered manatee and rare American crocodile, as well as many other species of marine animals and fish. Expect to spend at least three hours here. *Open daily 9:30–6.* ☎ *361-5705.* &. *Adults $18.95, seniors $16.95, children 3–9 $13.95.*

Crandon Park (25), at 4000 Crandon Boulevard, is a large public park situated along the eastern shores of Key Biscayne where you could easily spend an entire day outdoors. There's plenty to do and enjoy for the whole family. Facilities include a really nice picnic area with shelters and barbecue

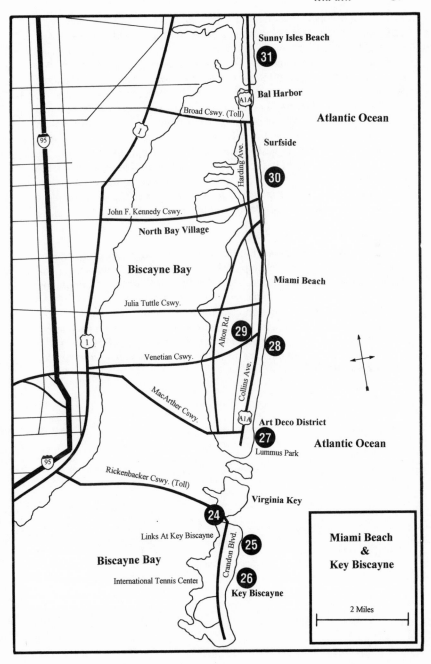

grills, a food concession stand, a swimming pool, freshwater showers, a playground for the kids, boat rentals, a baseball/softball field, and even a golf course. Best of all are the miles of sandy beaches where you can swim, sunbathe, surf, wade, and fish the hours away. Don't be surprised if a planned short visit turns into a day-long outing. *Open daily 8–sunset.* ☎ *361-5421.* ♿. *Admission $3.50 per car, $6 per recreational vehicle.*

  *The Biscayne Nature Center (26), part of the Crandon Park complex, is another not-to-be-missed experience. It's a hands-on marine exploration through the coastal hammocks, rock reefs, and beaches in the form of guided walks conducted by experienced naturalist guides. Allow plenty of time; the experience is well worth it. From the naturalists, you'll learn all about the environment, in-shore marine life, and the formation of the beaches and coral reefs. *You'll need to call for hours, specific tour information and rates; tours are by reservation only,* ☎ *642-9600.*

ADDITIONAL ATTRACTIONS:

  The **Links at Key Biscayne,** 6700 Crandon Boulevard, Key Biscayne, is a monster golf course. The championship, 18-hole course measures 6,457 yards for a par of 72 from the white tees, but from the blue tees it's whopping 7,099 yards for a par of 74, and every hole is its own unique experience. As you'd expect, all the facilities and amenities of a major complex are available for you to enjoy, including an excellent restaurant. *Green fees during the winter season are $68 per person, including the cart; $37.50 during the summer; special twilight rates are available. Call in advance to reserve a tee time.* ☎ *635-9129.*

ADDITIONAL SPORTING ACTIVITIES IN GREATER MIAMI:

Here are a few sporting activities that don't fit in with any of the Miami area daytrips, but which may be of interest to you:

Pari-Mutual Horse and Greyhound Racing, with five parks in the Greater Miami area is, of course, a major pastime in southern Florida. There are tracks at Miami Shores (Biscayne Greyhound Track, ☎ 800-432-0232), North Miami (Calder Race Course, ☎ 625- 1311) and at the Airport (Flagler Greyhound Track, ☎ 649-3000), but the two flagship courses are at Hialeah Park, "the world's most beautiful track," and Gulfstream Park, home of the Florida Derby. For race dates and schedules at Hialeah ☎ 885-8000, and at Gulfstream ☎ 931-RACE.

Miami Jai-Alai, at 3500 NW 37th Avenue in the Airport area, is the other pari-mutual attraction. Here you can visit the nation's oldest Jai-Alai fronton and watch the action of the world's fastest game. You can also enjoy a good dinner in the Courtview restaurant. *Jai-Alai is open nightly the year-round except Tues. and Sun., 7–midnight. Matinees Monday, Wednesday and Saturday noon–5.* ☎ *633-6400.* &. *General admission $1, reserved seats $3, Courtview Club $5, matinees $2, valet parking $2, self parking $1. Children allowed, but must be accompanied by an adult.*

Boating and Fishing. How can any visitor go to southern Florida and not get out on the water? Anglers, perhaps, have the best opportunities to take to the water. There are a half-dozen large charter boat operators and a half-hundred smaller, one-boat captains offering everything from a couple of weeks deep-sea fishing to a half-day of inshore trolling. You might like to try one of the following:

Three Captains Inc., Miami Beach Marina at Slip A-5, offer off-shore sport fishing and sightseeing for groups or individuals aboard the ***Reward II***, a 60-foot fishing vessel that holds up to 48 people. *Daily 8:30–7:30.*

The Kelly Fishing Fleet, Haulover Marine Center, 10800 Collins Avenue, North Miami Beach, offers half and full-day deep-sea fishing trips, as well as two and three-day fishing or diving cruises to the Bahamas. Five diesel-powered vessels are available for individuals on a per person basis. Refreshments and fishing equipment available. *Trips daily 9 a.m. to 12:30 p.m., 1:45 to 5:50 p.m., and 8 p.m. to midnight.* ☎ *800-330- 3483, fax 757-2870.*

Miami Beach

Miami Beach is a bustling, hustling tourist center with sun and sand thrown in for good measure. Hundreds of hotels, large and small, form the nucleus of a great autonomous city clustered from one end of the 10-mile-long island to the other, and it's here that visitors come by the hundreds of thousands from the cold climates around the world to enjoy the sun and fun of southern Florida. By day the city, the historic districts, and the beaches are crowded with people from almost every nation in the world.

GETTING THERE:

Depending upon where you're staying, to get to Miami Beach you'll take one of the seven bridges either from the downtown area, or elsewhere in Greater Miami. If you're coming in from out of town on Interstate 95, the chances are you'll take either I-195 (Julia Tuttle) or I-395 (MacArthur Causeway).

GETTING AROUND:

Most of the time you'll need your vehicle close by, but the Art Deco District is best seen on foot. In fact, an organized walking tour is offered. Contact the Art Deco Welcome Center (see below) for more information.

TOURIST INFORMATION:

Miami Beach Information Center, 1920 Meridian Avenue, in the Art Deco District of Miami Beach. ☎ 672-1270, fax 538-4336.

Miami Beach Visitor Information Kiosk, Washington Avenue and Lincoln Road Mall, in the Art Deco District, ☎ 672-6222.

Art Deco Welcome Center Miami Design Preservation League, Oceanfront Auditorium, 1001 Ocean Drive. ☎ 672-2014, fax 672- 4319.

FOOD AND DRINK:

Nick's Miami Beach (300 Alton Road on the second floor) is a popular spot; the service is good, the decor nautical, and the food outstanding. Lots of fresh seafood is on the menu, including peppered swordfish and blackened grouper. Open for lunch from noon until 3 p.m., and dinner from 6–11 p.m. $$–$$$.

The Art Deco District

Rascal House (17190 Collins Avenue, in Sunny Isles) is a Jewish, deli-style café open for breakfast lunch and dinner. The food is good and the prices are easy to live with. Specializes in stuffed cabbage, pastrami and corned beef. 947-4581. $.

SUGGESTED TOUR AND LOCAL ATTRACTIONS:

See map on page 37. Miami Beach's **South Beach** extends southward from the vicinity of Dade Boulevard, but is centered mostly around and along Ocean Drive and the Art Deco District. It's an area that was spared from destruction by the efforts of citizens and local designers who began painting and restoring the beautiful Art Deco buildings of a bygone, pre-World War II era. Today, subsequent redevelopment of the area has turned the gaily painted buildings into an eclectic collection of restaurants, hotels, nightclubs, galleries, and boutiques, most of which overlook the ocean.

The Art Deco District (27), the signature section of the South Beach, encompasses an 18-block square mile area from 6th to 23rd streets, and from Lenox Court to Ocean Drive. Designated a National Historic District, it's a vast collection of Art Deco, modern, and Spanish Mediterranean Revival architecture, the likes of which you won't find anywhere else in the United States. One-time Art Deco apartment houses and warehouses have been restored and repainted in bright pastel colors and are now the delight of artists and photographers alike. Stop in at the Welcome Center for information, gifts, books, maps, posters, and tee shirts. If you like, you can join a guided walking tour of the district on Saturday morning at 10:30, or a bicycle tour on Sunday, also at 10:30. Multilingual tours are available by reservation. ☎ *672- 2014.*

Bass Museum of Art (28), at 2121 Park Avenue in the Art Deco District, houses a permanent collection of Old Master paintings, sculptures, antique and period furniture, memorabilia, *objets d'art,* religious artifacts, and textiles. In addition, special exhibits and collections focus on contemporary American, Hispanic, and European art, as well as from many other areas of the world. *Open 10–5 Tues.–Sat., 1–5 Sun., closed Monday.* ☎ *673-7533.* ♿. *Adults $5, seniors and students $4, children 6–12 $2, children 13–17 $3.*

Miami Beach Garden Center and Conservatory (29), at 2000 Convention Center Drive, is not quite what its name implies. More a botanical garden than a retail outlet for plants and trees, the center is housed under a 35-foot-high dome and contains more than 200 varieties of tropical plants. If you like color, you'll love the special displays they put on at Easter and Christmas. *Open 10–5 Mon.–Sat. Closed major holidays.* ☎ *673- 7720. Free.*

From South Beach, go north on Highway A1A; the next stop is located east of Collins Avenue, between 79th and 87th Streets. The **North Shore State Recreation Area** (30), 3400 NE 163rd Street just north of the public beach, is a small park compared to most state-owned recreation areas. But, like most of its big sisters, it, too, is an oasis of lush, green, tropical vegetation, the deep blue sea, and wide sandy beaches surrounded on three sides by the urban sprawl of Miami and the Beaches. The 40-acre park was originally laid out in 1972 as the North Shore Open Space, but was taken over by Florida's State Park Service in 1987. Today, the park offers an opportunity for a few quiet hours of sunshine, sand, and sea, just beyond the concrete towers and busting tourist centers of Florida's largest city, but still close enough to stay in touch. It's a popular lunch-time get-away. *Open 8– sunset daily.* ☎ *940-7439.* ♿. *Admission $3.25 per vehicle.*

Continue north on Highway A1A to **Sunny Isles Pier** (31), 16701 Collins Avenue at Sunny Isles, built as a tourist attraction for the new Sunny Isles development. Originally it measured more than 1,000 feet in length, but a 1947 hurricane lopped off the end section. For many years the old pier lay neglected, and it fell into disrepair. Recently restored, it is once again open to visitors and fishermen. *Daily.* ☎ *949-1300.* ♿. *Nominal fee.*

*The Everglades

There's a choice of ways to experience the Everglades: you can drive in by car, from the east or west, or you can take an airboat ride. If you do it yourself, you'll find it to be a somewhat haunting experience. The drive is a fairly long one, but you have the freedom to stop and smell the roses, or swamp, so to speak. The airboat ride can last up to two or three hours and is an exhilarating experience, very much in the tradition of the great wilderness. Also available are guided tours. However you do it, the Everglades are a must-see.

GETTING THERE:

There are no regularly scheduled public transport bus tours to or within the park, but a number of private operators offer guided tours. These are quite good and will take you to most of the major attractions. Trips are not expensive, but they are restrictive.

There are three entrances to the Everglades: **Park Headquarters** at Homestead on Route 9336; **Shark Valley** 35 miles west of downtown Miami on Highway 41 (the Tamiami Trail); and **Everglades City**, on the west coast some 35 miles south of Naples, also on Highway 41 (more about Everglades City in Section IV).

AIRBOAT OPERATORS:

Miccosukee Indian Village & Airboat Tours, Mile Marker 70, Highway 41, PO Box 440021, Miami, FL 33144. ☎ 223-8380.

Valentine Tours, 3271 NW 7th Street, Suite 203, Miami, FL 33125. ☎ 541-0847. Airboat Tours depart daily at 10 a.m., includes expert guides and an alligator wrestling show; $49 per person.

TOUR OPERATORS:

Flamingo Lodge Marina & Outpost Resort, Flamingo, FL 33034, ☎ 253-2241, fax 941-695-3921, is located on Florida Bay in the heart of the Everglades. They offer tram tours and sightseeing cruises.

Gatortrax Adventure Tours, One 40th Street, ☎ 571-1897, offers two-day adventure trips into the Everglades.

ME Productions, 2000 SW 30th Avenue, Pembroke Pines, ☎ 800-544-0033. Offers a four-hour Everglades Tour, including an airboat ride.

Meier Tours, 2699 Collins Avenue, ☎ 800-551-0285: Everglades Tours depart daily at 8 in the morning; $40 to $50 per person.

Everglades National Park Boat Tours, Everglades City, ☎ 813-695-2591.

Wooten's Swamp Boat Rides, 35 miles south of Naples in Ochopee on Highway 41, ☎ 813-695-2781.

Shark Valley Tram Tours, Highway 41 in East Miami, ☎ 221-8455.

PRACTICALITIES:

Special Services: Most self-guided nature trails are wheelchair access-ible. Wheelchairs can also be accommodated on most tour boats, and assistance will be provided when getting on and off. For more information, contact the National Park Headquarters, ☎ 242-7700.

Safety: Swimming in the Everglades is not encouraged. Freshwater ponds are full of **alligators**, and the saltwater areas are shallow, muddy, and infested with **sharks and barracudas**. **Do not feed the wildlife**, especially **alligators** which, though they may seem slow and sluggish, can move with incredible speed. They are skilled, carnivorous predators. The Everglades are home to four **poisonous snakes**: diamond back and pigmy rattlers, the coral snake—it has colorful rings—and the water moccasin that swims on the surface.

The **sun** is intense, so use a sunscreen and wear sunglasses, long sleeves, long pants and, most important, a hat. Finally, watch for **changes in the weather**. Severe storms and high winds can develop very quickly, especially if you are on the water.

Pets must be kept on a leash at all times and are not allowed on the trails; they can, however, be taken on board boats.

Fishing is permitted, but you must have a valid saltwater or freshwater fishing license.

Fires are not allowed.

Fees: A vehicle permit good for seven days is available for $5 at the main entrance ($4 at Shark Valley), and $3 per person for pedestrians and cyclists ($2 at Shark Valley).

TOURIST INFORMATION:

The Everglades National Park, 40001 State Road 9336, Homestead, FL 33034. ☎ 242-7700.

FOOD AND DRINK:

Once you get into the Everglades you'll have only two dining options. The first is to pack a lunch and bring it with you along with bottled water, the second is to drive on to Flamingo at the southern end of the Everglades and

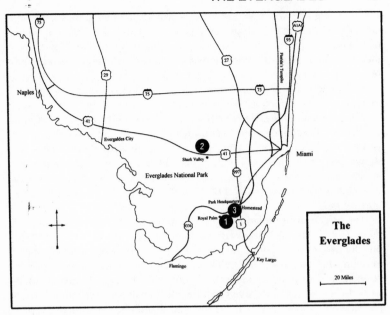

The Everglades

20 Miles

dine in relative luxury at the **Flamingo Lodge Restaurant**: breakfast is served 7–10, lunch 11:30–3, dinner 5–9. Reservations for dinner are a must. The menu includes lots of fresh seafood, chicken, and a variety of vegetarian dishes. ☎ 800-600-3813 and ask for the restaurant. $$.

From the west, Everglades City and Flamingo provide your options:

> **The Oyster House** (three miles south of Everglades City on Highway 29) is open for lunch and dinner from 11–10. The menu includes fresh local seafood, Florida gator, and stone crabs. ☎ 695-2073. $$.

SUGGESTED TOUR:

The Everglades encompass most of the southern tip of Florida, a vast subtropical wilderness of saw-grass prairie, hammock, and mangrove swamp that stretches from Lake Okeechobee to the Florida Keys and Cape Sable, and from Everglades City to the visitor center at Royal Palm near Homestead. Most of the water in the Everglades, so essential to its delicate ecosystem, comes from Lake Okeechobee. Since the 1930s, however, with the buildup of southern Florida, the supply has dwindled to desperately low levels. Canals, levees and dikes, land reclamation, and drainage have increasingly diverted the water, and vast commercial agricultural enterprises have spread right up to the park boundaries. Now the National Park's mission is to save the vast wetlands from further deterioration and preserve it as a wildlife habitat.

The Everglades are a unique blend of tropical and temperate plant and animal life. More than 700 species of plants, and 300 of birds, along with a number of endangered animals—manatee, Florida crocodile, Florida panther, etc.—make their homes among the swamps and jungles of what has become known around the world as the "International Biosphere Reserve."

Before you head southeast from Miami into the heart of the Everglades, there are several attractions worth including in your daytrip:

The **Everglades Alligator Farm** (1), at 40351 SW 192nd Avenue in Homestead, offers the chance to get to know the Everglades and its wildlife before you go forth on your own. Here you can take an airboat ride, enjoy live shows every hour that feature alligators and snakes, and venture into the hammock to see the osprey, great blue heron, anhinga, and the rare roseate spoonbill. *Open 9–6 daily.* ☎ *247-2628.* ᕒ. *Adults $11, children 4–12 $5, under 4 free.*

The **Miccosukee Indian Village** (2) is in the heart of the Everglades, 25 miles west of Florida's Turnpike on the Tamiami Trail. You can drive out there on your own or sign up for a guided tour. The Miccosukee Indian tribe has a museum that features many exhibits and artifacts. You can see the Miccosukee Indians in traditional garb demonstrate the age-old arts of patchwork doll making, wood carving, beadwork, and alligator wrestling. Visitors can ride an airboat deep into the Everglades and visit an authentic Indian encampment; it's an unusual experience that's well worth the relatively small fee. *Open 9–5 daily the year round.* ☎ *223-8380.* ᕒ. *Adults $5, seniors $4, children 5–12 $3.50, airboat rides $7.*

The **Fruit and Spice Park** (3) is a 20-acre botanical garden in Homestead at 24801 SW 187th Avenue. Established in 1944, the park is, as the name implies, a wonderland of exotic fruits and spices and, at $1 per person, a visit is a real value for the money. More than 200 species and 500 varieties of fruit, nuts, herbs and spices from every far-flung corner of the world can be found in this unique garden. You can even buy some of the exotic goodies to take home. It's fun to take time out here for a picnic, as the air is sweet and heady and lunch under the trees is an experience you're not likely to forget. *Open 10–5 daily.* ☎ *247-5727.* ᕒ. *Adults $1, children under 12 50¢.*

From here, it's off into the great unknown, the Everglades. From the east take Highway 9336 southwest out of Homestead to the entrance of the Everglades National Park and the main Visitor Center at Royal Palm. If you're coming in from the west, take Highway 41 from Naples or Everglades City, and then turn south on 997 into Homestead. It's a long drive, so you may prefer to take a guided your. There's plenty to see and do in and around Everglades City, and you can take another guided tour into the Everglades from there. At Royal Palm, you can buy film for your camera, insect repellents, postcards etc. It is worthwhile to purchase a comprehensive guide to the Everglades.

From Royal Palm, take either the Main Park Road (Route 27) west and

Airboat on the Everglades

then go south to Flamingo, or head south on Ingraham Highway, then west to Route 27 where you'll turn south and drive to Flamingo. Either way, it's a journey through the vast wilderness of only 38 miles or so, but do it properly by stopping frequently along the way to see the sights or stroll the board-walks. It will take at least three hours to reach Flamingo.

To try to describe the journey here would be an impossible task. The things you'll see, the things you'll do when you stop along the way, the animals and the wildlife, the scenery, the scent in the air, the heat in the middle of the day, the heavy silence broken only by the sounds of the birds, crickets, frogs, and the wind rustling the grasses, all defy description. The Everglades are a world apart. It's a subjective experience with a different meaning to each person. There's nowhere else like it in the entire United States, perhaps the world.

When you reach the end of your drive south, you'll be in Flamingo on the shores of Florida Bay, almost surrounded by water and in the heart of some of the most breathtaking countryside on Earth. Here you can rent a bike or boat, take a sightseeing tour, a dip in the swimming pool, eat lunch in the Fla-mingo Lodge Restaurant, or simply sit and relax for a while before starting back.

The Florida Keys

To most people who've never been there, the Florida Keys mean sunshine, the endless sea, Key West and Ernest Hemingway, and Key Largo and Humphrey Bogart and Lauren Bacall. And it's true, the Keys are all those things, but they are also much more. Key West, though now very much the "in place" to be, is one of the most unusual places on Earth. The rest of the chain of tiny islands, along with Key West, is 120 miles of perfect balance between extraordinary natural beauty, high times, relaxation, and non-stop activities. Getting there is a drive in the sunshine under a great open sky like no other in the world, and one you'll remember for many years to come.

GETTING THERE:

The jumping-off point to the Florida Keys is Key Largo, 42 miles south-west of Miami, and there's only one way to get there. Take Interstate 95 south at its junction with US-1 in downtown Miami, then US-1 south to Key Largo; you can't miss it. From Key Largo the **Overseas Highway**, the southern leg of US-1, follows a trail originally blazed in 1912 when Henry Flagler extended his Florida East Coast Railway from Miami to Key West. The Highway is 113 miles of roadway with 42 oversea bridges, including the famous Seven Mile Bridge at Marathon. And what will you see along the way? Endless seascapes as colorful as any artist's palette: the colors of a shimmering sea from the palest turquoise to the deepest blue, landscapes of russet browns and deep greens, swaying palms, silver buttonwoods and mangroves, all serene under a horizon-to-horizon blue sky dotted with fleecy white clouds.

You can make it from Miami to Key West in something less than four hours, but it's best if you allow more time. On your return to Miami, you'll want to take time out to enjoy the dramatic sunset. When the great ball of the sun falls into the sea, it sends radiant pink, orange, purple, and blue fingers stretching across the sky.

The **Mile Markers** are the keys to the Florida Keys. Often called mileposts, the markers may be seen, as the name implies, each mile along the Overseas Highway. They appear on the right shoulder or the median as small green signs with white numbers and begin with number 126, just south of Florida City, ending with the zero marker at the corner of Fleming and Whitehead Streets in Key West. Most locations of the stops, attractions, on the way south are identified by a mile marker number, i.e. 96.3. When asking directions in the Keys, you'll likely be given what you need as a mile marker reference, "just before or just beyond . . ." It's neat, and extremely practical. Better yet, the markers tell you exactly where you are, how far you've already traveled, and how far you still have to go.

GETTING AROUND:

The roads will take you almost everywhere you want to go. In some cases, a special attraction might require that you take a boat ride, especially if you want to visit one of the smaller, more inaccessible keys.

PRACTICALITIES:

The **Area Code** for the Florida Keys is 305.

Most of the attractions are open daily. A few do close on Sunday, and some open late and close early on the Sabbath, but not enough to make a difference. You can head south any day you like, but do watch the weather reports: it's always best to go when the sun shines, as the Overseas Highway can be quite a trial on a windy day, and even more so in a storm.

The **climate** is something of an enigma. You might think, that because a visit to the Keys will take you much farther south than often-sweltering Miami and the Beaches, the weather will be unbearably hot. Not so. True, it can get pretty warm down there, but you'll find that Mother Nature has provided her own air conditioning. Cooling breezes blow in off the ocean most of the year round, thus keeping the Keys' climate surprisingly temperate. The average daytime temperature in Key West is 81.9° F, with similar readings for the rest of the islands. During the late evening, when the temperature in Key West reaches its average low of 73°, the balmy weather creates an atmosphere for partying, and party they do, often into the wee hours.

There are basically two seasons in the Keys: winter and summer, or dry and wet, depending upon your outlook. Winter brings day after day of short-sleeve weather and blue skies, while the summer brings the rain: usually merely showers, short and sweet that provide sudden shade from the sun.

TOURIST INFORMATION:

The Florida Keys and Key West, PO Box 866, Key West, FL 33041-0866. ☎ 296-1552 or 800-FLA-KEYS.

Key Largo Chamber of Commerce and Florida Keys Visitor Center, 105950 Overseas Highway, Key Largo, FL 33037. ☎ 451-1414 or 800-822-1088, fax 451-4726.

Islamorada Chamber of Commerce: ☎ 800-322-5397.

Greater Marathon Chamber of Commerce: ☎ 800-262-7284.

Lower Keys Chamber of Commerce: ☎ 800-872-3722.

Key West Chamber of Commerce: ☎ 800-648-6269.

FOOD AND DRINK:

Seafood, always abundant in the Keys, is the highlight of the local cuisine. Grilled, sautéed, baked or boiled, or cold with a mayonnaise sauce, it's all exceptional gourmet fare, and any visit to the islands must include at least one seafood meal. But there's more; almost every ethnic group is represented, and you can dine on just about anything you like from fast foods to the finest fare prepared by the best chefs from Europe.

Key Largo:

The Italian Fisherman (10400 Overseas Highway at mile marker 104). The food is good, reasonable, and includes fresh seafood with a variety of pasta and other Italian dishes. ☎ 451-4471. $$.

Islamorada:

Whale Harbor Inn (on the Overseas Highway at mile marker 83.5) is open from 6 a.m. until noon for breakfast and lunch, and from 4–9 p.m. for dinner. The specialty is local seafood, and they have an outdoor raw bar and a nice nautical atmosphere. ☎ 664-4959. $$.

Marathon:

Perry's (6900 Overseas Highway at mile marker 51) is open for lunch and dinner from 11 a.m., and specializes in the inevitable fresh seafood, as well as steaks. ☎ 743-3447. $$.

Key West:

A & B Lobster House (700 Front Street) is open for lunch and dinner and specializes in fresh Florida lobster and prime rib. The restaurant overlooks the bay and harbor. ☎ 294-2563. $–$$.

Louie's Backyard (700 Wadell Avenue) is a neat experience. Open for lunch and dinner from 11:30 a.m., here you'll find some of the best seafood in Key West here. Dinner can be a little expensive, but lunch is quite reasonable, for the high standard of the food and the chance for outdoor dining on the oceanfront. Reservations accepted. ☎ 294-1061. $$–$$$$.

Kelly's Caribbean (301 Whitehead Street) is open for lunch and dinner from 11 to 1 a.m., and serves great Caribbean food, especially seafood and beef, and you can enjoy your meal outdoors in a shaded garden or in a treetop. ☎ 293-8484. $$.

SUGGESTED TOURS AND LOCAL ATTRACTIONS:

You could easily spend many days out in the Keys. Each Key is a world unto itself, and very few can be fully explored in a single day. The two trips described here and beginning on page 58 are extensive, so you'll need some pre-planning. There will be stops of interest that will appeal to some, but not to others. For the first trip you should include all the Keys from Key Largo to Big Pine. You might prefer to start early in the morning and drive southward all the way to Big Pine Key, begin the daytrip there and work your way back to Miami. If you don't complete the tour, you can resume the next

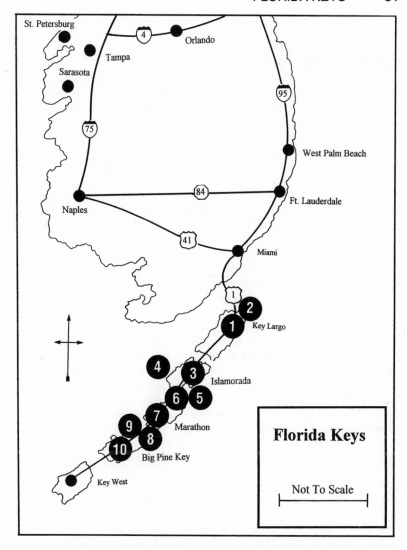

day at the point where you left off, without the long drive south.

For the trip to Key West (see page 58) you also have a several options: the first is to start out extremely early, say 5 a.m., and drive south without a stop, which should bring you into the city no later than 9. The other alternative is to allow two days for the trip and stay overnight on the Key. Either way, you should be able to cover most of the important stops. Finally, you can take an airplane, the flight is only 45 minutes. If you do you'll miss a great adventure and fail to savor the pleasures of one of America's most rewarding drives.

THE NORTH END TOUR:

This first trip will take you south as far as Big Pine Key, almost into Key West, but not quite. The tour is described as you would make it traveling from north to south, but you may want to consider driving to the southernmost point, begin the trip there, and take the stops in reverse order.

Key Largo (1) is the Florida Keys' largest island. Twenty miles long, but rarely more than two miles wide, its name means "long key" in Spanish. Humphrey Bogart is as much responsible for what Key Largo is today as is any other major influence.

In a time before man arrived on the islands south of the mainland, Key Largo was a string of islets. At first, bridges were built to connect them together, then, when the railroads came, the channels were filled and Key Largo became a single unit, one long Key that stretches all the way to Tavernier with a four-lane highway right down its center. Before Humphrey Bogart and Lauren Bacall made it famous, the island was called Rock Harbor, but enterprising businessmen, seeking to cash in on the publicity generated by the dynamic duo, decided to change it; in 1952, Rock Harbor became Key Largo.

If you like, you can check out the **Caribbean Club**; it provided the locale where Bogart's movie was filmed. Another little chunk of memorabilia: Key Largo, at the Holiday Inn Marina, is the present home of **The African Queen**, the actual boat used in Bogart's movie of the same name. You can even go aboard for a 45-minute ride; it will cost you $15 per person and there'll need to be at least two passengers. ☎ *451-2121 for reservations.*

Key Largo, however, is best known for its vast undersea preserve, **John Pennekamp Coral Reef State Park** (2) (on US-1 at Mile Marker 102.5, north of Key Largo). Here you can snorkel, scuba dive, or explore all the wonders of the only living coral reef in the continental United States, and do it from the comfort of a glass-bottom boat.

The park covers some 70 nautical square miles of seagrass beds, mangrove swamps, and coral reef. Coral reefs are many thousands of years in the making, being constructed from the skeletal remains of the living corals and other plants and animals, all cemented together by limestone secretions and calcareous algae. It's an extremely fragile world, easily damaged by the interference of humans, and, more recently by man-made, chemical pollution that kills the coral, turning the reef into a dismal, gray, and desolate world.

More than 53,660 acres of the park are submerged, 2,350 more are what the naturalists call uplands: a varied, natural habitat for many rare and endangered plants and marine animals.

There are so many activities, more than could be accomplished on one

The original African Queen *at Key Largo*

flying visit, that visitors often return to go snorkeling, swimming, picnicking, boating, sailing, windsurfing, fishing, studying nature, bird watching, and even camping.

Glass-bottom boats are available to ride out over the reefs. You might also join a snorkeling tour of the underwater park, or take scuba diving lessons. Canoes, motor boats, and sail boats are available for rent. *Open daily 8–sunset. PO Box 487, Key Largo, FL 33037.* ☎ *451-1202.* ♿. *Admission is $3.75 per vehicle and driver plus 50¢ per person. Boat rides are extra, reservations suggested,* ☎ *451-1621.*

The next stop is **Islamorada** (3), just 75 miles from Miami but a whole world apart. It's the centerpiece of a natural coral and palm-fringed group of islands called "the Purple Isles" that include Plantation, Windley, and Upper and Lower Matecumbe Keys. The name, Islamorada, is something of an enigma, variously attributed to Spanish explorers who are thought to have named the island for the heavy concentrations of violet snails they found on the seashore. Other local versions have it that the island was named for a small wildflower, railroad vine, or goatweed of the morning glory family that covers the island. Still others claim the Spanish meaning of the word "morada" means homestead. No matter, Islamorada is a tropical paradise with an underwater sea garden ripe for exploration, four magnificent state parks within easy reach, and a reputation as one of the finest sport fishing grounds in the United States.

Perhaps Islamorada's best known attraction is the 280-acre **Lignumvitae Key** (4) at Mile Marker 78.5. The Key was acquired in 1919 by William J. Matheson, a wealthy chemist from Miami. It's a remote island, isolated and serene, supporting many rare and endangered plants and trees indigenous to tropical forests. These include the gumbo limbo, mastic, Jamaica dogwood, poisonwood, strangler fig and, of course, the lignumvitae, for which the island is named.

The Key is accessible only by private or charter boats that are available at any of at nearby marinas. You can, however, take a three-hour round-trip boat ride to Lignumvitae Key, which departs daily at 1:30 p.m., from the Indian Key Fill on US-1 ☎ *451-7617 for rates).* If you go by private boat, you must notify the park rangers before you embark for the island; you'll be met at the dock. *Guided one-hour nature walking tours are given 10:30, 1, and 2:30, Thurs.–Mon. The park is closed on Tues. and Wed. PO Box 1052, Islamorada, FL 33036.* ☎ *451-7617. The fee is $1 per person.*

Islamorada's second state park is the **Indian Key State Historic Preserve** (5) at Mile Marker 78.5. It's a tiny Key, a little more than ten acres in size, and is separated from the Overseas Highway by open water. It is accessible only by private or charter boat.

Though you might not think it at first, Indian Key has a colorful history, and has passed through some very turbulent times. Archaeological excavations prove that the site was occupied by Indians several thousands of years before the arrival of the Spanish conquistadors. Exciting times at Indian Key, however, really began when the wrecking and salvage industry came to the keys in the late 1700s as commercial ships began using the Gulf Stream and the Bahama Channel, which lie perilously close to the great coral reefs. In 1831, Jacob Houseman bought the tiny island and made it headquarters for his wrecking business. During the years that followed, Houseman and the Key prospered. Soon there was a hotel on the island, warehouses, wharves, and a permanent population that fluctuated between 60 and 70 persons; life was good on Indian Key.

Then, on August 7, 1840, everything abruptly changed when the community was burned to the ground by Indians during the Second Seminole Indian War. The community never recovered from the catastrophe. Today the site has become something of a vacation spot for visitors to the Florida Keys. It is well worth a visit if only for a picnic and a short rest during the long journey southward. If you have the time you can go fishing, snorkeling, or swimming. *Open daily 8–sunset.* ☎ *664-4815. $1 per person. Three-hour boat tours to Indian Key depart Indian Key Fill on the Overseas Highway at 8:30 a.m., Thurs.–Mon.* ☎ *664-4815 for rates.*

The **Long Key State Recreation Area** (6) at Mile Marker 67.5 is the third park in the Islamorada area.

Long before it was acquired by the Florida Park Service between 1961 and 1973, the sub-tropical climate and the clear waters attracted explorers to the area. Long Key was home to the Calusa Indians, then to Spanish settlers. By 1912, with the establishment of the Key West expansion of the Florida East Coast Railroad, it was no longer inaccessible for travel. Long Key became an important depot for the railroad, and when its owner, Henry Flagler, established the Long Key Fishing Club, it became a popular attraction for some of the world's greatest salt water fishermen. Unfortunately, Long Key's era of prosperity met a violent end when a hurricane destroyed the railroad depot and the fishing club in 1935.

With the Florida Park Service's acquisition of the Key it was opened to the public in 1969. It took on a new life as one of the state's premier recreation areas, with lots to see and do. There's a campfire circle, three nature trails where you can see a wide variety of wading and shore birds, a canoe trail, an observation tower that offers spectacular views over most of the island, and a beach-side picnic area; just the spot to take a break. *Open daily 8–sunset. PO Box 776, Long Key, FL 33001.* ☎ *305-664-4815.* &. *$3.25 per vehicle.*

The **San Pedro Underwater Archaeological Preserve** is the fourth of Islamorada's state parks. It's not really a park, and it's not really accessible if you're trying to pack a lot into a single day.

The *San Pedro* was a 280-ton, Dutch-built ship that sailed as a part of the fleet of New Spain in 1733. In 1960 its remains were discovered in the Hawk Channel, close to Indian Key, in 18 feet of water. During the years that followed, several massive salvage expeditions stripped the carcass of the once-proud ship of all but a large pile of ballast stones. The wreck site covers an area some 90 feet long by 30 feet wide.

The once-bare underwater site has been enhanced by the addition of several replica cannons, an anchor, and a plaque offering wreck-site information. Unfortunately it's accessible only by private boat so, for nautical types, the site sits in 18 feet of water 1.25 nautical miles south from Indian Key at LORAN coordinates 14082.1 and 43320.6. *Long Key State Recreation Area, PO Box 776, Long Key, FL 33001.* ☎ *664-4815.*

From Islamorada you'll continue south on the Overseas Highway to **Marathon** (7). Beside its new concrete counterpart, the old Seven Mile Bridge juts into the sea like a giant fishing pier, inviting all anglers, walkers, and nature lovers. From the bridge, you can take in one of the world's great seascapes: a blue-green panorama of gulf and ocean, dotted with lobster traps and sailboats. Off the Key north of the bridge is some of the best fishing and sport diving in the world. Nestled below the old bridge, Pigeon Key, a tiny five-acre island, was the one-time home of the men who built Henry Flagler's Overseas Railroad. All this, along with the world famous Dolphin Research Center and the Turtle Hospital, is Marathon, the "Heart of the Florida Keys."

Ever since marine researchers discovered that dolphins may rival humans among the world's most intelligent mammals, they have become a continuing source of fascination. At the **Dolphin Research Center**, on Grassy Key near Marathon, they are studied the year-round, and you have a unique opportunity for a close encounter if you chance to swim with the gentle creatures. It will cost you $90 to do so, but it's tax deductible, and a rare experience, one you're not likely to forget. The ever-curious dolphins use their sensitive bottle-shaped noses to give you the once-over, often presenting their chins to be scratched or, occasionally, even kissed. They are affectionate and enjoy contact with people. *Open 10–5 Wed.–Sun. for guided tours.* ☎ *289-1121. Adults $9.50, seniors $7.50, children 4–6 $6.*

At Mile Marker 50, the **Museum of Natural History of the Florida Keys** (8) features 20 major exhibits and a half-dozen rotating displays that interpret the evolution of geography, botany, and zoology in the Keys, as well as the 5,000-year history of our habitation of the region. It's part of a 64-acre wilderness sanctuary know as Crane Point Hammock where you can experience first-hand some of the most sensitive ecological and archeological sites in Florida. Rare artifacts of gold and silver, cannons and hand weapons, and a vast display of everyday objects, all brought up from ships wrecked on the nearby reefs, are one of the highlights of a visit to the museum. The hammock itself can be experienced by taking a guided tour. *Open 9–5 daily except Sun., when the hours are noon–5.* ☎ *743-9100.* ♿. *Adults $5, seniors $4, students $2, under 12 free.*

*Bahia Honda State Park (9) is 12 miles south of Marathon. The park is unique to the area in that it features extensive sandy beaches and deep waters close enough offshore to provide exceptional swimming and snorkeling opportunities. The sub-tropical climate has created a natural environment found nowhere else in the United States. Bahia Honda Park is home to numerous rare and unusual plants including the yellow satinwood, gumbo limbo, silver palm, and the endangered small-flowering lily thorn. A specimen of the yellow satinwood, and one of the silver palm, have been named as national champion trees. You can see them all by taking a walk along the nature trail that follows the shore of a tidal lagoon at the far end of the Sandspur Beach.

Bahia Honda's geological base is limestone produced by a build-up of pre-historic coral formations similar to those found on the living coral reefs. When the sea level dropped thousands of years ago, the reef that became Bahia Honda emerged from the sea. It is the southernmost key where the reef formation is exposed.

Because of its unique swimming and snorkeling opportunities, the facilities at Bahia Honda are extensive. There are public restrooms; a concession facility that offers a limited range of groceries and camping and fishing supplies, and you can rent diving equipment at the dive shop. There are also freshwater showers on the beach, two boat launching ramps, and two picnic areas with shaded tables and barbecue grills.

Outdoor types will love Bahia Honda. You can go hiking, take a guided walk along the nature trail, enjoy a swim, snorkel, sun bathe, go fishing from the beach, or you can charter a deep water boat and go fishing for tarpon. All this, and the fact that it has been named one of the nation's "Best Beaches," make Bahia Honda a stop you mustn't miss. *Open daily 8–sunset.* ☎ *872-2353.* ♿. *$3.25 per vehicle.*

Big Pine Key (10) represents the end of your daytrip, or the beginning, depending upon how you decided to approach it. If you love the sea and all things in and under it, this is the place to visit. Some of the best diving opportunities in America are right here on Big Pine. Fishing is also one of the tiny island's premier sports. Of course, you can park the car and just walk because the scenery is spectacular and breathtaking. Just a few miles off-shore, **Looe Key Marine Sanctuary,** a protected reef area, offers a brilliant display of underwater landscapes with seafans and coral canyons that host a multitude of brightly colored fish. The shallow depths make a trip to the coral reef as much fun for beginner snorkelers as it does for pro scuba divers. Inland from this small island, the Blue Hole is the largest body of fresh water in the Keys. It is a former stone quarry which provides a source of drinking water for the many species of wildlife that lives on Big Pine, and nearby Watson's Hammock has primitive trails through the tropical forests of poisonwood, gumbo limbo, guava, acacia, and strangler fig. But something special to see is Big Pine's most famous inhabitants, the Key Deer. At home in the **National Key Deer Refuge,** there are now only some 300 of the tiny creatures left. Each is no bigger than a medium-sized dog. You'll find them waiting for you at the roadside, waiting for a handout. Please don't feed them or give them sweets. *Open daily during daylight hours.* ♿. *Nominal fee.*

Trip 9

Key West

This second daytrip to the Florida Keys takes you all the way south to Key West.

GETTING THERE:

Take Interstate 95 south to its junction with US-1 in downtown Miami, and then US-1 south to Key Largo; you can't miss it. From Key Largo the **Overseas Highway**, the southern leg of US 1, will take you all the way into Key West, some 160 miles southwest of Miami.

GETTING AROUND:

Getting around is easy in Key West: you can walk almost everywhere as the island is three-and-one-half miles by one mile in size. There are many little cafés and restaurants where you can take time out for a cup of coffee and sandwich. Or you can take a taxi. Another alternative is the **Old Town Trolley Fleet**, which provides transportation to and from the hotels and also offers narrated tours of Key West's historic landmarks. Many people rent a bicycle or moped, but most just walk. If you decide to use Shank's pony (walk), be careful, use a sunscreen, wear a hat, and don't try to take in too much at once. Although the sea breeze keeps the temperature at a comfortable level, the sun is still tropical and can quickly wear you down.

PRACTICALITIES:

The **Area Code** is 305.

Most of the attractions are open daily. A few do close on Sunday and some open late and close early on the Sabbath, but not enough to make a difference. You can head south any day you like, but do watch out for bad weather, Key West is always best seen when the sun shines. Remember: the Overseas Highway can be difficult during heavy weather.

FOOD AND DRINK:

Besides those listed on page 50, here are a few more good Key West eateries:

Bagatelle Restaurant, 115 Duval St. American cuisine in a 19th-century captain's house. ☎ 296-6609. $$.

Croissants de France, 816 Duval St. This sidewalk café specializes in seafood crêpes. ☎ 294-2624. $–$$.

El Siboney, 900 Catherine St. Try the authentic Cuban dishes. ☎ 296-4184. $–$$.

Turtle Kraas, 1 Lands End Village, Margaret St. at the waterfront. Once a cannery, it now serves seafood and other dishes. ☎ 294-2640. $–$$.

SUGGESTED TOUR:

Key West is a tiny tropical city with brightly painted shops and stores and neat little restaurants. It has more attractions to see and enjoy than do many tourist centers twice its size. Your first impression of the city will probably be one of awe. First-time visitors, regardless of what they've been led to expect, usually are taken by surprise when they enter the city at the end of the world. It's not so different from other small coastal cities in Florida, but it generates the feeling that it shouldn't be there. And, for such a small city, there's more to see and do than one can possible manage in a single day. Not all attractions are listed here, only those considered to be "must sees." A good place to start is at the junction with Highway 1 and Whitehead Street where you'll find the **Ernest Hemingway Home, Museum and Gardens** (1). Located at 907 Whitehead Street, this was home to one of America's most renowned writers. Here Ernest Hemingway penned some of his most famous works: *For Whom the Bell Tolls, Green Hills of Africa, A Farewell to Arms, The Fifth Column, and Snows of Kilimanjaro.* Of the house and grounds? Well, it's almost a spiritual experience. One can never seem to get rid of an overwhelming feeling that Hemingway still lives here, that any minute Papa is going to walk in and surprise you looking through his things. *Open 9–5 daily the year round.* ☎ *294-1575. ♿. Adults $6.50, children 4–12 $4.*

The **Key West Lighthouse Museum** (2) at the end of the world—938 Whitehead Street—and just across the street from the Hemingway Home, is the third-oldest brick lighthouse in Florida. Built in 1847, it has some 88 steps leading to the observation level and offers a magnificent view of the island and surrounding oceanscape. The museum housed inside the old lighthouse interprets its own history and the lighthouse history of the rest of the Keys. The climb to the top will take your breath away, but so will the view when you get there. *Open 9:30–5 daily.* ☎ *294-0012. Adults $5, children $1.*

The **Audubon House and Gardens** (3) at 205 Whitehead Street is a lovingly restored old house full of fine 18th- and 19th-century furnishings. John James Audubon, the world-famous naturalist, spent much of his life painting and cataloging wild birds in their natural habitat. His visit to Key West wasn't an extensive one, but it was significant. While there, he stayed at the home of Captain John H. Geiger, a salvage operator and harbor pilot. Each day, Audubon would explore the mangroves in search of new subjects to paint. Often he would leave the house as early as three o'clock in the morning and stay out until long after dark. More than 130 years later, Mitchell Wolfson acquired the old house and donated it as a public museum. The eclectic furnishings are of no particular style, and came to Key West from England, France, Italy, and Spain. *Open 9:30–5 daily.* ☎ *294-2116.* ♿. *Adults $7.50, children 6–12 $4.*

Surrounded as it is by the bluest, most densely populated waters in the world, it seems strange that Key West should bother with an aquarium. The **Key West Aquarium** (4) at 1 Whitehead Street, is the place where landlubbers can go to see all the wonders of the reef and never get their feet wet. Opened in 1932, it was the first tourist attraction in the Florida keys, and the first open-air aquarium in the United States. One of its most popular attractions is a great 50,000-gallon tank that exhibits a cross section of a near-shore mangrove environment with a variety of tropical and game fish, sea turtles, and birds. You can watch as guides feed the sharks, rays, and turtles, and even get a chance to pet a shark, if you feel so inclined. *Open 9–6 daily.* ☎ *296-2051.* ♿. *Adults $6.50, children 8–15 $3.50.*

Conch Train Tours, though not a stop on your tour, are worthy of a mention. If you want to see Key West quickly, this is the way to do it. The train rides on rubber wheels and follows the roadways, taking you on an exciting, historical 90-minute ride around all that's beautiful in the southernmost city in the United States. *Operates 9–4:30 daily from 1 Key Lime Square.* ☎ *294-5161. Adults $14, children 6–12 $6.*

*The Mel Fisher Maritime Heritage Society Museum (5), at 200 Green Street just off Whitehead Street, is where you can see some of the priceless artifacts Mel gathered from the sunken ships of the old Spanish treasure fleets. He recovered more than $400 million in gold, silver, and jewels from the *Nuestra Señora de Atocha* alone, and you can see much of it on display in the museum, including gold and silver bars, doubloons, chains, rings, and much more. *Open 9:30–5 daily.* ☎ *294-2633.* ♿. *Adults $6, children 4–12 $2.*

The **Harry S. Truman Little White House Museum** (6), close to the Mel Fisher Museum at 111 Front Street, is where President Truman spent 11 working vacations. Extensive renovations have returned the old home to its condition during the White House years of the 1940s. And it's crammed full of original furnishing, memorabilia, antiques, and other interesting presidential artifacts. Be sure to take the guided tour and watch the video; you'll enjoy the house all the more if you do. *Open 9–5 daily.* ☎ *294-9911.* ♿. *Adults $7, children and students $3.50.*

The **Donkey Milk House** (7), at 613 Eaton Street, was the home of U.S. Marshal "Dynamite" Williams, a hero of the Great Fire, and is now a "truly tropical version of Classic Revival" full of antiques and interesting artifacts,

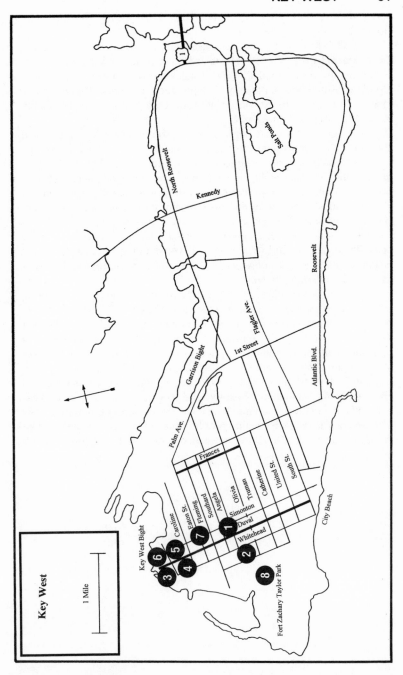

Key West

1 Mile

and with verandahs off every room. *Open 9:30–5 daily.* ☎ *296-1866. Adults $5, seniors $4, children 5–12 $1.*

No visit to Key West would complete without a visit to the **Fort Zachary Taylor State Historic Site** (8) on Southard Street. As far back as 1836, before Florida achieved statehood, the United States knew that the protection of the Florida coastline was of paramount importance. So, it was decided that a chain of forts should be established along the eastern seaboard, one of them at Key West to protect the harbor.

Construction of the fort began in 1845, shortly after Florida achieved statehood. Five years later the fort was named after Zachary Taylor, the president who died in office earlier that year. Construction was slow and, by the time the Civil War broke out the project was still incomplete. Construction was further slowed by outbreaks of yellow fever, shortages of men and materials, hurricanes, and by the very remoteness of the location. The three-story fort was finally finished in 1866, some 21 years after work on it began.

The fort is landlocked, but you can tour the battlements and see a number of authentic cannons and ammunition recovered during the excavations that began in 1968. *Open 8–sunset daily.* ☎ *292-6713.* ♿. *Admission $3.25 per vehicle plus 50¢ per person.*

One of the most exciting aspects of a daytrip is that you can go exploring on your own. And there's no better place to do it than in Key West. Another defensive bastion, Fort Jefferson, the "Gibraltar of the Gulf," lies on Garden Key in the heart of the Dry Tortugas. You can take a ride over the reefs in a seaplane, visit the southernmost point in the United States, the Wrecker Museum (the oldest house in Key West), the Heritage House, Mallory Market, and Ripley's Believe-it-or-Not Odditorium; you can even take a cruise on a sea-going catamaran or explore the reef from the safety of a glass-bottom boat. Finally, all summer long there are the **Sunset Celebrations**. As that sun goes down each evening people come out to play, eat, and drink in the streets; it's party time with a vengeance in Key West, and you shouldn't miss it.

Fort Lauderdale

Less than 100 years ago, Fort Lauderdale was little more than a trading post and ferry landing on the edge of the New River. In fact, until the turn of the 20th century, the only residents in the area were runaway slaves, Indians driven south from Georgia and the Carolinas who later became known as the Seminoles, and a handful of white settlers. During the mid-1800s, three Seminole Indian Wars brought three wooden forts called Lauderdale, named for the first military commander, William Lauderdale. None of these survived. In 1892, when Dade County built the first paved road on Florida's east Coast, things began to happen and the area, then known as the New River Settlement, opened up. In 1893, Frank Stranahan started the first Indian trading post, general store, and post office. It is the redoubtable Henry Flagler, however, to whom much of the credit must go for bringing the world to Fort Lauderdale. His Florida East Coast Railroad established the first easy access to the area and since then the city-by-the-sea prospered. But perhaps it was Connie Francis in the 1950s movie, *Where The Boys Are*, that brought Fort Lauderdale to the attention of the vacationing world. For a long time it was infamous as the Spring Break Capital of Florida. But those days are gone, as are the thousands of kids who frolicked on one of Florida's most beautiful beaches. Today, Greater Fort Lauderdale remains a popular destination. The forts are gone and the Indian canoes have been replaced by water taxis, but there's still a great deal of the town's historic past left to explore. The beaches are enticing and the shopping second to none. If you're a water baby, you'll find the ocean blue and inviting, the reefs colorful, and the sand soft and warm.

GETTING THERE:

By Road, from Miami you have a couple of options: you can take the scenic route and drive north along the coast on Highway A1A, or you can take the fast route via Interstate 95. Either way, it's a drive of only 25 miles or so.

By Air, the Fort Lauderdale/Hollywood International Airport is served by most major domestic airlines, and many more out of Canada and Europe.

By Rail, Amtrak provides long distance service into Fort Lauderdale. The station is at 200 SW 21st Terrace, ☎ 587-6692 or 800-USA-RAIL.

Local train service between Miami and Greater Fort Lauderdale is provided by Tri-Rail, ☎ 1-800-TRI-RAIL. This commuter system operates some 15 stations in Dade, Broward, and Palm Beach counties, and services the area between Greater Miami and the Beaches and West Palm Beach. Tri-Rail connects directly to Metrorail for convenient access to or from the downtown area and south Miami at no additional cost. Call for fares. A 50% discount applies to seniors, students, and persons with disabilities. Trains operate daily except Christmas and Thanksgiving.

By Bus: The Greyhound/Trailways terminal is at 513 NE 3rd Street, ☎ 764-6551 or 1-800-231-2222.

GETTING AROUND:

Driving in the city is not a problem, but try to avoid Interstate 95 and all major roads during weekday rush hours. There's plenty of parking available; some convenient, some not quite so handy. Parking on the streets downtown is metered at 75¢ per hour. Municipal parking at the beaches costs between $3 and $5 per day, depending upon the location.

Most avenues in Fort Lauderdale run north and south; streets run east and west.

Interstate 95 is the north-south expressway along the eastern edge of the city. Florida's Turnpike, a toll road, also runs north and south. Other major roadways include US-1 and Highway A1A, the scenic route beachfront route north and south. Interstate 595 is the principle east-west expressway.

The easiest and least expensive way of getting around Greater Fort Lauderdale is the Broward County Mass Transit bus system (☎ 357-8364). Some 190 buses operate 36 different routes on weekdays, 34 on Saturdays and 21 on Sundays, covering an area of more than 300 square miles. You're never far away from a bus stop, and the busses run frequently.

Broward County Transportation Authority also operates a free downtown trolley system from 7:30 a.m. to 5:30 p.m. on weekdays; ☎ 429-3100. The trolley also offers sightseeing tours on Tuesdays through Sundays.

Taxis operate throughout the county, but they are not the least expensive form of transport. ☎ 765-4455 for details.

The **Water Taxi** at 1900 SE 15th Street, ☎ 565-5507, is an exciting way to tour Fort Lauderdale. You can jump aboard, seven days a week, at various landmarks throughout Broward County. The yellow craft carry about a dozen people in relative comfort; it's a fine and relaxing way travel the city.

Wheelchair Accessible Van Rentals: Wheelchair Getaways (West Palm Beach) offers full-size mini-vans equipped with lifts and tie-downs. Free airport delivery and pickup. Services in Miami, Fort Lauderdale, and West Palm Beach; ☎ 800-637-7577.

PRACTICALITIES:

The **Area Code** is 954.

The Climate. The sun shines most days in Greater Fort Lauderdale. The average year-round temperature ranges from a low of 71°F to a high of 90°. Sometimes it rains, especially in the late spring and late summer, and you can expect afternoon showers even the middle of summer. The sun here is hot so don't over-expose your skin. Use a sunscreen with an SPF factor of at least 15, more if you have sensitive skin, and don't stay on the beach too long during the hours 11–3.

Most of the attractions in the area are open seven days a week. The streets and beaches are crowded practically all of the time, especially so during the winter months, and there's no real let-up, so you can more or less pick your day and visit whenever you like.

TOURIST INFORMATION:

Greater Fort Lauderdale Convention & Visitors Bureau, 200 East Las Olas Boulevard, Suite 1500, Fort Lauderdale, FL 33301. ☎ 765-4466; fax 765-4467.

Greater Fort Lauderdale Chamber of Commerce, 512 NE 3rd Avenue, Fort Lauderdale, FL 33302, ☎ 462-6000.

FOOD AND DRINK:

Sunny playground that it is, it's no wonder that those with a taste for the finest, or with an adventuresome palate, will find the gastronomic delights of Greater Fort Lauderdale all they could wish for. From mom-and-pop specialty cafés to elegant restaurants serving the finest of international cuisine, you'll find it all here. Even getting to the restaurant of choice can be an adventure. Many of them overlook the Intracoastal Waterway and are accessible by water taxi. The trip will cost $14, but what an experience. As it is almost everywhere in Florida, fresh seafood, caught right off the beach, is sensational. You can also enjoy splendid meat dishes, many varieties of pasta, and home-cooked delights such as only mom can make. And, as you might expect at one of Florida's premier vacation spots, there are hundreds of places to find them all. The choices are endless, and often bewildering. Here are a few suggestions—you won't be disappointed:

> **Café Seville** (2768 E. Oakland Park Boulevard at Bayview Drive) is a Spanish-style restaurant with a menu to match. Open for lunch and dinner Monday through Saturday; closed Sunday; reservations accepted. Specialties include paella. ☎ 565-1148. $$.

> **Chameleon** (1095 SE 17th Street Causeway) is open for dinner from 6–10:30 daily. Reservations required for Friday and Saturday. The cuisine is continental, and the specialties include fresh seafood, game, and rack of lamb. ☎ 522-6795. $$$.

> **Charley's Crab** (3000 NE 32nd Avenue) is a delightful place to eat. Open for lunch and dinner from 11:30-11 daily; reservations accepted. Fresh seafood is the specialty here, including stone crab

and lobster, with a variety of pasta thrown in for good measure. ☎ 561-4800. $–$$$.

Cypress Room (in the Westin Hotel at Cypress Creek). If you're looking for an elegant evening, this is the place. Open for lunch from 11:30 and dinner from 5:30, but it's best that you make a reservation. The cuisine is regional American (southern) with a dash of the continental. Jackets required for men. ☎ 772-1331. $$$.

Kelly's Landing (1305 SE 17th Street in the Southport Shopping Center) is a family-style restaurant with a New England flavor. Open weekdays and Saturday for lunch and dinner from 11, and on Sunday from noon. Good, old-fashioned seafood, steak, and chicken are the specialties, and all at prices that won't hurt the pocketbook. ☎ 670-7009. $.

Sage (2378 N. Federal Highway) is open for lunch and dinner— brunch on Sunday—from 11 a.m. The specialties include braised lamb, roast pork, and a fine salad bar. Totally non-smoking. ☎ 565-2299. $.

SUGGESTED TOUR:

If you were to take in all of Greater Fort Lauderdale's more than 300 miles of navigable waterways, 23 miles of Atlantic beaches, and its many tourist attractions, it would take more than a month, and there would still plenty left over for another visit. What follows, then, barely samples the treasures; even so you probably won't be able to do them all. Be sure to visit the **Public Beach** and, if you can find three hours to spare, take a cruise on the **Jungle Queen**.

The **Bonnet House** (1), 900 N. Birch Road, is a good place to begin. Once the winter home of artists Frederick and Evelyn Bartlett, it stands on a 35-acre beach-front estate that features beautiful landscaped gardens, lagoons, and an art gallery. Many of the pieces were created by the Bartletts. These include small, unconventional works, as well as the hand-painted ceilings. You'll need to allow at least 90 minutes. *Open May through November; closed during the winter. Tours of the house are given Wed.–Fri. at 10 and 1, and Sat.–Sun. at 1 and 2.* ☎ *563-5393. Adults $7, seniors $6, children 6–18 $5.*

The 180-acre **Hugh Taylor Birch State Recreation Area** (2), at 3109 East Sunrise Boulevard, lies inside the city limits close to the Bonnet House between the Atlantic Ocean and the Intracoastal Waterway. It's a tropical wonderland with four distinct biological communities that provide a home for an abundance of local wildlife. Popular activities include fishing, hiking and jogging along the 1.7-mile course that rims the park, swimming, canoeing (rental canoes are available), and picnicking. *Open daily from 8–sunset.* ☎ *564-4521.* &. *Admission $3.75 per vehicle.*

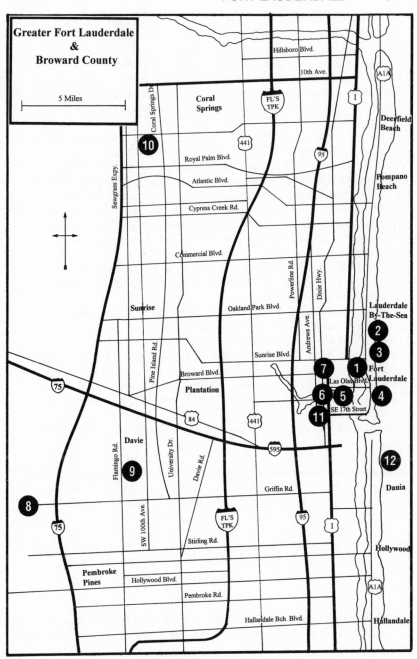

Go south from Hugh Taylor Birch on Highway A1A and you'll arrive at the **Public Beach** (3) on Atlantic Boulevard. No trip to Fort Lauderdale would be complete without a visit to its famous beaches, and there are more than 23 miles of them. The Public Beach is a newly renovated mile-and-a-half of sand and sea that stretches from Sunrise Boulevard to Seabreeze Boulevard. It features a wide promenade, bicycle lanes, lots of palm trees, and a picnic area. The water is clear, shallow and inviting, and the swimming is great; don't miss it.

Continue south on Highway A1A and you'll arrive at the junction with Las Olas Boulevard. A little farther south on the south side of Bahia Mar Yacht Basin is the berth of the **Jungle Queen** (4). A morning or afternoon sightseeing cruise down the New River aboard the Jungle Queen takes at least three hours of your daytrip; an evening dinner cruise four hours.

The evening cruise includes a stop at an island for an "all-you-can-eat" barbecue and shrimp dinner. The daytime cruises include a visit to an Indian village and an alligator wrestling show. The views along the way are splendid, and the whole experience is delightful. *Sightseeing cruises leave daily at 10 and 2; dinner cruise daily at 7.* ☎ *462-5596.* ♿. *Morning or afternoon cruise $9.95; children 2–10 $7. Dinner cruise $22.95, children under 10 $11. Reservations required.*

Return to Las Olas Boulevard and turn west. The **Stranahan House** (5), at 335 SE 6th Avenue, is on the New River just south of the boulevard. Originally a trading post for the Seminole Indians, it became the home of the Stranahans in 1906. Today, it's an historical museum with antique furnishings, art work, and lots of artifacts and memorabilia. Tours of the home are conducted by volunteers in period costumes. The landscaped gardens overlook the river. If you can, try to visit on Friday evening; it will cost you a little more, but you can join in and enjoy the "Social." *Open 10–4 Wed.–Sat., Sun. 1–4.* ☎ *524-4736.* ♿. *Adults $5, seniors and students $3, children under 12 $2.*

Continue west on Las Olas Boulevard to 2nd Avenue. The **Fort Lauderdale Historical Society Museum** (6), 219 SW 2nd Avenue, is part of a complex containing three of the city's oldest structures: the New River Inn, the King-Cromartie House, and the Philomen Bryan House. All three were built around the turn of the 20th century. The site also features a replica of Fort Lauderdale's first schoolhouse, and a modern museum that houses the Society's archives. Exhibits depict local history, but there are also some special displays that include Seminole Indian art work, artifacts from the Seminole Wars, a collection of historic photographs, and an exhibit that interprets the history of baseball. *Open 10–4 Tues.–Sat.* ☎ *463-4431.* ♿. *Adults $2, children $1.*

Museum of Discovery and Science and Blockbuster IMAX Theater (7) is a little farther north at 401 SW 2nd Street, and is one of Florida's premier creative learning centers. The brand new, 85,000-square-foot museum fea-

The Museum of Discovery and Science

tures seven interactive exhibits on two floors. These include the **Florida EcoScapes**, **KidScience**, and **Space Base** featuring an exciting five-minute space flight. There's also a unique exhibit called **Sound**, where you can learn to more fully understand its workings and principles. But the jewel in the museum's crown is the **Blockbuster IMAX Theater** with its vast five-story, 80-foot-wide screen and 14,000-watt, six-channel, four-way, 42-speaker sound system; that's quite a mouthful, but it has to be experienced to be believed. *Open 10–5 Mon.–Fri., 10–8:30 on Sat., and noon–5 on Sun.* ☎ *467-6637.* ♿. *Adults $6, seniors and children 3–12 $5. IMAX admission: Adults $9, seniors $8, and children 3–12 $7. Discounted combination tickets available.*

Everglades Holiday Park and Airboat Tours (8), at 21940 Griffin Road west of the city, is Fort Lauderdale's own version of the great wilderness excursion, and the airboat is, of course, the traditional way to see it. If you have the time, you'll be able to visit a Seminole Indian settlement, and see all the wonderful wildlife of vast swamp as well as an alligator wrestling show. *Tours 9–5 daily.* ☎ *434-8111.* ♿. *Call for rates.*

***Flamingo Gardens and Arboretum** (9), west of the city via SE 24th Street at 3750 Flamingo Road in Davie, is a tropical garden with all sorts of unusual things to see and do. You can ride a tram for a mile-and-a-half through citrus groves, a rain forest, and a natural hammock. You'll also see flamingos on their island habitat, otters, alligators, and a variety of other wildlife, wet and dry. Visit the free-flight aviary, the birds-of-prey exhibit, and a museum that interprets Everglades history. You could easily spend a half-day here, but it is one of Fort Lauderdale's must-see attractions. *Open 9–5 daily. The last tram leaves one hour before closing.* ☎ *473-2955.* ♿. *Adults $8, seniors $6.50, children 3–11 $4.50.*

Butterfly World (10), in Tradewinds Park, also west of the city via Sunrise Boulevard at 3600 W. Sample Road in Coconut Creek, comprises some three acres of tropical gardens and many thousands of brilliantly colored butterflies. The grounds include several nature walks, including an English rose garden, a water garden, a vine walk, and a tropical rain forest. There's also an insectarium and a museum. It's an unusual attraction and, though a little pricey, one well worth seeing. *Open Mon.–Sat. 9–5, Sun. 1–5.* ☎ *977-4400.* ♿. *Adults $9.95, seniors $7.95, children 4–12 $5.*

Ocean World (11), just south of the city at 1701 SE 17th Street via Highway A1A, is yet another version of the Sea World experience. Here you can enjoy continuous shows featuring dolphins, sea lions, all sorts of exotic birds, and watch as divers play and interact underwater with the dolphins. You'll also see alligators and a wide variety of tropical fish, including sharks. You can even take a sightseeing cruise along the Intracoastal Waterway if you like. It's a fun show, and one the whole family is sure to enjoy. *Open daily 1–6.* ☎ *523-6611.* ♿. *Adults $15, children 3–12 $11.*

The **John U. Lloyd State Recreation Area** (12), is also south of the city in Dania, off Highway A1A. The 250-acre beachfront park is located on one of Florida's barrier islands, just off the Intracoastal Waterway. John U. Lloyd Beach is one of Broward County's most important sea turtle nesting areas. More than 10,000 hatchlings are produced on the beach each year, and there's an ongoing program to ensure that as many of the babies as possible survive.

On the west side of the park, along the Intracoastal Waterway, a man-made wetland is slowly, but surely, bringing back the red mangroves that were lost during the port expansion of 1989. These wetlands provide a natural nursery for all sorts of fish and other marine life. Another interesting area, a long strip of tidal waterway known as the New River Sound, is a protected area for the endangered manatee and other marine and animal life. The mangrove-lined sound is a place of wild and scenic beauty where you can take to the waters in a canoe and observe the wildlife in its natural habitat.

Facilities at the park are extensive. There's a paved, lighted jetty at the north end of the park that provides excellent fishing opportunities and is a good spot to watch the ships entering and departing Port Everglades. You can walk for miles along the park's broad sandy beaches, swim and fish the hours away, or eat a quick lunch in a shaded picnic area on the beach. *Open daily from 8–sunset.* ☎ *923-2833.* ♿. *Admission $3.25 per vehicle.*

West Palm Beach

Palm Beach County is a class act, as the rich and famous have known for many a year. Today, West Palm Beach and its surroundings are growing with the rest of southern Florida's resort kingdoms. True, the great mansions are still very much a part of the Palm Beach experience, and to travel the waterways in search of a glimpse of an unwary celebrity is always fun, but there's much more to savor. It's the ocean with its slate blue waters, warm in winter and cool in summer. It's the playful dolphins in the shallows, the great sea turtles, and the giant marlin offshore. It's the unbeatable climate, uncrowded beaches, and waving palms. Is it for everyone? No. But, if you're searching for something a little different, Palm Beach County will provide you with just the daytrip you're looking for.

GETTING THERE:

By Road, from Miami you have several options: you can take the scenic route and drive north along the coast on Highway A1A, you can take the fast track an go via Interstate 95, or you can go a little farther west and take Highway 441. Whichever you decide, it's a drive of about 70 miles.

By Air, Palm Beach International Airport is served by most major domestic airlines, and many more out of Canada and Europe.

By Rail, Amtrak provides long distance service into West Palm Beach, ☎ 1-800-USA-RAIL or 832-6169.

Local train service between Miami and Palm Beach County is provided by Tri-Rail (☎ 800-TRI-RAIL). This commuter system operates some 15 stations in Dade, Broward, and Palm Beach counties, and services the area between Greater Miami and the Beaches and West Palm Beach. Tri-Rail connects directly to Metrorail for convenient access to or from the downtown area and south Miami at no additional cost. Call for fares. A 50% discount applies to seniors, students, and persons with disabilities. Trains operate daily except Christmas and Thanksgiving.

By Bus: Greyhound/Trailways, ☎ 800-231-2222 or 833-0825.

GETTING AROUND:

As always, your first and most convenient option is your own motor vehicle. The roads are busy at times, especially during rush hour, but rarely does the traffic become a problem. There's adequate parking wherever you go, both on meters and in city-owned lots; the beaches are especially well provided for. Parking on the streets downtown is metered at 75¢ per hour. Municipal parking at the beaches costs between $3 and $5 per day, depending upon the location. The major highways north and south are the Florida Turnpike, Interstate 95, and Highway A1A which hugs the seashore. The main route east and west is Highway 98.

There are two public transport systems available in Palm Beach County: **Cotran Bus Service** operates routes county wide; **Lolly The Trolley** provides service in Lake Worth. Travel on Cotran is inexpensive, but not as convenient as you might wish.

Wheelchair Accessible Van Rentals: Wheelchair Getaways (West Palm Beach) offers full-size mini-vans equipped with lifts and tie-downs. Free airport delivery and pickup. Services in Miami, Fort Lauderdale, and West Palm Beach. ☎ 800-637-7577. **Dial-A- Ride** also provides a door-to-door van service for the elderly and handicapped, ☎ 689-8961.

PRACTICALITIES:

The **Area Code** for Palm Beach County is 561.

The Climate. The average year-round temperature in Palm Beach County ranges from a low of 71°F to a high of 90°. The sun shines the year-round. You can expect some rain, especially in the late spring and late summer, and you might experience showers in the late afternoon even the middle of summer. The sun here is very hot, so don't over-expose your skin. Use a sunscreen with an SPF factor of at least 15, more if you have sensitive skin, and don't stay on the beach too long between 11 a.m. and 3 p.m.

Most of the attractions in the area are open seven days a week.

TOURIST INFORMATION:

Palm Beach County Convention & Visitors Bureau, 1555 Palm Beach Lakes Boulevard, Suite 204, West Palm Beach, FL 33401. ☎ 471-3995, fax 471-3990.

Chamber of Commerce of the Palm Beaches, 401 N. Flagler Drive, West Palm Beach, FL 33401. ☎ 833-3711, fax 833-5582.

FOOD AND DRINK:

As in the other resort areas of south Florida, Palm Beach County is a land of gastronomic delights. You'll find everything from fast food to fine dining, from the one-of-a-kind specialty café to the top-flight elegant restaurant of international reputation.

Fresh seafood is the mainstay of the restaurant industry in Palm Beach, and so it should be, because most of what you'll eat is caught locally at one of the small fishing towns such as Jupiter or Stuart. Even so, you can still enjoy a good steak or prime rib in any one of more than 100 establishments.

Basil's Neighborhood Café (771 Village Boulevard, West Palm Beach) is open for lunch and dinner from 11:30 to 10, Monday through Saturday, and for dinner only on Sunday. The menu includes lots of fresh seafood with specialties that include tuna, and wood-oven roasted salmon and pizza. ☎ 687-3801. $–$$.

Greek Village (6108 S. Dixie Highway, West Palm Beach) is open weekdays for lunch and dinner, and dinner only on Saturday and Sunday. Greek cuisine, including great salad and moussaka. ☎ 582-1666. $.

Morton's of Chicago (downtown in the Phillips Point Building, just off Flagler Drive) is open only for dinner. If you like fine dining, elegance and opulent surroundings, this is the place for you. The cuisine is traditional American with specialties in grain-fed, aged beef. Fresh seafood is also on the menu, along with whole spring chicken. Reservations are a must, and gentlemen must wear a jacket. ☎ 835-9664. $$$.

Parker's Lighthouse (2401 PGA Boulevard, Palm Beach Gardens) specializes in fresh seafood, including crunchy grouper and seafood linguine. Open daily for lunch and dinner from 11 a.m. You can eat indoors or outdoors, and the view over the marina through floor-to-ceiling windows is spectacular. ☎ 627-0000. $$.

River House (2373 PGA Boulevard, Palm Beach Gardens, on the Intracoastal Waterway) is open for dinner from 5-10:30. The specialty is seafood, but the menu also includes lamb chops, steak, and prime rib. ☎ 694-1188. $$–$$$.

Waterway Café (2300 PGA Boulevard, Palm Beach Gardens, on the Intracoastal Waterway) is open for lunch and dinner from 11:30. The specialties include such innovations as shrimp fettucine Alfredo, lump crab cakes, and teriyaki swordfish. ☎ 4694-1700. $$.

SUGGESTED TOURS AND LOCAL ATTRACTIONS:

A two-hour cruise on *The Star of Palm Beach* (1), 900 E. Blue Heron Boulevard at Singer Island, should be the core of your daytrip to West Palm Beach. The boat, which can carry up to 300 passengers in air-conditioned comfort, is a replica of a Mississippi paddle-wheeler and, while a ride aboard such a craft would be a treat in itself, the journey past the spectacular backyards of the mansions of West Palm Beach is an experience not to be missed. *Cruises depart daily at 10, 12:30, and 3.* ☎ *848-7827.* ♿. *Adults $9.95, children 3–12, $5.*

Dreher Park Zoo (2), 1301 Summit Boulevard, east of Interstate 95, houses more than 500 animals and birds on its 22 acres, including a rare Florida panther, Bengal tigers, giant tortoises, wallabies, and kangaroos. All of the residents are kept in natural settings or special encounter areas. You can walk the Cornell Nature Trail, an elevated boardwalk, visit the Australian Outback, and spend time with the kids at the children's zoo, featuring small animals they can get to know personally. *Open daily 9–5; Sat. and Sun. 9–7, mid–April through mid-October. Last admission is 45 minutes before closing.* ☎ *533-0887.* ♿. *Adults $6, children 3–12 $4.*

The **South Florida Science Museum, Planetarium and Aquarium** (3) is at 4801 Dreher Trail North. As with most museums of this type, the experience is one of interactive, hands-on exploration. The Light and Sound Hall includes exhibits that interpret visual media, while the Aquarium plunges you to the bottom of the ocean to examine the wonders of the coral reef. Winding its way through a tropical jungle, the Native Plant Center is part exhibit and part nature trail. The planetarium takes you outside the Earth's atmosphere, beyond the outer reaches of the Solar System to the center of the galaxy. *Open daily 10–5.* ☎ *832- 1988.* ♿. *Adults $5, seniors $4.50, students $3, children 4–12 $2. Planetarium shows $1.75, Laser shows extra.*

*Lion Country Safari (4) lies 16 miles west of West Palm Beach on Southern Boulevard and, though it's a bit out of the way, it's another one of those "not-to-be-missed" experiences. You'll head out into the veldt on a mini safari, a drive through the 500-acre park and its more than 1,000 wild animals. This is as close to Africa as you can get without actually traveling there. The animals you'll see along the way include most of the exotic beasts you would associate with the great continent. There are lions, wildebeests, giraffes, and rhinoceroses all wandering freely in simulated habitats with strategically placed, landscaped barriers to separate the predators. You'll drive your own car, unless it's a convertible—you can rent a suitable vehicle there—along a paved road through five distinct regions: Lake Nakaru, the Serengeti Plain, the Great Plains, the Wakie National Park, and the Gorongosa Preserve, and you can make the drive as many times as you wish all for the one entrance fee. Also included in the park is a boat ride, petting zoo, paddle boats, carousel, jungle golf, dinosaur exhibit, reptile park, and a gift shop. There's even a free kennel where you can leave your pet. Allow at least three hours. *Open 9:30–5:30 daily.* ☎ *793-1084.* ♿. *Adults $13.95, seniors $8.95, children 3–15 $9.95.*

Norton Gallery of Art (5), at 1451 South Olive Street, is one of southern Florida's premier cultural attractions. It features an outstanding permanent collection, as well as a full schedule of temporary exhibitions. The extensive American collection features works by such notables as Georgia O'Keeffe, while the international collections include paintings by Picasso and Degas. *Open 10–5 Tues.–Sat., 1–5 Sun. Guided tours are conducted daily at 2, Dec.–March.* ☎ *832-5194.* ♿. *Donations.*

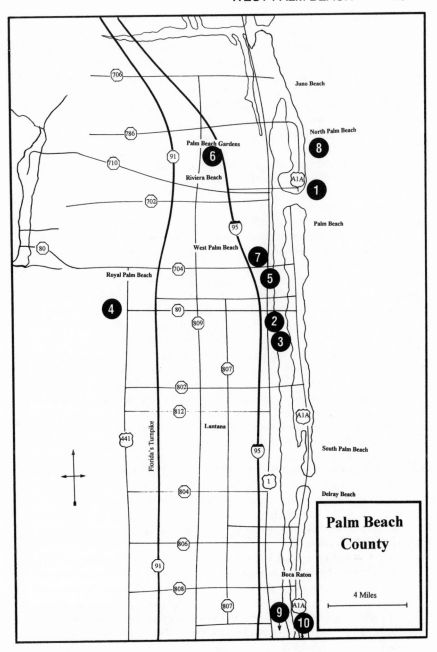

The PGA National Resort and Spa (6) in Palm Beach Gardens has been the national headquarters of the PGA for more than 25 years and, even if you aren't a golfer, it's well worth seeing. Visit the pro's shop to browse the huge selection of golfing attire, all monogrammed with the exclusive PGA logo. If you play, it will take your entire daytrip to get in a round, and you'll have to book your tee time well in advance. You can even take a lesson at the Jack Nicklaus/Jim Flick Golf School. ☎ *626-3900.*

The Flagler Museum (7), Coconut Row, is the lovingly restored home of railroad magnate Henry Flagler. This is how the rich and famous lived at the turn of the 20th century. All of the furnishings are original, as are the decorations including paintings, silver, china, and oriental rugs. You can also see authentic clothing and costumes dating from the early 1800s. *Open 10– 5 Tues.–Sat., and noon–5 on Sun.; closed Mon.* ☎ *655- 2826.* &. *Adults $7, children 6–12 $3.*

From downtown Palm Beach, take Highway 1 north to Riviera Beach and the junction with Route 708. Turn right there, go to Highway A1A and turn north to **John D. MacArthur Beach State Park** (8), on Highway A1A in North Palm Beach. This is one of Florida's finest state-owned recreation areas, a barrier island in northern Palm Beach County, and a tiny oasis of great natural beauty in the midst of southern Florida's vacation strip. The small area set aside by the state to preserve the natural heritage of a sub-tropical coastal habitat that once covered southeast Florida. It offers a pint-sized refuge far away from the crowded vacation hot-spots.

The park encompasses some 225 acres of uplands, a mixture of maritime hammock and mangroves surrounding Lake Worth Cove, and another 535 acres of submerged terrain. This is one of the finest examples of a sub-tropical habitat to be found anywhere in the South, a home to a wide variety of flora and fauna including herons, ibis, roseate spoonbills, osprey, fiddler crabs, pelicans, tern, sandpipers, and many other species of shorebirds. It's also one of the few places where you can still find sea lavender, cabbage palms, mastic trees, gumbo limbos, strangler figs, and beach star.

MacArthur Beach is a prime nesting area for sea turtles. During the summer months you can see large numbers of loggerhead, green, and leatherback turtles. Ranger-led turtle-watching walks are usually held in June and July. The park also has a nature center featuring exhibits and a video that interprets the barrier island habitat, its rare and varied plant life, and its animal communities.

A 1,600-foot boardwalk spans Lake Worth Cove from the park's nature center to the Atlantic beaches where the sea is almost always warm and the sand is soft and inviting. Popular activities include nature study and bird watching. John D. MacArthur is the perfect place to go hiking along the beaches, surf fishing, swimming, shell collecting, snorkeling, and pic-nicking. *Open 8–sunset daily.* ☎ *624-6950.* &. *Admission $3.25 per vehicle.*

From MacArthur, drive north on Highway 1 to Hobe Sound; the **Jonathan Dickinson State Park** (9) is on your left to the east. Covering more than 11,000 acres, this is one of the largest parks in south Florida. It's a vast natural resource with a great many distinct plant and wildlife communities, including an area covered with coastal pine scrub—a biological community so rare that it's been designated as "globally imperiled."

The Loxahatchee River, now one of the nation's "Wild and Scenic Rivers," winds its way through the park beneath a great green canopy of lush vegetation, creating a truly remarkable, natural world. The park's dunes, coastal hammock, mangroves, and the rich environment of the Loxahatchee riverbank, provide rare opportunities for you to observe some of Florida's most endangered animals, including the gopher tortoise, scrub jay, and Florida sandhill crane.

There are public restrooms, a picnic area with tables and grills, and, if you feel so inclined, you can rent a canoe or rowboat and take to the waters on your own. If you like to walk, there are many miles of nature and hiking trails, several of which meander through the endangered scrublands. To learn more about the park and its workings, join one of the ranger-led park tours or take a boat ride on the *Loxahatchee Queen. Open 8–sunset daily.* ☎ *546-2771.* ♿. *Admission.*

The final stop on this daytrip is some 25 miles to the north of Jonathan Dickinson on Highway A1A. The **Fort Pierce Inlet State Recreation Area** (10) is a 340-acre park located on the north shore of the Fort Pierce inlet. This is where you'll find nearly-deserted beaches with miles of rolling sand dunes and coastal hammocks where you can spend a lazy afternoon sun bathing in the hot Florida sunshine, far from the crowds farther south. It's also one of those idyllic, hard-to-find romantic spots where you can share a few quiet moments with someone special. If you can be there at dawn, when the sun breaks over the horizon in a blaze of golden glory, you'll see a spectacle you'll never forget. The sea and sand turns into a jeweled, glittering wonderland. Fort Pierce Inlet was, in 1995, designated one of the nation's "Best Beaches," and rightly so. You can walk for miles along the shore, fish in the surf, swim, or enjoy a picnic. *Open 8–sunset daily.* ☎ *468-3985.* ♿. *Admission, $3.25 per vehicle.*

Cinderella Castle in the Magic Kingdom of Walt Disney World

Section III

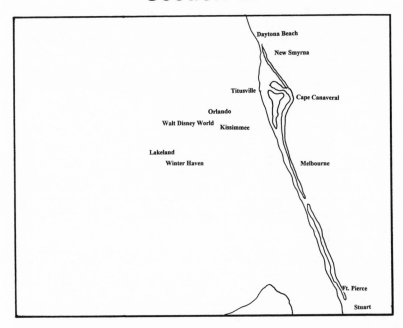

ORLANDO, CENTRAL FLORIDA AND THE CENTRAL EAST COAST

Central Florida is where you'll find the nation's number-one tourist attraction, plus a half-dozen more that are almost as popular. The great theme parks are Walt Disney World (The Magic Kingdom, EPCOT, and MGM Studios), Sea World, and Universal Studios—each a daytrip by itself. They draw more visitors to central Florida than all other attractions combined. To the east, the beaches and temptations of the Space Coast offer even more excitement and opportunities. To the south and west, still more.

Orlando is the center of this exciting world. Kissimmee and St. Cloud just to the south represent Florida's equestrian heritage. Ocala, to the north, is where you'll find Florida's great flatlands and the Ocala National Forest, a vast wildlife refuge and the largest sandpine forest in the world. In Lake County, you can taste the best locally-produced wine in the state, or spend a quiet hour or two horseback riding through Florida's most scenic countryside. Farther south, the roar of racing engines might draw you to the famous Sebring Motor Racing Circuit. For the outdoor sportsman, there are hundreds of lakes, rivers, and creeks that offer the finest freshwater fishing in the nation. This is particularly so in Lake County, where you can fish for world-class bass and other species.

Orlando was first settled in the early 1840s by army volunteers who liked the area so much that they remained after the Seminole Indian Wars ended. By 1860 it became a thriving little community in the center of a great cotton plantation. The Civil War brought hard times to Orlando and central Florida. With the slaves gone, and no way of transporting cotton to the markets, the industry collapsed.

To make matters worse, in 1871 an intense rainstorm washed away the crops, leaving cattle as the only industry in the area. And so Orlando became a frontier town in the tradition of the Wild West. The streets turned into war zones, where the actual number of people killed remains unknown. Rustling became a major enterprise. So bad was the situation that to restore order martial law had to be declared. By the late 1800s a new industry was introduced to Orlando, the citrus groves, the first of which were planted in 1865 and showed some promise. But it wasn't until the Kennedy Years in the middle of the 20th century that things really took off when space exploration came to Cape Canaveral, just 50 miles to the east. This was the event that changed the course of Orlando's history. By 1965 Walt Disney announced his plans to convert more than 27,000 acres of swampland into a "Magic Kingdom." Walt Disney World opened in 1971 and the city's growth took off like one of the rockets blasting off at neighboring Cape Canaveral.

Today, Orlando is among the world's top tourist destinations, always bustling and crowded, where long lines of waiting people are the norm rather than the exception. Perhaps that's as much a part of the magic as the famous little cartoon characters that brought them here.

GETTING THERE:

By Air: Almost all major airlines, domestic and worldwide, serve Orlando International Airport, south of the city at the junction of Highway 436 and the Bee Line Expressway.

By Car: Interstate 4 serves the city east and west, connecting Orlando with Tampa and St. Petersburg, and with Daytona Beach where it connects with Interstate 95, the main route north and south along the east coast. Interstate 4 also provides a fast route through the city. Florida's Turnpike—a toll road—links Orlando with West Palm Beach, Ft. Lauderdale, and Miami. To the north, the Turnpike connects with Interstate 75, the main route into Florida from the north. The Bee Line Expressway—another toll road—makes the connection between Orlando and Cape Canaveral. Highway 50—Colonial Drive—is an east/west route that passes through the downtown area connecting the smaller cities on the Gulf Coast to those on the Atlantic coast. Finally, Highway 436—Semoran Boulevard—swings in a great arc northwest from the airport and the Bee Line Expressway in the southeast to Highway 441 near Apopka; it's an alternative route to Interstate 4.

By Bus: The **Greyhound/Trailways** bus terminal is off Highway 50 and the John Young Parkway at 555 Magruder Avenue. ☎ 800-231-2222, or 292-3422.

By Train: There are two **Amtrak** stations: one at 1400 Sligh Boulevard, the other 150 West Morris Boulevard in Winter Park. **Auto Train,** which brings both passengers and their cars from Lorton, Virginia, uses Sanford station 22 miles north of Orlando. ☎ 800-USA-RAIL.

GETTING AROUND:

Although navigating Orlando is usually easy, it can also be a hectic, sometimes hair-raising, experience. Rarely are the roads quiet. The downtown area is laid out in a grid, with north/south numbers starting at Central Avenue, and east/west numbers beginning at Orange Avenue. **Rush hours** are 6:30–9, and 4–6:30. If you can, stay off the roads, especially the urban freeways, during those times.

Parking is rarely a problem. Metered spaces are available on the streets, and there are plenty of commercial garages and lots. Charges run from $1 per hour to $12 for a full day.

Public Transport—often the cheapest, but not always the most convenient way of getting around—is handled by **Lynx,** a tri-county authority that operates buses over more than 30 routes throughout the region. The basic fare is 75¢; transfers cost 10¢. ☎ 841-8240 for schedules. **I-Ride** is a new public transport service operating in and around the International Drive area on a circular route that begins at Sea World and runs north just past Wet 'n Wild at American Way. the adult fare is 75¢ per ride, and children under 12 can ride free if accompanied by an adult.

Rental Cars are available from most of the national companies. Rates, however, vary with the seasons, so be sure to reserve early to get the best deal.

Taxis are plentiful, but expensive: a trip to or from the airport will cost $22, but trying to get from one side of the city to the other is costly. The charge is $2.65 for the first mile and $1.40 for each additional mile. Yellow, ☎ 422-4455; Checker, ☎ 699-9999; City, ☎ 422-5151; Ace Metro, ☎ 855-0564.

ACCOMMODATIONS:

Though there are more than 83,000 hotel rooms available in the Orlando area, unless you make a reservation you might not be able to find a place to stay. Plan early and be sure to reserve well in advance. Accommodations range from neat little mom-and-pop bed & breakfast inns to the vast resort complexes of the major hotel chains. The price you can expect to pay depends on the season and the type of accommodations you're looking for. You might prefer a room out of town, or at a budget motel, for as little as $40 per night. For a room close to the center of the action, say on Republic Drive in Orlando, you can expect to pay between $90 and $120 per night. A room at Disney's Contemporary Resort at the Magic Kingdom will cost upwards of $150 per night. It pays to shop around; there are some great deals to be had if you take the time to dig a little. Visit in the fall and you can get a room at the Hampton at Universal Studios for as little $54 per night for two persons.

PRACTICALITIES:

The **Area Code** for Orlando is 407.

The **climate** inland is usually hot and humit, except during the winter months, December through February, when it's quite comfortable with daytime highs in the low 70s. During the summer, however, things can become decidedly sticky and the fiery sun will quickly burn unprotected skin. Afternoon rainstorms are frequent.

Opening times are in sync with the experience. Most attractions are open daily the year round, although a some do close early on Sundays.

Entrance fees run from very reasonable to expensive, but then, this is the entertainment capital of Florida, so be prepared to spend on a grand scale.

TOURIST INFORMATION:

Orlando/Orange County Convention and Visitors Bureau, 6700 Forum Drive, Suite 100, Orlando, FL 32821-8087. ☎ 363-5800, fax 363-5899.

The Tourist Information Center at the Mercado Mediterranean Village, 8445 International Drive is open daily 8–8.

Greater Orlando Chamber of Commerce, 75 East Ivanhoe Boulevard, Orlando, FL 32804, ☎ 425-1234.

FOOD AND DRINK:

Dining out is an important part of the total Orlando experience. There are hundreds of restaurants and cafés to choose from, many are good, some are just average. Some of the better choices are listed with each daytrip. While these are a good place to start, half the fun on any vacation is discovering something new, so don't be afraid to explore.

Downtown Orlando

SUGGESTED TOURS AND LOCAL ATTRACTIONS:

First, let's begin by saying, "you can't do it all." There's so much to see and do, so many exciting attractions, and so many compelling areas in west central Florida that it would take forever to experience them all. So how to do it? When you decided on Orlando you did so for a reason, and that was very likely to visit Walt Disney World. These three parks will probably loom large in your plans and account for several days. To make the best of the rest takes serious planning. This section of the book contains 10 great daytrips for your consideration, including the Magic Kingdom and EPCOT. Browse through them first to see what takes your fancy. Some daytrips feature only a single attraction, such as Sea World. Most of them include several stops, along with some special attractions that you can manage in a single day. You don't have to visit them all, just select the stops that interest you. To help, there's an estimate of the amount of time you're likely spend at any given location.

Trip 12

Orlando

There are a great many attractions in the Orlando area; many are located on International Drive. Only the smaller ones are described below, and there are plenty more for you to discover for yourself. The large operations, such as Universal Studios, are listed separately as each is a complete daytrip in itself.

GETTING THERE:

PRACTICALITIES:

TOURIST INFORMATION:
   See pages 80–82.

FOOD AND DRINK:
   Orlando abounds in interesting restaurants; here are just a few:
   La Normandie, 2021 E. Colonial Drive (SR-50), east of US-17. French cuisine, reservations suggested, ☎ 896-9976. $$–$$$.
   Pebble's Downtown, 17 West Church St. near Orange Ave. A casual, lively place for American cuisine. ☎ 839-0892. $$.
   Café Europa, Church Street Market, upper level. Eastern European dishes in a café setting. ☎ 872-3388. $$.
   Crabby Bill's, 925 N. Semoran Blvd., SR-436 near SR-50. Crabs and all other kinds of seafood in a casual setting. ☎ 273-4422. $–$$.

LOCAL ATTRACTIONS:
   A good place to begin is located five miles south of the Bee Line Expressway, on Highway 441 at 14501 South Orange Blossom Trail. **Gatorland** (1) is a theme park where Florida's most famous resident is king. Here you'll find marshes and swamps, the natural habitat of the alligator—and there are more than 5,000 of them here—along with crocodiles, snakes, and numerous other reptiles. Your visit will include three exciting shows: Gator Jumparoo, Gator Wrestlin' "cracker style," and Snakes of Florida. You'll also visit the Alligator Breeding Marsh and observation tower, ride a narrow-gauge railway and, if you feel so inclined, visit Pearl's Smokehouse for some smoked gator ribs and deep-fried gator nuggets. If you've never seen an alligator close-up and ugly, you should definitely give this attraction a try.

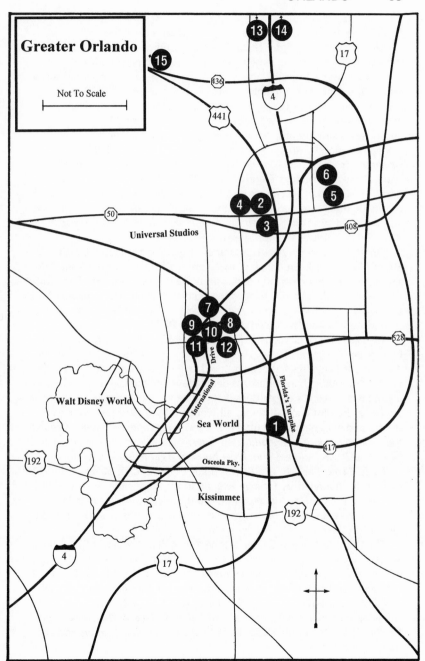

Open 8–dusk daily; allow at least three hours. ☎ *855-5496 or 800-393-JAWS.* & *Adults $11.95, seniors $9.56, children 3–9 $8.95.*

Church Street Station (2), at 129 West Church Street, is downtown Orlando's flagship dining, entertainment, and shopping complex.

At the corner of Church Street and Orange Avenue, **Terror on Church Street** (3) is a high-tech haunted house with a difference. Fun? Yes. Scary? Yes. It would be difficult to imagine that even the most skeptical visitor could get through all 23 rooms without being startled a few times. There are no real ghosts, ghouls or goblins, but the clever use of special effects and trained actors, combined with the element of surprise, make the tour one full of suspense and fright. Each room has its own theme. Some feature famous scary characters, such as Freddy from *Nightmare on Elm Street*, and Hannibal "The Cannibal" Lechter from *Silence of the Lambs*, while others rely on scenes of shock and terror to do the work. Children under 10 must be accompanied by an adult. *Open 7 p.m.–midnight daily. Allow up to an hour.* ☎ *649-3327. Adults $12, children under 17 $10.*

On the same street, between Orange Avenue and Garland, the **Church Street Market** (4) is an enticing, two-story marketplace with 17 specialty shops and six restaurants, all situated around a central courtyard. The courtyard itself is a pleasant diversion with street lamps, benches, fountains, and cobbled brick walkways. The Market connects to Church Street Station via a second story footbridge. *Open daily 10–late.* ☎ *872-2300.*

The **Harry P. Leu Gardens** (5) are just north of the Church Street Historical District and Highway 50, at 1920 North Forest Avenue—go via Virginia Avenue. The Leu home has been restored to its original condition, that of the late 1800s. Although the house, its decorations and furnishings are interesting in themselves, it's the gardens that will be the focus of your visit. There are more than 50 acres of them, all wonderfully landscaped with plants, shrubs, and trees native to central Florida. *Gardens open 9–5 daily. Guided tours of the house are conducted Tues.–Sat. Allow at least an hour.* ☎ *846-0770.* &. *Adults $3, includes house and gardens; Children 6–16 $1.*

Loch Haven Park (6) is also just north of the Church Street Historical District. It's bounded by Orange Avenue to the west, Mills Avenue to the east, and is bisected by Princeton Boulevard, which is how to enter the area. The park contains three museums and a theater, and is considered to be Orlando's cultural center. The museums are:

The Orlando Science Center & John Young Planetarium, at 810 Rollins Street, houses a hands-on natural history and physical science complex with exhibits that include Space, Waterworks, the Trading Center, the Tunnel of Discovery, and Nature Works. The Planetarium pretty well takes care of the world of space exploration and the stars. *Open 9–5 daily, noon–5 on Sun. Allow at least two hours, more if you intend to take in the planetarium.* ☎ *896-7151.* &. *Adults $6.50, includes the planetarium; seniors and children 3–11 $5.50.*

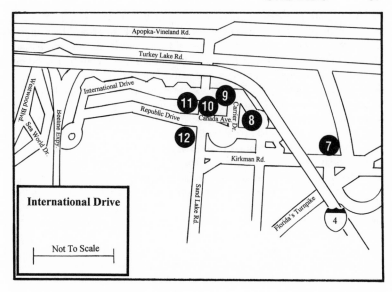

The **Orange County Historical Museum** is at 812 Rollins Street. Here you'll find a great number of Victorian exhibits, artifacts, and memorabilia that interpret the history of Orange County and Orlando. There's a rendering of a turn-of-the-century country store, a hot-type newspaper print shop, and other period exhibits. There's also a fully restored fire station with trucks and equipment, all circa 1926. *Open 9–5 daily, Sun. noon–5. Allow at least an hour.* ☎ *897-6350.* &. *Adults $2, seniors $1.50, children 6–12, $1.*

The **Orlando Museum of Art**, at 2416 Mills Avenue, offers its permanent collection of 19th- and 20th-century paintings and sculpture, as well as a number of exhibits containing some fine examples of African and pre-Columbian art. For the kids, the Art Encounter presents an enjoyable hands-on approach. *Open 9–5 Tues.–Sat., noon–5 Sun. Allow at least an hour.* ☎ *896-4231. Adults $4, children 4–11 $2.*

From Orange Avenue, travel west on Highway 50 to Kirkman Road and turn south toward the International Drive district; the **Mystery Fun House** (7) is just across the way from the Universal Studios main gate. The 15-room building features a miniature golf course called Jurassic Putt, a shooting gallery, a trolley ride, a game room, an Old Tyme Photo, a restaurant, and a gift shop. Also featured are the Forbidden Temple and Starbase Omega "The Ultimate Laser Game." *Open 10–9 daily. Allow at least two hours.* ☎ *351-3355.* &. *Admission charge.*

Wet 'n Wild (8) is at 6200 International Drive, off Interstate 4 at Exit 30A. Not an attraction for everyone, but more for the young and young at heart, this water park features a variety of waterslides and flumes, a giant wave pool, a water playground, and a cable-operated surf board ride. The "Surge" is something special: a multi-passenger slide that hurtles around more than 600 feet of curves and bends for a ride that should make your hair stand on end. For the kids, there's a playground with miniature versions of the attractions in the rest of the park. There's also a restaurant on the property, picnic facilities, showers, and locker rooms. *Open daily, but you'll need to call for times. Allow at least a half-day.* ☎ *351-3200 or 800-992-WILD.* ⚇. *Adults $23.95, seniors over 54 $11.98, children 3–9 $18.95.*

Ripley's Believe it or Not—Orlando Museum (9) is just down the road on International Drive at number 8201. There's always something new inside, from the odd to the unusual to the bizarre and the macabre. The Moving Bridge is not moving at all, but the pictures on the wall are, thus giving the illusion of motion. It's great. *Open 9–11 daily. Allow at least an hour.* ☎ *363-4418.* ⚇. *Adults $9.95, children 4–12 $6.95.*

If you're a railway enthusiast, you won't want to miss **Trainland of Orlando** (10) just across from Ripley's at 8255 International Drive. Here, a one-half-inch scale model railway layout winds its way through a wonderful world in miniature in an indoor garden complete with a seven-foot waterfall, trestles, tunnels, and bridges, with sound effects and lighting. There are also displays and exhibits featuring model toy trains and rolling stock from the turn of the century up to the present. The Trainland Express, an old steam train, leaves the station for a 20-minute tour of the complex and a number of nearby buildings on International Drive. *Open 10–10 daily, 10–6 on Sun. Allow at least an hour.* ☎ *363-9002.* ⚇. *Adults $6, seniors $5, children 3–13 $4, train rides $2 extra.*

ORLANDO AT NIGHT:

Your daytrip around Orlando doesn't have to end early. There are a number of attractions that open only when the sun goes down. These will usually include dinner and a show. You might like to try one or both of the following:

King Henry's Feast (11) is just down the road from Trainland at 8984 International Drive. If you've never been to one of these period dinner theaters, you've missed a special treat. Here, you're transported back in time to the Merry Old England of King Henry VIII. The feast takes place in the banqueting hall of a great castle, and is presided over by the king himself. It seems it's his birthday, and he's looking for a seventh wife so, ladies, watch out. The festivities include a court jester—lots of fun and comedy—a sword and fire swallower, and other court entertainers; all very much in the tradition of the late Middle Ages. And the food is good, too. *Open nightly the year-round but times vary with the season;* ☎ *351-5151 for schedules and reservations. Allow at least three hours. Adults $34.95, children 3–11 $21.95.*

If you're a "who-done-it" fan (and even if you're not), an evening at **Sleuths Mystery Dinner Theater** (12) is an experience you won't forget. Take Carrier Drive from International Drive, go two blocks east to Republic Drive and turn right. Sleuths is at 7508 Republic. The three-hour show features a murder mystery that's played out while you eat dinner; the audience participates in solving the puzzle. It's a fun experience with lots of laughs, and the ending is never quite what you expect. *Shows 6 and/or 9 p.m. daily. Allow three hours. Reservations are required.* ☎ *363-1985.* ♿. *Adults $34.95, children 3–11 $22.95.*

ADDITIONAL ATTRACTIONS:

Take Interstate 4 north out of downtown Orlando and drive 15 miles to the junction with Highway 46, where you turn left. The 4,636-acre **Lower Wekiva River State Reserve** (13) is five miles to the west on the St. Johns Creek, the Blackwater Creek, and the Wekiva River. The park maintains a wide variety of plant and wildlife communities. It's a place where lovers of nature and the great outdoors can find all sorts of rare species not readily found elsewhere. The unique feature of the reserve is its system of backwater creeks, streams, and wetlands that provide habitats for alligators, otters, wood storks, sandhill cranes, and even black bears. Activities you can enjoy include hiking, canoeing, bird watching, and wildlife photography. *Open 8– sunset daily.* ☎ *330-6725.* ♿. *Admission $3.25 per vehicle.*

Take Interstate 4 north from downtown Orlando to its junction with Highway 434, then go west on Wekiva Springs Road to **Wekiva Springs State Park** (14); it's just beyond the city limits, 10 miles from the city center. The park encompasses an area of wild and scenic beauty resembling the central Florida that was home to the Timucuan Indians of long ago. It's the headwater of the Wekiva River in an area full of lush, green vegetation. Here you can observe nature in all its natural splendor. From wetland forests bordering the creeks to the dry, sandy pinelands, the area teems with plant and animal life. The Wekiva River flows eastward for a short distance where it is joined by the Rock Springs Run. Together they flow 15 miles to meet the St. Johns River to the northeast. The spring is formed by the rushing waters of underground rivers flowing through limestone caverns beneath Florida's central ridge.

Facilities include restrooms, some 13 miles of nature and hiking trails, picnic areas with tables and grills, and a concession stand where you can get a snack and soft drinks.

If you like to fish you'll find there are plenty of largemouth bass, bluegill, and redbreast sunfish, both in the Wekiva River and the Rock Springs Run. You can rent a canoe or head out on foot, hiking or bird watching. Picnickers won't find a more pleasant spot than this. *Open 8–sunset daily.* ☎ *884-2009.* ♿. *Admission $3.25 per vehicle.*

From downtown Orlando, take Highway 441 northwest to its junction with Highway 435 just beyond the city limits and turn north. **Rock Springs Run State Reserve** (15) is five miles farther on. The more than 12 miles of river frontage, loaded with sand pine scrub, pine flatwoods, bayheads, and swamps here on the Wekiva River provide the varied and diverse range of natural habitats that are strictly managed so as not to endanger the fragile ecosystem. It's a wild and woolly natural area. If you're the outdoorsy type, a visit to the Reserve is a must. Hiking, canoeing, and backpacking are part of the reserve's recreational activities, but you'll also find plenty of solitude.

Hunters might be interested to know that from time to time, special deer hunts are organized by the Florida Game and Freshwater Fish Commission. ☎ *the Park Service at 383-3311 for details and reservations. Open 8–sunset daily. Admission $3.25 per vehicle.*

*Walt Disney World: The Magic Kingdom

Walt Disney World is much more than Mickey and his friends. It's a world apart, divided into three parts: The Magic Kingdom, EPCOT, and MGM Studios. Each is brilliantly innovative in its own way. It would be easy to get carried away with flattering descriptions of these magnificent attractions, but the following pages will stick to practical advice for visitors. To appreciate these wonders, you'll just have to see them for yourself.

Taken in its entirety, Walt Disney World is hardly a daytrip; rather it's a vacation all its own. You could, however, experience one or possibly two of its components in a single day, and have a great time doing it. For that reason, each of its segments is treated here as a separate one-day adventure, beginning with The Magic Kingdom and continuing with the others on pages 96 and 99.

GETTING THERE:

From Orlando, you can enter Walt Disney World either from Interstate 4 or Highway 192 in Kissimmee. For the latter, take Highway 17 south and then turn west to the main entrance.

GETTING AROUND:

Navigating the complex and properties is fairly easy, given that everything is clearly posted. Transport is provided from the parking areas to the entrance at Disney-MGM Studios and EPCOT, as well as to the Transportation and Ticket Center at Walt Disney World. From there, you can hop on the monorail or shuttle coaches for transportation between all areas.

PRACTICALITIES:

The **Area Code** is the same as for Orlando, 407.

Parking and Pets: Parking is $5 per day. Free transport is available from the parking areas to the Transportation and Ticket Center. There are kennels located at the Magic Kingdom where, for a nominal fee that includes care and food, you can leave your pet, knowing that it will be well looked after.

Cost: The following prices **do not** include taxes:

A one-day, one-park ticket is $38.50 for adults, $31 for children ages 3–9. It covers admission to all the attractions in the Magic Kingdom, EPCOT, or Disney-MGM Studios.

A four-day Park Hopper Pass is $144 for adults, $115 for children ages 3-9. It includes unlimited admission to all the attractions in the Magic Kingdom, EPCOT, and Disney-MGM Studios for four days with any combination of parks per day.

A four-day Value Pass is $129 for adults, $103 for children ages 3–9. It provides admission for one day at the Magic Kingdom, one day at EPCOT, one day at Disney-MGM Studios, and one day at any park of your choice.

A five-day World-Hopper Pass is $196, $157 for children ages 3–9. It provides unlimited admission to all the attractions in the Magic Kingdom, EPCOT, and Disney-MGM Studios on any five days and any combination of parks. It also includes admission to Disney's other attractions: Typhoon Lagoon, River Country, Blizzard Beach, Discovery Island, and Pleasure Island for a seven-day period beginning on the first day you use the pass.

Unused tickets to attractions are valid for an unlimited period of time. No refunds for any reason at all, including bad weather, so take note of the forecast before you go.

Opening hours: The three major parks—The Magic Kingdom, EPCOT, and Disney-MGM Studios—open daily at 9. Closing times vary from park to park.

Expect large crowds and long lines, especially when school is out and over holiday periods.

Physical considerations: A day, let alone four days, at any of the major Disney parks can be physically exhausting, so take it easy and rest often. Of the eight or ten hours you might spend at The Magic Kingdom, seven to nine will be outdoors under a hot sun. Therefore, it's essential that you wear a hat and use a heavy sun screen.

Children: If you are traveling with youngsters, place an ID card in each child's pocket. These should include the child's name, parent or guardian's name, hotel or residence and the phone number. You should also make arrangements to meet them at the Information Counter should you become separated.

Tourist Information: Walt Disney World Resort Information, PO Box 10040, Lake Buena Vista, FL 32830-0040, ☎ 824-4321.

FOOD AND DRINK:

No problems here, just bring plenty of cash and take your pick from one or more of the many restaurants and cafés scattered around the Kingdom; however there's one restaurant you shouldn't miss. If you can, make a dinner reservation at **Cinderella Castle**, and do it as early as possible. It's quite an experience to eat in the Great Hall.

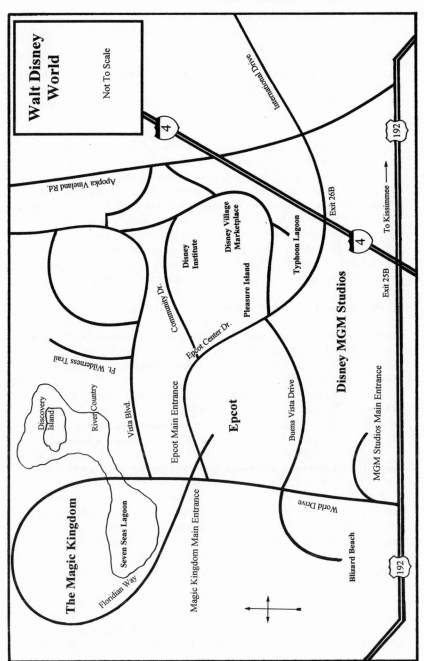

SUGGESTED TOUR AND ATTRACTIONS:

Of all the advice you may receive from friends and travel agents, there's one bit of information that can help you avoid the large crowds inside the Magic Kingdom and make your day a little less hectic. **Get there early, before it opens and when you enter the park go straight to the far side, then work your way back toward the entrance.** Most people begin on Main Street and work their way in, but that's where the crowds are. If you start there you'll spend most of the day waiting in line at one attraction after another.

As you probably already know, the Magic Kingdom is devoted mainly to the world of Disney's animated cartoons and their characters. It includes 41 major adventures on the 100-acre site: seven lands with attractions, restaurants and shops based on favorite Disney themes of fantasy, yesterday and tomorrow. These are **Adventureland, Liberty Square, Frontierland, Main Street USA, Fantasyland, Tomorrowland, and Mickey's Toontown.** And, with each new movie, so the Kingdom expands to include it.

You'll arrive at the Magic Kingdom either by ferryboat or monorail train. You'll then pass through the turnstiles and make your way past the old-fashioned Main Street Railroad station. From there it's onward to one of the seven happy lands of yesterday, tomorrow, and fantasy. Here's what you can expect:

Main Street, USA: This is America as it was 100 years ago with a glitzy movie house and Ice Cream Parlor. At one end of the street is the Town Square, with its City Hall and tree-shaded areas for concerts by the Walt Disney World Band. At the other end, beautiful Cinderella Castle—a fairytale palace brought to life—towers 18 stories above Central Plaza and the entire Magic Kingdom.

Adventureland: Here, you'll visit the Gigantic **Swiss Family Robinson Treehouse**, re-created from the movie, board a boat for a **Jungle Cruise**, see the amazing Tiki birds and singing flowers in **Tropical Serenade**, and enjoy the greatest swashbuckling adventure of all as you explore a battered fort and discover **Pirates of the Caribbean**. There, you'll board a buccaneer launch, travel through a mysterious grotto and plunge down a waterfall to find yourself in the midst of a pirate battle for control of a harbor town.

Frontierland: Beside the Rivers of America is the land of frontier America—the Old West with its boardwalks, brass-railed saloons, and wooden forts. It features the **Country Jamboree,** the zaniest troupe of singing bears ever assembled, with real old-time music and a foot-stomping beat. In the **Diamond Horseshoe Saloon Revue & Medicine Show** you can see dance-hall ladies and elegant gents sing and dance. There's **Tom Sawyer Island** with Injun Joe's Cave, the Magnetic Mystery Mine, and the old Fort Sam Clemens, all reached on a log raft. **Big Thunder Mountain** takes you for a wild ride on a runaway mine train, and young frontiersmen and frontierswomen can try their hand in the **Big Thunder Shooting Gallery**. The tallest peak in the Magic Kingdom, **Splash Mountain**, features a log ride with one of the world's longest flume drops—a five-story, 47-degree descent reaching speeds of 40 miles per hour that plunges into the Disney classic, **Song of the South**.

Liberty Square: The true spirit of America is brought to life in the shadow of a giant oak known as Liberty Tree. Here, you'll visit the **Hall of Presidents** to experience some of the most significant moments in American history through the magic of three-dimensional Audio-Animatronics. Nearby on a graveyard hill is the ominous **Haunted Mansion** with the liveliest collection of ghosts you could ever imagine. You'll explore the house and its ancient rooms in a "doom-buggy." After that, you can board an old-time stern-wheeler or a Davy Crockett canoe to make the journey 'round the bend past the Indian camps and the settler's shack.

Fantasyland, perhaps the happiest of all the Disney lands, is the one inspired by the animated film classics. Here, in the courtyard of Cinderella Castle are the **Mad Tea Party, Dumbo the Flying Elephant, Snow White's Adventures, Peter Pan's Flight,** and **Mr. Toad's Wild Ride.** In the center of it all is the magnificent, gigantic **Cinderella's Golden Carrousel**. Most charming of all is **It's a Small World** where hundreds of doll-like figures sing and dance in their native costumes.

New Tomorrowland features a glimpse into a city of the future as envisioned by the science-fiction writers and movie makers. The main thoroughfare of this city is the **Avenue of Planets**, home to the **Tomorrowland Interplanetary Convention Center** where the X-S Tech, a mysterious corporation from a distant planet, is displaying a new teleportation device that brings the audience face-to-face with an alien in **ExtraTERRORestrial Alien Encounter**. Across the way, **The Timekeeper** takes you on a hysterical blast through time in Circle-Vision 360 format. High above Rockettower Plaza, you'll board a rocket on the **Astro Orbiter** for a ride through space. Then, if action, speed, and perpetual motion is what you're looking for, you can blast off into the night skies of **Space Mountain** for a twisting, diving "return-to-earth" ride aboard a miniature space shuttle.

Mickey's Toontown Fair is the newest attraction in the Magic Kingdom. It brings the fair to Mickey's neighborhood located between Fantasyland and New Tomorrowland. Here you'll have opportunities to meet and pose for pictures with Mickey and all his friends. And you can enjoy the charms of Mickey's bungalow, Minnie's House, Donald's Boat, and Goofy's Coaster.

All of this is only the beginning of a daytrip to the Magic Kingdom. There's also live entertainment in every land, lots of fascinating shops and stores where you can buy souvenirs, and more than 30 restaurants and cafés. At the end of the day, the concept of Mickey Mouse and all his friends, cartoon and historical characters, is celebrated daily in the **Mickey Mania** Parade. You daytrip ends with a magnificent display of fireworks against the backdrop of Cinderella Castle.

Walt Disney World: EPCOT Center

The acronym EPCOT stands for Experimental Prototype Community of Tomorrow. It's the name of another Disney World park, three miles south of the Magic Kingdom, that encompasses two major themed areas: **Future World** and **World Showcase.** In one, guests can shrink in horror in their theater seats as well as try out the latest in technology, including personal communicators, high-definition TV, and virtual reality. In the other, they can sample the sights and cultures of countries around the world as they stroll from continent to continent. There's something exciting around every corner at EPCOT, from "Honey, I Shrunk the Audience" to visits to exotic destinations.

GETTING AROUND:

Navigating the complex is fairly easy as everything is clearly signposted. Transport is provided from the parking areas to the entrance at Disney-MGM Studios and EPCOT, and to the Transportation and Ticket Center at Walt Disney World. From there, you can hop on the monorail or shuttle coach. Once inside EPCOT, walking is the way to go.

PRACTICALITIES:

For entrance fees and transportation information, see page 91–92.

You can receive updated information about waiting times for EPCOT shows on the **Tip Board** located in the southwest quadrant of Innovations Plaza, near the Future World fountain.

Because entertainment in the World Showcase countries is an important part of the experience and is constantly changing, be sure to pick up the "**EPCOT Guidemap**" at the park entrance and try to time your daytrip around the "don't miss" shows. One of the best is "IllumiNations," a nightly fireworks and laser light show launched from the World Showcase Lagoon.

World Showcase and Future World have different opening hours. Future World, at the front of EPCOT, opens earlier in the morning and closes in the mid-evening. World Showcase opens in the late morning and stays open until IllumiNations begins.

EPCOT Center

TOURIST INFORMATION:

Walt Disney World Resort Information, PO Box 10040, Lake Buena Vista, FL 32830-0040, ☎ 824-4321.

FOOD AND DRINK:

The restaurants of World Showcase offer cuisine from around the globe, from traditional Italian fare at Alfredo's in the Italy Showcase to chicken couscous in Morocco's Restaurant Marrakech.

In Future World, the restaurants feature regional American favorites from gourmet pizza to fresh seafood.

All EPCOT restaurants offer children's value meals and can accommodate special dietary needs with advance notice.

If all you're interested in is a quick bite, there are plenty of fast-food outlets, from Mexican tacos at a waterside dining area to grilled chicken in The Land pavilion food court.

For serious dining, reservations are a must. Your first stop should be at Guest Relations to make lunch or dinner arrangements. On some days, restaurants may be fully booked by 10 a.m.

SUGGESTED TOUR:

Future World: Spaceship Earth, a shiny 180-foot-high geosphere, is Future World's landmark behind which is a showplace for human achievements. Inside, scenes depict life as it might appear in the 21st century's "Global Neighborhood." Crescent-shaped buildings just beyond Spaceship Earth to the south house **Innovations**, a showcase for future gadgets and gizmos, with hands-on exhibits that constantly change as new products and technologies are developed.

West of Spaceship Earth, **The Living Seas** offer a ride through a Caribbean coral reef contained in a tank 200 feet in diameter and 27 feet deep. **The Land** features the motion picture *"Circle of Life,"* an environmental fable starring several characters from *"The Lion King."* *"Living With the Land"* is a boat ride through greenhouses of the future, and the zany *"Food Rocks"* concert is all about good nutrition. **Journey Into Imagination** includes a new high-tech 3-D misadventure *"Honey, I Shrunk the Audience"*.

To the east, **Universe of Energy**, is a re-creation of the primeval world, complete with life-size dinosaurs and a look at sources of energy for the future. **Wonders of Life** features *"Body Wars,"* a flight-simulator thrill ride, and a variety of shows and activities that focus on and around human life. **Horizons** showcases scientific visions of the future, while the **General Motors Preview Center** provides a sneak peak at the development of an all-new automobile attraction scheduled to open in 1997.

World Showcase: Across World Showcase Lagoon, 11 nations offer distinctive wares, ethnic cuisine, shows, entertainment, and architecture representing their various cultures. Even the landscape changes from country to country as you make your way around the 1½-mile promenade.

Going in a clockwise direction: **Mexico** offers a boat ride through Mexican history accompanied by live mariachi bands. **Norway** takes you on a voyage through time beginning in a 10th- century Viking village. **China**, with a Circle-Vision 360 film, whisks you away to exotic sites such as Beijing's Forbidden City, Mongolia, and Shanghai. **Germany** feature towns along the Rhine river, while **Italy** provides a reproduction of the Doge's Palace and an outdoor theater. Next, **American Adventure** offers an ambitious show celebrating important moments in US history. Tranquil Oriental gardens and dancing are showcased in **Japan**. **Morocco** is where 19 Moroccan artists spent months re-creating the intricate, colorful tile-work of the North African country. **France** is the setting for a film tour through its cities and countryside, while the **United Kingdom** exhibits its flower gardens and cobbled streets. Finally, **Canada**, with entertainment by a bagpipe band and a Circle-Vision 360 film, takes you through some of its most picturesque regions.

Walt Disney World: MGM Studios

More than just a theme park, Disney-MGM is also a working TV and film studio. While the park's Hollywood Boulevard celebrates the dreamy era of Tinseltown's booming commercial district of the 1930s and '40s, Sunset Boulevard pays tribute to the theater district with colorful facades derived from famous landmarks such as the Beverly Wilshire Theater and Carthay Theater, where "**Snow White and the Seven Dwarfs**" premiered. Add the **Twilight Zone Tower of Terror** along with several other mind- blowing rides and thrills and you're in for a daytrip with a real difference.

GETTING AROUND:

Navigating the complex is fairly easy as everything is clearly marked. Transport is provided from the parking areas to the entrance at Disney-MGM Studios and EPCOT, and to the Transportation and Ticket Center at Walt Disney World. From there you can hop on the monorail or shuttle coach. Once inside the Studios, walking is the main mode of transportation.

PRACTICALITIES:

See pages 91–92.

TOURIST INFORMATION:

Walt Disney World Resort Information, PO Box 10040, Lake Buena Vista, FL 32830-0040, ☎ 824-4321.

FOOD AND DRINK:

The restaurants and cafés within the park are all a part of the adventure through Hollywood history and lifestyle.

> **The Brown Derby** faithfully recalls the landmark Hollywood restaurant and meeting place of the stars where gossip is accompanied by Cobb salad and fruitcake.

> **California Crazy**, on a quiet, lake serves snacks and desserts from buildings created in the form of a tramp steamer and a life-size dinosaur.

> **The Prime Time Café** takes you back into the kitchenettes of the 1950s sitcoms for dining atop laminated tables next to old-fashioned TVs tuned to reruns of long-ago shows.

Other themed restaurants include the **Sci-Fi Dine-In Theater Restaurant, Hollywood & Vine Cafeteria of the Stars, Mama Melrose's Ristorante Italiano, Backlot Express** and the **Disney-MGM Studios Commissary and Soundstage Restaurant** where you can meet with the stars of "*Aladdin*" and "*Pocahontas.*"

SUGGESTED TOUR:

Once beyond the massive gates and into the park, we recommend that you take the **Backstage Studio Tour**. It presents many aspects of film production in detail, along with sneak previews of the shows and films you'll be seeing on the screen and TV the following year. The innovative design of the park allows you to peek in at the shooting on state-of-the-art soundstages where such popular TV shows as "Full House" and "Wheel of Fortune" are made, along with feature films.

From the moment you enter the park, you'll feel as if you're right into the middle of the action. As you stroll along "Golden Age" Hollywood Boulevard the fine line between fiction and reality begins to blur. You'll meet detectives, starlets, cabbies, and cops. Even superstar memorabilia salesman Sid Cahuenga can be found wandering the street. All these "streetmosphere" actors are there to get you involved in their many tongue-in-cheek story plots throughout the day.

As for rides and thrills, there are enough to keep the family entertained all day.

A full-scale reproduction of the famous **Chinese Theater** is the gateway to the **Great Movie Ride**, Disney's most elaborate ever. That will immerse you into the charm, romance, intrigue, suspense, and blazing six-shooter action of some of Hollywood's most memorable action films.

You'll experience what it must be like to be the size of an ant as you wander through the giant blades of grass in the **Honey, I Shrunk the Kids Movie Set Adventure**. It's a jungle with hidden slides, caves, spider webs, a leaky hose, tunnels, ants and bees just as in the hit movie.

The Monster Sound Show features dozens of crazy contraptions and thingamajigs, each capable of producing a distinctive sound. They become tools of "audio artists" selected from the audience. The challenge is to add sound effects to a short movie mystery-comedy.

In the **Indiana Jones Epic Stunt Spectacular**, you'll see professional stunt men and women in a live action-packed show that re-creates the death-defying heroics of the classic adventure films starring Harrison Ford.

Star Tours is where you'll embark on the wildest galactic journey ever. The ride combines flight-simulator technology and a thrill-a-second motion picture to create a "Star Wars" experience that transforms the audience into passengers aboard an intergalactic spacecraft on a flight to the Moon of Endor.

The Twilight Zone Tower of Terror

Towering above it all at the end of Sunset Boulevard is Disney's newest attraction, **The Hollywood Tower Hotel and Twilight Zone of Terror.** It stands like an ominous beacon straight out of an episode of a television thriller, beckoning you to experience a mind-boggling plunge from the 13th floor right into the "Twilight Zone" itself.

Then there are the live shows to see, such as "Beauty and the Beast Live on Stage" and "Voyage of the Little Mermaid," which features dazzling special effects combined with puppets, Audio-Animatronic figures, live performers, and clips from the actual films.

Finally, the perfect end to a perfect day, the **"Toy Story Parade"** takes over Hollywood Boulevard daily in a combination of dance and humor with a brigade of larger-than-life classic toys including Mr. Potato Head, the Green Army Men, Woody the Cowboy, and Buzz Lightyear—all from Disney's completely computer-animated hit film.

Trip 16

*Sea World

Sea World of Florida is the world's most popular marine life park. Through the presentation of marine animal shows, hands-on attractions, and other programs, the park features more than 20 major attractions and entertaining exhibits, and is a window to the mysteries of the sea. Like all the major theme parks in the Orlando area, a visit here is a complete daytrip in itself.

GETTING THERE:

Sea World is at the intersection of Interstate 4 and the Bee Line Express, just 10 minutes south of downtown Orlando.

GETTING AROUND:

A daytrip to Sea World is strictly a walking tour. Many of the exhibits are indoors, but the major encounters take place outside so that much of your time will spent in the sunshine.

PRACTICALITIES:

Park Hours: Open the year-round from 9–7, with extended hours during the summer and holidays. Allow eight hours for the full tour.

Admission: Adults $39.95, children 3–9 $32.50, two and under free.

Parking is $5 per car, $8 per RV or camper. Discounts are available for AAA members, seniors, and military personnel. Take note of the exact location of your vehicle; the themed signs will be helpful.

Services: Strollers, lockers, and indoor climate-controlled pet kennels are available for rental.

Handicapped accessible: Wheelchairs are available for rental.

Clothing: Casual and comfortable dress is recommended. While Sea World is not a water park, you can get wet, especially at the Shamu Stadium.

Cameras and other electronic equipment should be protected from the salt water in all the animal pools.

Show Schedules are distributed at the Information Counter. To ensure a good seat, arrive at the shows at least 20 minutes before starting time.

Children: Those traveling with youngsters should place an ID card in each child's pocket. These should include the child's name, parent or guardian's name, hotel or residence, and the phone number. You should also make pre-arrangements to meet them at the Information Counter if you become separated.

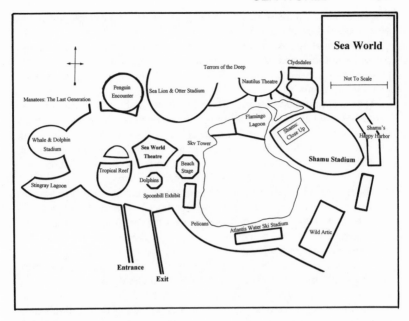

TOURIST INFORMATION:

Sea World, 7007 Sea World Drive, Orlando, FL 32821, ☎ 407-351-3600.

FOOD AND DRINK:

There are seven restaurants—**Mango Joe's, Buccaneer Barbecue, Bimini Bay Café, Chicken 'n Biscuit, Mama Stella's Italian Kitchen,** The **Dockside Grille,** and **Treasure Island Ice Cream**—and a number of snack bars and kiosks are scattered throughout the park.

The Aloha Polynesian Luau Dinner and Show is a South Seas themed evening out complete with traditional music, songs, dance, and fare from the islands of Hawaii. Reservations are required, ☎ 407-351-3600 or 800-227-8048.

SUGGESTED TOUR:

Pick up your show schedule at the Information Counter by the entrance. From there, you'll make your way around in a clockwise direction. The major attractions are, in no particular order:

Wild Arctic is a thrilling, motion-based flight over the frozen north where you'll be exposed to the beauty and dangers of Arctic exploration. Stepping down from a simulated helicopter ride, you'll enter the frozen world of Base Station Wild Arctic and encounter the real animals that live there, including beluga whales, walruses, harbor seals, polar bears, and two playful polar bears named Klondike and Snow.

Baywatch at Sea World brings the television screen to life in an action-packed water show featuring personal watercraft, water ski and aerial stunts, pyrotechnics, acrobatics, and musical numbers all set within a Baywatch-themed adventure.

Shamu Stadium and Shamu: Close Up! Here, at the 1.7- million-gallon natural killer-whale habitat, you'll enjoy watching the great black-and-white whale and his friends perform—you're sure to get wet in the process—and get closer to Shamu than you ever thought possible. You'll learn about playtimes and training sessions, and experience the successful breeding program in killer whales at the marine mammal nursery.

Shamu: World Focus combines live action and video imagery in a powerful new killer whale presentation. Through the use of ShamuVision, visitors are transported to remote locations around the world to observe killer whales in the wild, and then treated to a spectacular underwater ballet.

Mermaids, Myths and Monsters is Sea World's high-energy, nighttime extravaganza, choreographed to festive music, which combines state-of-the-art fireworks, laser and laser-graphics animation with waterscreen technology. Check your show schedule for performances.

Pacific Point Preserve is a 2½-acre natural setting that closely duplicates the rocky, northern Pacific coast. It's also home to California sea lions as well as harbor and fur seals.

*Hotel Clyde and Seamore features an encounter with the park's hilarious sea lions, otters, and walruses in their comic show. The antics of the animals and their human counterparts are an experience you don't want to miss.

The **Whale and Dolphin Stadium** is where you can see false killer whales and Atlantic bottlenose dolphins perform amid funky tropical sets.

Manatees: The Last Generation? features an underwater look at Florida's most endangered species.

Dolphin Cove is the attraction's two-acre centerpiece, and home to a large community of Atlantic bottlenose dolphins. Featuring two-foot-high waves, a sandy beach, underwater viewing, and a man-made coral reef, this is without doubt the most innovative dolphin facility in the world.

Sea World's newest attraction, **Key West at Sea World**, presents all the entertainment, beauty and charm of the nation's southernmost city in a five-acre section designed to re-create the lush environment of the Florida Keys.

Other attractions include **Penguin Encounter**, home to hundreds of penguins. You can sit for hours and watch them play, dive, swim, and interact. **Shamu's Happy Harbor** is one for the kids, a three-acre playground. **Terrors of the Deep** features eels, barracuda, venomous and poisonous fish, and sharks. **Window to the Sea** takes you for a look at Sea World behind the scenes.

Visitors encounter a manatee

Two guided tours—each lasts 60 minutes—offer a little something extra, beyond the attractions at Sea World:

The **Polar Expedition Tour** takes you on an adventure from the North Pole to the South featuring a face-to-face encounter with a magellanic penguin, a visit behind the scenes at Sea World's Penguin Research Facility, and an exclusive view of the Wild Arctic support areas.

Bird's-Eye View is a stroll through the park that stops at more than 10 rare-bird habitats with a close-up look at the exotic birds, including a laughing kookaburra and a Tocco toucan; you'll be able to feed some of the birds, including ibis and geese, along the way.

Universal Studios

Universal Studios Florida is a major theme park, a venture of MCA Inc. and the London-based Rank Organization. It is also a working motion picture and television studio. The production facilities and movie-themed attractions place you right into the heart of the movies. Here, you'll experience the famous "Back Lot," the sound stages, realistic street scenes, and special movie sets. King Kong is here to astound you, an earthquake that rivals the real thing will shake you up, and "Jaws," the mighty white shark that terrorized Amity, haunts the waters of the lake, just as he did off the beaches in the famous movie. Add some interactive entertainment, a dozen or so movie character look-alikes, and some fine dining opportunities, and you have all the makings of a memorable daytrip. Allow at least eight hours.

GETTING THERE:

Universal is located in Orlando near the junction of Interstate 4 and the Florida Turnpike. The main entrance is approximately one-half mile north of I-4 on Kirkman Road (Highway 435). Take Interstate 4 to Exit 30-B to reach Kirkman Road. Another entrance is located on Turkey Lake Road, taking Interstate 4 to Exit 29 (Sand Lake). If traveling westbound on I-4, make a right on Sand lake and then a right onto Turkey Lake Road. If Traveling eastbound on I-4, make a left onto Sand Lake and then a right onto Turkey Lake Road.

GETTING AROUND:

As usual in a major theme park, once you get inside you'll probably have to walk, although strollers, wheelchairs, and electric carts may be rented. Being on your feet so long can make for a tiring day, so take it easy and don't rush. There's plenty see and do, and a whole day to do it in.

PRACTICALITIES:

The park opens daily at 9; closing times vary with the seasons.

Admission: One-Day Ticket: Adults $38.50 plus tax, children 3–9 $32.86, under three free. **Two-Day Ticket**: Adults $55 plus tax, children 3–9 $44, under three free.

Parking: $5 for cars, $7 RVs and trailers, valet parking $11.

The sun is hot and often overpowering, so be sure to use adequate sunscreen and wear sunglasses plus a hat.

Children: Those traveling with youngsters should place an ID card in each child's pocket. These should include the child's name, parent or guardian's name, hotel or residence and the phone number. You should also make arrangements to meet them at some specific location within the park should you become separated.

TOURIST INFORMATION:

Universal Studios Florida, 1000 Universal Studios Plaza, Orlando, FL 32835, ☎ 407-363-8000.

FOOD AND DRINK:

There are at least 18 restaurants and cafés, all at strategic locations around the park, so finding a place to eat will not be a problem. The amount of food you consume, however, might be. You'll find something to suit just about every taste, including fresh seafood, ethnic cuisine, ice cream, and snacks. Especially recommended are the **Chez Alcatraz**, the **Hard Rock Café**, the **Cartoon Café**, and the **Studio Stars Restaurant.**

SUGGESTED TOUR:

There's no one good way to experience a hassle-free visit to Universal Studios. To avoid the crowds, you might start at the far side of the park and work your way back toward the entrance, but that will only help in the short term. Here are the main attractions and what you can expect from them:

*Jaws: Well folks, you've suffered along with Chief Brody in the movie, now you can experience the great white shark for real. "Jaws" uses space-age underwater technology never before employed in any other attraction in the world. You'll not only be thrilled by the physical reality of the beast's attacks, but experience dramatic, multi-sensory special effects. The seven-acre lagoon holds five million gallons of water. The 32-foot, 3-ton killer shark is made of steel and fiberglass and has been outfitted with realistic latex skin. During relentless attacks throughout the six-minute adventure, it moves through the water at realistic speeds of up to 20 feet per second and attacks with power equal to that of a 727 jet engine. This ride presents an adventure that's as about real as it can get; don't miss it.

Back to the Future—The Ride: Known as a simulator ride, "Back To The Future" combines film with kinetic motion for realism and excitement. The combination of 70mm film, 80-foot- diameter hemispherical screens, multi-channel surround-sound, special effects, and hydraulically-activated dynamic motion creates a total multi-sensory experience like no other. The ride is the only attraction in the world to use two specially designed domed theaters with seven-story-high OMNIMAX screens adjacent to each other. The domes provide the largest projected image ever used in conjunction with a motion simulator. You'll ride through time in a DeLorean sports car— just like the one in the movie—surrounded by liquid nitrogen fog—a first in special effects—that gives the feeling of traveling through space.

Kongfrontation: King Kong is made from tons of steel, plastic, fabric, and 7,000 pounds of fur. He stands four stories tall and weighs six tons, and with an arm span of 54 feet is the largest computer-animated figure ever built. The giant ape performs 46 terrifyingly realistic motions. He can simulate a smash of his fist onto the top of the aerial tramway, the destruction of a flying helicopter, and lifting your tram car high into the air. Leading-edge technology enables the aerial tramway to drop downward, plummeting at 12 feet per second with 1.75 G's of acceleration through a set designed around Manhattan's lower east side as it was in 1976, the year of the second King Kong movie starring Jessica Lange and Jeff Bridges.

E.T. Adventure: Steven Spielberg created a host of new characters for this ride where 80 animated figures, 558 trees and bushes, and more than 300 plants inhabit the Green Planet. There are more than 3,300 miniature city buildings, 250 cars on the streets, 4,400 twinkling stars above, and 140 street lights illuminating the vast city beneath you as you take your flight. The thin line between reality and fantasy blurs, then disappears, as you soar home on a star-bound bike with E.T. to save his planet. It's an awesome and thrilling experience.

Earthquake: The Big One: This ride has all of the visual effects of a full-blown earthquake, and resets them every two minutes. More than 65,000 gallons of water are released and recycled every six minutes. The crashing subway train is the only one of its kind in the world. The falling roadway slab weighs 45,000 pounds. All in all, it's a shattering experience that registers 8.3 on the Richter scale.

The Funtastic World of Hanna Barbera: In more than 50 years of working together, Bill Hanna and Joe Barbera have created 300 specials, series and films, plus some 3,000 30-minute cartoons. Their work has won seven Oscars and eight Emmys. The animation featured in this attraction marries two-dimensional character art with computer-generated, three-dimensional backgrounds, all programmed to motion-based seats in the largest cartoon spaceship in the world as Yogi Bear, Scooby Doo, the Flintstones, and the Jetsons lead you on a high-speed, non-stop chase where you actually become part of a cartoon.

Dynamite Nights Stuntacular presents death-defying stunts, cinematic special effects, and synchronized audio and lighting systems combined in this unbelievably realistic attraction that features an astounding 60-foot stunt-boat jump through a 2,000-degree, three-story wall of fire.

Ghostbusters offers the largest single magic illusion ever created in a full-scale, live action re-creation of the film sequence from *Ghostbusters* at the Temple of Gozer, an exact replica of Spook Central in the movie. The cast includes 14 larger-than-life spooks and several other unexpected guests from the netherworld. The use of both visible and non-visible light is part of the secret behind the eerie special effects.

Hitchcock's 3-D Theater: The world of Alfred Hitchcock is a special one, known everywhere through the gripping, terror-filled movies he made during his 43-year association with Universal that began in 1934. You can experience this suspense and horror first hand, and find it an encounter you'll never forget, especially at night when you can't sleep.

And there's much more. The kids will want to spend **A Day in the Park With Barney**, which brings to life the purple dino-star's make-believe preschool playworld. You'll want to take in one or two of the shows, perhaps **Bettlejuice's Graveyard Revue** or the ***Murder, She Wrote* Mystery Theater**. And, of course, you'll want to visit such street sets as Rodeo Drive, Fisherman's Wharf, Amity Harbor, and more than 30 others. If this daytrip doesn't wear you out, nothing will.

Dynamite Nights Stuntacular

Trip 18

The Central East Coast: Daytona Beach, Ormond Beach, and New Smyrna

This has long been one of Florida's most popular sections of coastline. Here, almost every vacation experience you can imagine is available, from the excitement of the great rockets blasting off from the Space Coast to the thrills of high-speed motor-racing at Daytona, from hunting sunken pirate gold on the beaches of the Treasure Coast to the fabulous beaches themselves, and on to the abundant wildlife in the great refuges and wetlands.

Daytona is the big town on Florida's East Coast. For many years it's been second only to Indianapolis as far as motor racing fans are concerned, and every year they descend on the city and its International Speedway by the hundreds of thousands. But Daytona is more than a racetrack. The beaches are world famous and have long been an important part of the East Coast's attraction. Daytona is also a major cultural center with a number of fine museums, theaters, and historical sites.

A little farther south, beyond Port Orange and New Smyrna, Florida's Space Coast tops the list of spectacular attractions. From the Kennedy Space Center to Spaceport USA and the U.S. Astronaut Hall of Fame, visitors to this section of the coast are treated to a panoply of tradition, patriotism, excitement, and the wonders of a dozen or more museums. Additionally, there are the theaters, galleries, and exhibits that provide a comprehensive look at our space program.

Just to the east, the Canaveral National Seashore and Merritt Island National Wildlife Refuge offer not only a wild and lonely area of great natural beauty for you to explore, but a vast natural habitat for hundreds of species of wildlife, including seabirds and turtles.

Even farther south, the counties of Indian River and St. Lucie have become famous as America's Treasure Coast. It was to this section of Florida's East Coast that the great Spanish treasure fleets, plying the heavy seas eastward to Cadiz laden with gold, silver, and gems were swept northward by hurricanes and lost on the rocks. And it's here that treasure seekers, beachcombers, anglers, and those who just need a little peace and quiet come to spend pleasant hours in the sunshine. The opportunities for outdoor recreation are unparalleled on the Treasure Coast. Diving, snorkeling, golfing, tennis, hiking, nature watching, dining, and baseball—this is where the Dodgers, Mets, Marlins, and Astros conduct their winter training—are just a few of the possibilities that await.

Indian River is where early settlers built their homes and vast plantations. Today, the river is just as beautiful and enticing as it was all those hundreds of years ago. Now visitors come from around the nation to enjoy the great outdoors. The fishing is superb, the scenery dazzling, and the magnificent off-shore reefs are a magnet for divers and snorkelers. If you like to windsurf, sail, boat, or fish, this is the place for you.

Vero Beach is another pleasant spot on the East Coast, but one virtually undiscovered by the great vacationing multitudes. For those in the know, it's a favorite spot to go to avoid the crowds, and to enjoy the peaceful sandy beaches, fine restaurants, and outstanding shopping centers. And they've done their best to keep Vero a secret. Because of that, it remains one of few unspoiled areas left on the central East Coast.

Stuart is the sport fishing capital of east Florida. It's a little town with a big reputation among the aficionados who know all about such things. A quaint little place where there seems to be more fishing boats than homes. It's a place where the sun goes down over the harbor in a blaze of red and gold and sets the atmosphere for a night of quiet reminiscence after a day on the ocean in search of the "big one."

Hobe Sound and Jensen Beach are Florida's favorite turtle spotting locations. From June through July, thousands of the faithful flock to the warm sands to join ranger-led nighttime expeditions and watch the loggerhead turtles' annual migration from sea to sand.

SUGGESTED TOURS:

There are two daytrips to the Central East Coast you should consider. One is to the north and covers a stretch of the coast from Ormond Beach to New Smyrna including Daytona and its beaches. The other, beginning on page 120, explores the Space Coast from New Smyrna through Titusville, Cocoa Beach, and south to the Sebastian Inlet, including the Canaveral National Seashore and the Kennedy Space Center. Whichever you decide on, there'll be more to see and do than can be accomplished in a single day, so you'll have to pick and choose from the wealth of attractions.

DAYTONA BEACH, ORMOND BEACH, AND NEW SMYRNA:

This whole area seems to be dedicated to the early days of motor racing. Ormond Beach is said to be the birthplace of the sport and Daytona is synonymous with it. The name conjures up all sorts of automotive sounds, most of them extremely noisy, along with images of sleek racing machines, suntanned drivers, and roaring crowds. You can't think of Daytona without thinking of motor racing, but that's not the only attraction here. The beaches are among the best in the world, as thousands of college students on spring break each year will attest. Unlike the narrow strips of sand found at most resorts, the beach here, besides being more than 23 miles long, is some 500 feet wide at low tide. There's plenty of room for everyone, even in high season. Port Orange is a small seaside community, very peaceful and quite unspoiled. New Smyrna, a little farther south, along with Ponce Inlet, is equally unspoiled, and virtually undiscovered. If you're looking for a day away from the hustle and bustle of Orlando and the major theme parks, the southern section of this daytrip might be just the place.

GETTING THERE:

There's really only one way to get there quickly, and that's to take Interstate 4 northeast from Orlando to its junction with Interstate 95. It's a fast drive of about 45 miles that shouldn't take much more than 50 minutes or so. From there, you can head out in whichever direction you like. Daytona is less than 10 miles farther east on Interstate 4, Ormond Beach is 12 miles to the north via Interstate 95 and Highway 40, and New Smyrna Beach is 15 miles to the south via Interstate 95 and Highway 44.

GETTING AROUND:

Your vehicle will take you almost everywhere you want to go, and where it won't you'll just have to walk. Some of the stops include nature walks and trails; try to get out and about on foot if you can. The experience is sure to be an enjoyable one. Just be sure to use adequate sunscreen and wear a hat.

PRACTICALITIES:

The **Area Code** is 904.

There's no best day to make this trip. True, you'll find some of the attractions open late and close early on Sundays, and Saturdays tend to get a bit crowded at the major attractions but, other than that, you can take pretty well your pick.

TOURIST INFORMATION:

Ormond Beach Chamber of Commerce, PO Box 874, Ormond Beach, FL 32175, ☎ 904-677-3454.

Daytona Beach Area Convention and Visitors Bureau, 126 East Orange Avenue, Daytona Beach, FL 32114. ☎ 904-255-5478 or 800-854-1234, fax 904-255-5478.

FOOD AND DRINK:

Daytona Beach:

Hungarian Village (424 South Ridgewood). They are open for lunch and dinner from 11 a.m., and the Hungarian/American menu makes for an interesting change; try the wienerschnitzel or the beef goulash. ☎ 253-5712. $$.

Port Orange:

Aunt Catfish's On The River (at the west end of Port Orange Bridge Causeway on the Intracoastal Waterway on Highway A1A) Although usually busy, it's a great place for lunch or dinner. As the name suggests, seafood is the main item on the menu. Try to get in early to avoid a wait. ☎ 767-4768. $–$$.

New Smyrna Beach:

Riverview Charlie's (at the east end of the North Causeway Bridge at the Riverview Hotel, 101 Flagler Avenue) is the place to relax at the end of a tiring day. Open for lunch and dinner from 11:30–10, the menu includes fresh seafood. If you get there early you might still find some room on the deck. ☎ 428-1865. $–$$.

SUGGESTED TOUR:

This daytrip takes in a section of the coastline and Intracoastal Waterway stretching southward from Ormond Beach through Daytona Beach to Ponce Inlet and New Smyrna. Because there are numerous stops and quite a bit of driving, you'll have to pick and choose carefully from among the many attractions if you're to complete it in a single day. Otherwise, you might prefer to stay overnight and do the trip slowly and in comfort. As always, it's a good idea to begin at the farthest point and work your way back toward home base.

At this point you have a couple of options to consider. First is the long route, which takes in three state parks before turning east to Ormond Beach. Secondly, you can give the parks a miss entirely. If you do this, you'll miss some wonderful countryside and three unique sites as you head straight to Ormond Beach. The following assumes you want to go the full route and begins at Hontoon Island State Park between Delray and DeLand, and proceeds north and then east to Ormond Beach. If you decide to go straight to Ormond Beach, skip the next few pages and go to the listing for Tomoka State Park on page 116.

From Orlando take Interstate 4 and drive northeast to its junction with Highway 17 where it crosses the St. Johns River. Depending on your starting point, it's a drive of about 15 miles. Head north on 17 toward Orange City and watch for French Avenue and a sign pointing west to the **Blue Spring State Park** (1); from there it's about two miles.

Blue Spring is well known as a winter home for the manatee, a large sea cow with big sad eyes and a gentle disposition. These endangered animals gather here in the warm waters of the spring during the winter months, seeking refuge from the cold St. Johns River. Will you see a manatee? If you do, you'll be lucky as there are very few of them left alive.

Three years after England acquired Florida from Spain, John Bartram, a prominent botanist, explored the St. Johns River to assess the resources that might have value to the British Crown. His written report of January, 1766, is extensive, and his description of the visit to Blue Spring vivid. Today, Blue Spring remains much as it was when Bartram traveled the area more than 200 years ago, and has become a popular outdoor and recreational center. You can swim and go snorkeling in the Blue Spring Run (Blue Spring has long been regarded as one of Florida's best snorkeling parks), canoe the waters of the St. Johns River, and go fishing. The waters within the park are well-stocked with largemouth bass, shellcrackers, speckled perch, bluegill, and channel catfish. There's also a picnic area with tables and grills, and a concession stand where you can buy gifts, food and drink, and rent a canoe. *Open 8–sundown daily.* ☎ *775-3663. Allow at least 90 minutes.* ⎣. *Admission $3.25 per vehicle.*

Although **Hontoon Island** (2) is just across the river from Blue Spring, you'll have to drive north on Highway 17 to DeLand, and from there take Highway 44 six miles to the west. Unfortunately, it's accessible only by private boat or by passenger ferry (see below). If you're a conservationist or if you simply enjoy beautiful solitary places, the island's inaccessibility makes it one of Florida's romantic and still largely undiscovered spots. Before its purchase by the State of Florida in 1967 it had a varied past. For eons it was home to the Timucuan Indians (their mounds can be viewed from the nature trail), then came pioneers, homesteaders, a cattle ranch and, finally, a boatyard.

Today, the island, bordered by the St. Johns River and the Huntoon Dead River, is one of Florida's less well-known state recreational areas, a microcosm of Floridian habitats and wetlands where the wildlife is as varied as the scenery. There are pine flatwoods, palm and oak hammocks, cypress swamps, marshes, river tributaries, even a lagoon. A self-guided hiking trail leads you along a two-hour walk beginning at the ranger station and following the Huntoon Dead River to a large Indian mound at the southwest corner of the park. An 80-foot-high observation tower provides a breathtaking view over most of the island. Nearby, there's a nice picnic area with tables and grills, the ideal spot for a late outdoor lunch or early evening cookout. You can rent a canoe and take to the waters, and you can go fishing. The waters hereabouts team with largemouth bass, bluegill, speckled perch, and channel catfish. *Open daily 8–sunset.* ☎ *736-5309. Allow at least 90 minutes. The passenger ferry operates free of charge from 9 in the morning until one hour before sundown. There's plenty of parking available on the mainland.*

From Hontoon Island, return to DeLand via Highway 44 and take Highway 17 north, then northwest, for about five miles. Watch for signs pointing the way to **De León Springs Recreation Area** (3); the park is at the corner of Ponce De León and Burt Parks roads.

De León Springs is another of Florida's many state parks that focus on a major natural spring system. At peak periods more than 19 million gallons of fresh water gush daily into the spring run, making it the centerpiece of an outstanding outdoor recreational facility.

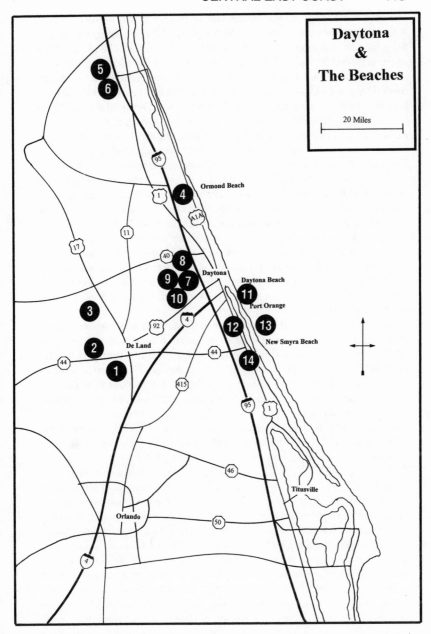

Daytona
&
The Beaches

20 Miles

The area has a long and sometimes violent history. It was home to Native Americans as far back as 8000 BC. By the early 1500s it belonged to Spain, then, for a short period in the mid-1700s, to the English. In 1783 it was once again acquired by Spain before becoming part of the United States. The American artist John James Audubon visited Spring Garden, a plantation owned by one Colonel Orlando Rees, in 1832. A few years later the plantation was sacked during the Second Seminole War. During the Civil War it was an important Confederate supply center until Union troops eventually captured it and destroyed most of the facilities. During the late 19th century it became a winter tourist resort and in 1982 was acquired by the State of Florida and turned into a recreation area, one of the finest in the state.

Today, DeLeón Springs is a great place to get out into the open air and relax. If love to swim or snorkel, you must take time out for a dip; the water of the spring is crystal clear and the temperature remains steady at 72 degrees throughout the year. You can rent a canoe, take a walk along a secluded nature trail, or enjoy a picnic lunch in a shady area set aside just for that purpose. *Open 8–sundown daily.* ☎ *985-4212. Allow at least 90 minutes, more if you decide to go for a swim.* &. *Admission $3.25 per vehicle.*

From De León Springs, continue north on Highway 17 to its junction with Highway 40. Turn right there and drive 24 miles to the junction with Route 5A, turning north to Tomoka State Park.

If you've decided on the direct route to Ormond Beach, take Interstate 4 from Orlando and drive northeast to its junction with Interstate 95, turn north, drive to the intersection with Highway 40 and turn east toward Ormond Beach. Continue east on 40 for 3½ miles, past the intersection with Highway 1/5. From there it's a short four-mile drive to **Tomoka State Park** (4).

Tomoka is near the junction of the Tomoka and Halifax rivers. Because of its location to the north of the popular beaches at Ormond, this beautiful, scenic park with its creeks, rivers and lagoons is still largely undiscovered— by-passed—by the crowds. You might like to stop on the way in and buy provisions for a picnic breakfast, or you can bring food with you to cook in the open air at one of the picnic area grills. The park museum offers real Florida gifts. If you're an angler, and you've brought along your fishing pole, you'll find there's plenty of sport to be had. The rivers, creeks, and lagoons abound with striped bass, speckled trout, bluefish, redfish, flounder, mullet, sheephead, and whiting. Food and drink is available in the museum block, where you can even rent a canoe. Energetic souls might go for a walk along the nature trail, where there's lots of wildlife to see. *Open 8–sundown daily.* ☎ *676-4050. Allow at least 90 minutes.* &. *Admission $3.25 per vehicle.*

Back in Ormond Beach, at 160 East Granada Boulevard, you'll find the **Birthplace of Speed Museum** (5). It was here, as early as 1902, on these beaches that motor racing in Florida is started. In those early days of the automobile, speeds were not quite what they were today. As technology improved, so did the performance of the pre-World War I cars. Today, the museum interprets the role played by the area in the development not only of motor racing, but of the automotive industry in general. Features include a replica of an early Stanley Steamer and several historic automobiles. *Open 1–5 p.m., Tues.–Sat.* ☎ *672-5657. Allow at least 60 minutes.* ♿. *Admission $5.*

Also in Ormond Beach, at 25 Riverside Drive, the **Casements** (6) is where John D. Rockefeller spent his winters from 1914 until his death in 1937. Extensively renovated and restored, the house now serves as the city's cultural center. Exhibits include items of Rockefeller furniture and mementos, an extensive art collection—including many historic pieces from Hungary—and Boy Scout memorabilia along with a variety of changing exhibits. Guided tours are available. *Open 9–7 Mon.–Thurs., 9–5 Fri., 9–noon Sat. Tours at 10 and 2:30.* ☎ *676-3216. Allow at least 60 minutes.* ♿. *Donations.*

After a quick look at Ormond's beaches and the site of original speedway—marked out during the **Antique Car Meet** held over Thanksgiving Weekend—it's time to head southward. Take the scenic route along Atlantic Avenue (Highway A1A), driving 4½ miles to its junction with International Speedway Boulevard (Highway 92/600), and turn right. Continue on for four more miles to the **Daytona International Speedway** (7), which will be on your left. Now, what can be said about the Speedway that you can't see for yourself? Not much; it's an extravaganza that speaks pretty well for itself. Be sure to take the guided tram tour of the racetrack, infield, pits, and garages, then stop in to see the extensive collection of motor racing memorabilia and photographs in the World Center of Racing Visitor Center. *Open 9–5 daily; tram tours depart the visitor center every 30 minutes between 9:30 and 4.* ☎ *254-2700. Allow at least 90 minutes.* ♿. *Admission to the Visitor Center is free; tram tours: adults $5, children under 6 free with a paying adult.*

If you like old cars, the **Klassix Auto Museum** (8) at 2909 West International Speedway Boulevard is well worth a visit. From the Speedway, continue west on Highway 92. The museum is about a half-mile beyond the Interstate 95 interchange. Of special interest here, besides the inevitable Daytona motor racing exhibits, is a complete collection of Corvettes dating from 1953 to the present, all displayed in period settings. There's also a fine collection of vintage motorcycles and a large number of specialty cars. Like ice cream? Don't miss the 1950s ice cream parlor. *Open 9–6 daily.* ☎ *252-3800. Allow at least 60 minutes.* ♿. *Adults $8.50, seniors over 55 $7.50, children 7–12 $4.25.*

When you leave the Klassix Auto Museum, take International Speedway Drive east, back through Daytona to Atlantic Avenue. **The Boardwalk** (9) will be just ahead of you. If you're traveling with kids, you should take time out and let them enjoy this entertainment center. There are all sorts of amusements, arcades, a bandstand featuring live concerts, a gondola skyride, and the Space Needle. *Open daily early 'till late. Allow at least a couple of hours.*

The **Halifax Historical Society and Museum** (10) is two blocks south of Highway 92 at 252 South Beach Street. Many dedicated people spent a lot of time making the society and its museum what it is today. From humble beginnings the center, housed in a former bank building, is the showplace of Daytona's historical past, not the least of which is its motor racing heritage. Here you can see displays of racing memorabilia, old postcards and photographs, and Indian artifacts from the days long before the European explorers arrived in the area. There is also a miniature replica of the Boardwalk as was in the mid-1930s, complete with vintage cars, a band, and lots of tiny people. *Open 10–4 Tues.–Sat.* ☎ *255-6976. Allow at least 30 minutes. Adults $2, children 50¢, free on Sat.*

Atlantic Boulevard—Highway A1A—runs the entire length from Ormond Beach through **Daytona Beach** (11) and on to Ponce Inlet. It borders the beaches to the east, and no visit to Daytona would be complete without a stop-off somewhere along the 23-mile stretch of sand and ocean. Your only consideration is do you want to mingle with the crowds? Or do you want to get out of town to a quieter spot? Whatever you decide, you're in for a treat. The sandy beaches are kept scrupulously clean, they're wide and inviting, and the sea seems to stretch away, north, south, and east almost forever.

There are a couple of other places in Daytona worthy of mention: the **Museum of Arts and Sciences**, at 1040 Museum Boulevard, has a number of interesting exhibits, including a the skeleton of a 13-foot tall, 130,000-year-old, giant sloth. *Open 9–4 Tues.–Fri., and noon–5 Sat. and Sun.* ☎ *255-0285. Allow at least 60 minutes. Adults $4, students $1, planetarium $2.* **The Southeast Museum of Photography**, at 1200 International Speedway Boulevard, is on the Daytona Beach Community College Campus. *Open 10–4 Tues.–Fri., and 1–4 on Sun. Donations. Allow at least 30 minutes.*

From Daytona, take Highway A1A south from the Boardwalk for 2½ miles and turn west into Port Orange; **Sugar Mill Gardens** (12) is a mile west of Highway 1 off Herbert Street on Sugar Mill Road. The gardens cover more than 12 beautifully landscaped acres surrounding the ruins of an mid-18th century English sugar mill, which was destroyed by Indians during the Seminole Wars. The combination of ruins and gardens offer a scene of serene beauty. A stroll through them is like no other, especially when you encounter the four stone dinosaurs strategically placed along the way. *Open 8–5 daily.* ☎ *767-1735. Allow at least 60 minutes.* ♿. *Donations.*

Return to Highway A1A—Atlantic Avenue—and proceed southward to Ponce Inlet, taking South Peninsula Drive to the ***Ponce De León Inlet Lighthouse** (13). This is the one stop you won't want to miss. For more than 100 years the old lighthouse has stood guard over the water of the inlet, warning sailors of the dangers inshore. Today, it is a museum and historic monument, fully restored to working order and open for you to enjoy. The climb to the top is strenuous, so you'll need to be sound of wind if you are to make it. But once at the top, you're in for a rare experience. The view over Daytona Beach, the inlet and the surrounding area is nothing short of spectacular. The cooling wind blows through your hair, the air is fresh and sweet and, on a clear day you can see forever. The park at the base of the structure has an attractive picnic area and you can buy gifts and souvenirs at the shop. The lighthouse keepers' cottages are now museums with all sorts of nautical and lighthouse artifacts on display. *Open 10–8 daily during the summer, 10–4 winter.* ☎ *761-1821. Allow at least 60 minutes.* ♿. *Adults $4, children under 11 $1.*

The final stop on your daytrip is across the inlet in New Smyrna. From the lighthouse take Atlantic Boulevard north to its junction with Highway 421 and turn west to Highway 1. Turn south on Highway 1 and drive 13 miles to the junction with Highway 44; the **New Smyrna Sugar Mill Ruins State Historic Site** (14) is just to the west, south on Mission Drive.

This sugar mill was only one of ten that once thrived along the eastern coast of Florida. During the early 1800s the mill was the heart of a great southern plantation. Besides sugar, it produced a variety of other products for export to the northern states and to Europe. It was operated by slave labor. Today, there's not much left to see as the plantation was attacked and burned by Indians during the second Seminole War in 1835. The park is quiet and you'll enjoy your visit. *Open 8–sundown daily.* ☎ *428-2126. Allow at least 60 minutes.* ♿. *Admission $3.25 per vehicle.*

From here you can, if you have any time left, turn east and visit New Smyrna, or you can continue west on Highway 44 to its junction with Interstate 4, which will take you back to Orlando.

Trip 19

The Space Coast

You can't think of the Space Coast without recalling images of the great rockets that carried America's astronauts, first into orbit and then on to the Moon. Images of the Space Shuttle, still going strong after more than 20 years of service, and images of *Challenger* exploding over the sea in a great fireball. But the Space Coast—Brevard County—is much more than that. It means long, pristine, sandy beaches with tiny coastal towns and resorts, half-forgotten secluded parks and wildlife sanctuaries where you can spend time relaxing away from the big cities and the crowded theme parks. From New Smyrna southward along the Canaveral National Seashore, across Merritt Island to Titusville, and then on to Cocoa Beach and the Sabastian Inlet, it stretches for more than 70 miles. Other than the crowds that visit the Kennedy Space Center, the area is quiet, low in traffic and often wild and seemingly undiscovered. For mile after mile, the beaches continue ever southward, flanked by palm trees and dunes covered with seagrass, and punctuated by long piers where anglers reel in all sorts of finny catches from snapper to sharks. Visitors to the Space Coast can get close to nature, commune with giant turtles, even manatees, and see more than 500 species of wild birds and animals, 60 of which are on the endangered list, in eight refuges and preserves.

For more than 10,000 years before the first European explorers set foot in what is now Brevard County, Paleo-Indians and Archaic people wandered the shores and riverbanks, living in small groups on what they could hunt or gather, undisturbed through the eons until that first fateful moment when Juan Ponce de León landed just below Cape Canaveral. At the time, the area was inhabited by two major Indian tribes: the Ais and the Jeagas. So, due to a perceived threat of Indian attack and, to a lesser degree, heavy concentrations of mosquitoes, the would-be settlers moved on to more hospitable areas. But by the early 1700s, the tribes were facing extinction. Diseases carried in from Europe had taken their toll, as had attacks from other tribes. The English and second Spanish periods had little effect on Brevard County, and the American War of Independence almost completely by-passed the area, as did the Civil War. In the years following the Civil War, however, settlers from nearby southern states began to filter in, searching for a new beginning. Thus, in 1868, three Confederate officers and their families founded the Georgiana settlement on Merritt Island. By the 1880s, the cities of Melbourne, Rockledge, Cocoa, and Titusville were well established. And then came the railroad, opening up the area from Jacksonville to Key West through Titusville. The modern era began in 1940 with the establishment of the Banana River Naval Air Station, known today as Patrick Air Force Base. But it wasn't until the 1950s that Brevard County really made its mark by becoming home to the Kennedy Space Center. Overnight, the area turned into the high-profile, technological wonder of the world that it remains today.

GETTING THERE:

From Orlando it couldn't be easier. Take the Bee Line Expressway (Highway 528) east to highways 1 and A1A.

GETTING AROUND:

Your vehicle will carry you almost everywhere you want to go, and your feet will take you the rest of the way.

PRACTICALITIES:

The **Area Code** is 407.

Most of the sights and attractions are open daily, although some of the smaller ones do close on Sundays or Mondays. Almost any day is a good day to make this trip.

There are many stops included in this tour. As it would be impossible to complete them all in a single day, a little selective culling is called for. One or two of the attractions can take up a considerable amount of time. For example, the Kennedy Space Center could be treated as a daytrip all by itself.

As always, the sun is dangerous, especially on the beaches. Be sure to use an adequate sunscreen in addition to sunglasses and a head covering.

TOURIST INFORMATION:

Florida's Space Coast Office of Tourism, 2725 St. Johns Street, Melbourne, FL 32940, ☎ 800-USA 1969.

FOOD AND DRINK:

There are many quaint little eateries along the 72 miles of this trip. As always, fresh seafood is the mainstay of most menus, but you'll be able to find whatever else you might desire. For starters, there's:

Titusville:

Steamers Riverside Eatery (801 Marina Road) is open for lunch and dinner from 11–10. There's a rustic atmosphere about the place and it overlooks the Indian River. Lots of fresh seafood on the menu. ☎ 269-1012. $$.

Paul's Smokehouse Restaurant and Lounge (3665 Washington Avenue) is open for lunch and dinner from 11–9 and specializes in barbecue, prime rib, and fresh seafood. Here, you'll dine on the waterfront on the Indian River. It's a pleasant, friendly place with lots of memorabilia on display. ☎ 267-3663. $–$$.

Cocoa Beach:

The Pier Restaurant (on Cocoa Beach Pier at 401 Meade Avenue) is a great place to eat lunch or dinner. You'll need a reservation for dinner as it can get busy at times. The menu includes fresh seafood caught daily, and you eat in a dining room on the pier overlooking the ocean. ☎ 783-7549. $$.

Melbourne:

Banana Bay Waterfront Restaurant (2425 Pineapple Avenue on Highway 1 behind Philips Junior College) is open for lunch and dinner from 11–9, features outdoor and indoor dining on the Indian River, and a menu with lots of creative dishes including seafood. ☎ 242-2401. $$.

SUGGESTED TOUR:

When you arrive at the junction with Highway A1A you'll join and follow it for most of the way south. It's a fabulous drive, always scenic, light on traffic, with plenty of interesting places to stop along the way to enjoy a quiet moment or two, perhaps taking time out for some refreshment, or even a picnic. Mile after mile the road hugs the beach to the east and the Indian River to the west. Almost every mile, it seems, there's a pier jutting out into the water of the Atlantic or the river. If you're an angler you'll want to stop at least once and try your hand. You won't find any better beaches or more relaxing spots than these.

Before you set out you should be aware that if you intend to make the Kennedy Space Center a part of your daytrip you'll have time only for one or two of the other stops listed here. Your visit to the Space Center will take at least five hours—if you take in the Astronaut Hall of Fame and U.S. Space Camp as well it will take a full day—so it might be a good idea to split the daytrip in two and do it over a couple of days.

When you reach the junction with Highway 1, turn north and go to Highway 406. Turn right there and go to Route 3 and turn north again; the **Old Haulover Canal** (1) is on Route 3 on the narrowest section of Merritt Island. Built by the federal government in 1854, the canal linked Mosquito Lagoon to the east with the Indian River to the west. This was the traditional crossing point for travel down the waterway. Until the canal was completed goods had to be carried across the island and then loaded aboard boats to continue the journey southward. Just three feet deep and 14 feet across at its widest point, the canal was hand-excavated by slaves owned by a local citrus grower. For 30 years the canal served as an important link in Florida's

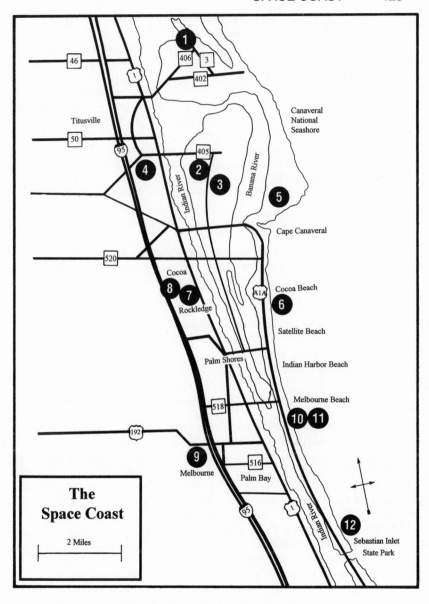

inland waterway system, but it was abandoned in 1884 when a new Haul-over was constructed just to the north.

From the Haulover, drive south again to Highway 402. Return to High-way 1 and turn south to Route 405 (NASA Parkway), heading east to the ***Kennedy Space Center and Launch Complex 39** (2). SPACEPORT USA is the visitor center, your lift-off point for a tour of the complex and the gateway to the Merritt Island National Wildlife Refuge. Leave your vehicle in the parking lot and take one of the two regularly scheduled bus tours: the Red or the Blue. Make sure you arrive early to avoid crowds. Buy your tickets for the bus tours and the IMAX theaters as soon as you get there. *Open 9–sun-set daily. Bus tours (see below) depart daily every 15 minutes from 9:45 until two hours before sunset.* ☎ *452-2121.* ♿. *Free wheelchairs and kennels are available. Admission is free. IMAX theater tickets $4, children 3–11 $2. Bus tours $7, children 3–11 $4.*

Construction of Launch Complex 39 was completed in 1968, and it has been the jumping-off point for all U.S. manned space missions since. Lo-cated at the northern end of Merritt Island, it remains in use today as the launch site for the Space Shuttle. It's also one of the nation's most historic sites: from here Apollo 11 set out on man's first voyage to the Moon. There were also three Skylab missions, the Apollo/Soyuz Test Project, and more than 40 Shuttle voyages.

SPACEPORT USA is where your visit to the complex begins. Here you'll find all sorts of interesting multimedia displays and two IMAX Theaters, both with five-story-high screens. Two IMAX movies, "the Dream is Alive" and "The Blue Planet," will absolutely take your breath away. They include actual footage shot by astronauts in space. The highlight of SPACEPORT USA is the rocket garden where you can see actual spacecraft and an assortment of space equipment.

The **U.S. Astronaut Hall of Fame**, at 6225 Vectorspace Boulevard, is the home of **U.S. Space Camp Florida**. Here, you can take a self-guided tour and see all sorts of space memorabilia, including Gus Grissom's space suit, the one he wore on his Mercury flight. But Space Camp is also the place where young people come from all over the nation to train like real astronauts, and you can watch them at work. You can also experience a voyage into space aboard a full-size space shuttle, simulated, of course. *Open 9–5 daily.* ☎ *269-6100.* ♿. *Adults $9.95, children 3–12 $5.95.*

The **Astronauts Memorial** is a Space Mirror inscribed with the names of U.S. astronauts who died in the line of duty. Each name has a reflective panel behind it and the mirror is computerized to keep it aligned with the sun so that its light shines through the names: it's very moving, emotionally. The mirror is visible from the approaches to Spaceport and is accessible through the entrance. *Free.*

Bus Tours: if you want to see everything, take one or both of the sched-uled tours. They depart every 15 minutes, include a live commentary, and are well worth the cost of the fare.

The Red Tour features a simulated countdown of the Apollo 11 launch. You'll see an authentic lunar lander on a moonscape, and a Saturn V rocket at the Vehicle Assembly Building. The tour also takes in Launch Complex 39 with a stop close enough to space shuttle launch pads A and B for you to take photographs.

The Blue Tour will take you to Cape Canaveral Air Force Station where the early launches took place. It includes a stop at the Air Force Space Museum and the mission control center for the Mercury and Gemini programs.

As for the **Merritt Island National Wildlife Refuge** (3), if nature conservancy is important to you, take the Black Point Drive, a self-guided, seven-mile driving tour through the refuge. Along the way you'll pass through a number of natural habitats, see lots of animals and birds, and enjoy a little time away from major traffic routes. *Open dawn–dusk daily. Free.*

When you've finished your tour of the Kennedy Space Center and/or the Merritt Island Wildlife Refuge, if you have time left, you'll need to rejoin Highway 1 and drive back toward the city of Titusville, with several stops along the way.

The ***Valiant Air Command Warbird Museum** (4) is at 6600 Tico Road at the Space Center Executive Airport; just follow the signs. This amazing place combines an historical flying museum with an operations center, and also serves as headquarters for the Valiant Air Command, an organization that preserves vintage aircraft dating from World War II. Since its formation in' 1977, the VAC has reached monumental proportions with more than 350 historic aircraft under its wing. Each year, in March, they host an air show at the Space Center Executive Airport, during which historic aircraft fly once again. *Open 10–6 daily. Allow at least an hour and a half.* ☎ *268-1941.* ♿. *Adults $6, seniors over 55, vets, and military personnel with ID $5, children under 13 $4.*

The **Canaveral National Seashore** (5) lies to the north of the Kennedy Space Center and Highway A1A hugs its extreme outer limits north and south. You can reach it via a number of feeder roads, but the Bee Line Expressway (Highway 528) is probably the best and most direct route. From Spaceport USA, drive south on Highway 1 to 528 and turn east. From there it's a short hop to A1A. Once there, turn north and follow the road beyond Cape Canaveral Air Force Station. The Canaveral National Seashore is a vast wilderness area stretching over some 57,000 acres, 25 miles of deserted barrier islands and beaches, tidal lagoons and mile after mile of dunes, all covered with waving seagrass. Here, it's still possible to encounter the endangered manatee as well as turtles, alligators, and other species of wild animals and birds. The beaches are almost always quiet—you'll have no trouble finding a secluded spot for a lunchtime picnic and a swim—and surf fishing is always inviting. If you'd like to find out more about the Seashore, you can join one of the ranger-led activities either at Playlinda Beach at the southern tip of the Seashore, or Apollo Beach at the northern end. *The*

Seashore is open 6–8 through the summer, and 6–6 the rest of the year. Some sections, however, are closed for the three days before a shuttle launch. ☎ 267-1110. Free.

From the Canaveral National Seashore it's but a short drive south on Highway A1A to Cocoa Beach. There are three interesting stops here, two of them are musts. For a long time the little city by the sea remained virtually undiscovered by the vacationing public. But, with the advent of the Space Program on Merritt Island, all that changed. Aside from its magnificent beaches, it's also just the spot to catch a glimpse of the space shuttle blasting off.

*Cocoa Beach Pier (6) extends for more than 800 feet into the Atlantic. It's a great place to visit for fishing, dining, dancing, and shopping. There's an 850-foot promenade leading down to the beach and an observation deck overlooking the ocean with a view north toward Merritt Island and the Kennedy Space Center.

The ***Astronaut Memorial Planetarium and Observatory** (7) is actually in Cocoa, not Cocoa Beach. If you'd like to visit, you'll need to take Highway 520 west to its junction with Highway 501 and then turn north. From there, drive 1.75 miles. You can't miss it. This is the largest public-access observatory in Florida, a must for stargazers. You can look through a 24-inch telescope and see the planets, stars, and other interesting objects in the far-off blackness of space. The planetarium offers a different view of the galaxy, and two theaters show space-related films. *Open 6:30–9:30 Thurs.–Fri. and 2–4 Sun.* ☎ *634-3732.* ♿. *The rooftop observatory and the exhibition hall are free. Admission to one show $4, children under 12 $2. Admission to two shows $7, children under 12 $4.*

Also in Cocoa, the **Brevard Museum of History and Natural Science** (8), at 2201 Michigan Avenue, is where you can explore prehistoric, historic, and natural science exhibits relating to Brevard County. There's also a children's discovery hall where the kids can interact with the exhibits, and some 22 acres outside with nature trails and walks, all of which are accessible to wheelchairs. *Open 10–4 Tues.–Sat., 1–4 Sun.* ☎ *632-1830.* ♿. *Admission $5.*

Head back to Highway A1A and turn south toward Melbourne where you'll find the **Space Coast Science Center** (9) at 1510 Highland Avenue. Here you can experience all sorts of strange scientific phenomena. For instance, you can play with colored shadows, see your shadow on a wall, and then walk away and leave it there. You can probe inside a giant kaleidoscope, fly in the Anti Gravity Mirror, or look into the workings of beehive or an offshore coral reef. It's lots of fun, and an educational experience the kids will love. *Open 10–5 Tues.–Sat., noon–5 on Sun.* ☎ *259-5572.* ♿. *Admission $5.*

No visit to Melbourne would be complete without a look at **Melbourne Beach and its Pier** (10). The old wooden structure was built between 1888 and 1889 by the Melbourne and Atlantic Railroad Company, which also founded the settlement of Melbourne Beach, the oldest beach community in Brevard County. If you brought your fishing pole, this is a good place to spend a quiet hour.

Melbourne Beach is also home to the oldest church in Brevard's barrier islands. The **Community Chapel** (11) at 500 Atlantic Avenue was built in 1892. It's a wood-frame structure, white, with a gabled roof topped with a belfry trimmed with wooden louvers. The little church has survived fires, floods, hurricanes, and hard times; it's worth a visit if you have the time.

From Melbourne Beach, continue south on A1A; it's a grand, scenic drive of about 15 miles.

The ***Sebastian Inlet State Recreation Area & McLarty Treasure Museum** (12) is the final stop on this daytrip. For anglers, there's no finer location to enjoy the sport. The surf fishing is exceptional. But the park has much more to offer than good times, sun, and recreation. It's a veritable time machine waiting to transport you back to the days when the Spanish treasure fleets loaded down with gold, silver, and jewels turned eastward toward Europe and their home port of Cadiz. And it was close to the Sebastian Inlet, in 1715, that a violent hurricane brought about the demise of an entire fleet of galleons returning to Spain from Mexico and Peru. More than a dozen great ships were driven off course and wrecked on the rocks in the shallow waters along the Treasure Coast. Those who survived swam ashore.

Today, the original site of the survivor's camp is home to the McLarty Treasure Museum, which houses a wealth of artifacts. Exhibits here tell the story of the shipwreck, the early attempts to salvage the treasure, and display valuable objects recovered during later expeditions.

The park itself is a part of one of the many barrier islands that protect Florida's southeastern shoreline from the ravages of nature. It's a complex world of sandy beaches, dunes and coastal hammocks, bordered by mangroves and forests that provide natural habitats for the wildlife community. It's also one of Florida's finest recreational facilities.

The Sebastian Inlet and the surrounding Atlantic waters provide some of the best saltwater fishing, shrimping, and clamming in the state. There are two Atlantic jetties, catwalks under the Inlet bridge, and more than three miles of beaches. All of them have access to the Indian River, the ocean, and an abundance of snook, redfish, bluefish, and Spanish mackerel.

Other activities at the inlet include swimming, snorkeling and scuba diving, hiking along the miles of sandy beaches, sun bathing, boating, bird watching, and nature study. This is a rare opportunity to observe the osprey, as well as many species of shore and wading birds, sea turtles and, at times, even the manatee. Sebastian Inlet is also rated among the finest surfing sites on the entire Atlantic coast, hosting several national surfing tournaments each year. If you visit during June and July, you might stay late and enjoy one of the ranger-led expeditions in search of nesting loggerhead turtles. If so, you'll need to contact the ranger station and make a reservation.

There are restrooms, a boat ramp and a dock, a picnic area with public rest rooms, and fresh water showers. Ample parking is provided, and there's a concession stand where you can eat breakfast and lunch daily, and rent beach chairs and fishing equipment. *Open 8–sundown daily.* ☎ *984-4852.* ♿. *Admission is $3.25 per vehicle.*

From Sebastian Inlet, it's best that you drive north, back to Melbourne Beach, and turn west on Highway 500, which will take you, via Kissimmee, all the back into Orlando from the south.

ADDITIONAL ATTRACTIONS:

Located on Taylor Creek Road in Christmas about 25 miles east of Orlando, off Highway 50, the 28,000-acre **Tosohatchee State Reserve** is the result of thousands of years of natural cyclical action of winds, floods, and fire. The reserve is home to several dozen varied and unique plant communities, marshes, swamps, flatwoods, and hammocks. These provide habitats for the reserve's teeming wildlife, including many rare and endangered species.

Tosohatchee borders some 19 miles of the St. Johns River in east Orange County. The land was purchased in 1977 under the Environmentally Endangered Lands Program in an effort to preserve the great natural beauty of the area and its extensive wetlands. The name, Tosohatchee, translates roughly from a Native American language to "fowl creek," the name of the creek which flows through the northern portion of the reserve.

The Tosohatchee marshes are a popular feeding ground for many species of wading shore birds and, during the winter months, a refuge for vast numbers of migrating waterfowl. The heavily forested uplands are home to a wide variety of wildlife, including the bobcat, gray fox, white-tailed deer, wild turkey, assorted hawks and owls, and various species of songbirds. Of the endangered species that live within the reserve, the eastern indigo snake, Florida panther, gopher tortoise, and bald eagle are just a few.

For those who enjoy hoofing it, Tosohatchee is regarded as one of Florida's "Best Hiking" areas. You can also go bicycling, fishing, and bird watching—Tosohatchee is a good place for wildlife photography. *Open 8– sunset daily.* ☎ *568-5893. Admission $3.25 per vehicle.*

*Cypress Gardens

Winter Haven is southwest of Orlando, set in central Florida about 75 miles from either coast. This is citrus country, home to some of the state's finest groves and the Florida Citrus Festival, held each year in nearby Auburndale during late January and early February. It's also sporting country, with fishing the premier outdoor sport. In the area there are numerous spring-fed lakes connected by a series of canals that form a 30-mile waterway teaming with trophy bass, blue gill, crappie, and catfish. But perhaps Winter Haven's main claim to fame is Cypress Gardens, a vast theme park and botanical garden renowned the world over.

GETTING THERE:

From Orlando, it's best to take Interstate 4 southwest to its junction with Highway 27. Head south on 27 for about 20 miles, then west on Route 540. Winter Haven is about 45 miles southwest of Orlando.

PRACTICALITIES:

The **Area Code** is 941.

Cypress Gardens is open 365 days a year, from 9:30 to 5:30. Try to visit when the weather forecast is good, and be sure to take along an adequate sunscreen lotion.

Kennels are available for a nominal fee.

The park is fully accessible to the handicapped, including parking and wheelchairs.

Admission: Adults $27.95 plus tax, seniors over 55 $22.95 plus tax, children 6–12 $17.95, under six free.

TOURIST INFORMATION:

Cypress Gardens, PO Box 1, Florida 33884, ☎ 324-2111 or 800-282-2123; fax 324-7946.

FOOD AND DRINK:

Everything you could ever want to eat you'll find right here in the park. There are restaurants, cafés, and walk-up stands serving everything from seafood to salads, burgers to pizzas and deli-style sandwiches to fresh-baked goodies.

SUGGESTED TOUR:

It's difficult to describe Cypress Gardens without sounding like a travel brochure. Edged by sparkling lakes and ancient cypress swamps, this is one of the world's premier botanical paradises. There's something magical about the atmosphere in the gardens, a feeling that all this splendor just can't be real, that, somehow, it's all an illusion. But it is real. More than 200 sprawling acres of gardens and lakes are filled with some 8,000 varieties of plants and flowers from around the world. Then there's the internationally-acclaimed water-skiing extravaganza, a vast conservatory full of exquisite butterflies, magnificent floral festivals, scenic floral boat rides, plus reptile and birds-of-prey shows. To top it off, there are museums, restaurants, shops, and authentically costumed southern belles. All together, Cypress Gardens draw almost as many people during the season as does Walt Disney World.

The original 16 acres of subtropical and tropical gardens were carved from the virgin cypress swamp by Dick and Julie Pope, and were opened to the public in 1936. Today, those first 16 acres are still the focal point of the entire garden complex. The trademark gazebo, surrounded by bougainvillea, still sits at the crest of a gentle rise, and it presents a scene that's exactly what comes to mind when one thinks of the pre-Civil War period of gracious living, southern hospitality, and great mansions.

Every year, the Gardens put on a series of new attractions complementing the permanent collection. Whatever new additions you find, and find them you certainly will, you should consider a bonus. The **Original Gardens**, mentioned earlier in this section, is where you should begin your tour.

"Wings of Wonder," The Butterfly Conservatory is a walk among more than 1,000 brilliantly colored butterflies in free-flight, untold numbers of exotic wildfowl, and 20 or so bright green iguanas. It's a small world within a world of waterfalls, jungle plants and flowers that provide both home and food for the brightly-colored residents.

Plantation Gardens is basically a herb-and-scent garden, but what a sweet-smelling experience it is. You can touch, snip and smell the exotic herbal plants. There's also a vegetable garden—the envy of all who would aspire to a green thumb—and a butterfly garden of nectar-filled plants and flowers especially attractive to the native variety of the gorgeous winged insect.

Magnolia Mansion: This ante-bellum-style mansion was built in the 1940s, and features a wonderful spiral staircase inside, graceful columns and verandah outside, all overlooking the Plantation Gardens and Lake Eloise. If you like, you can enjoy some light refreshment here before moving on.

Cypress Roots Museum houses memorabilia dating back to the park's origins. It chronicles the history of this, Florida's oldest theme park, through vintage photographs, original water skis, old-fashioned costumes, and candid snapshots of visiting celebrities.

The **Pontoon Lake Cruise** presents the "real" Florida as it might once have been. You'll take a leisurely cruise along the banks of Lake Eloise and on the way see all sorts of wildlife including snowy egrets, blue herons, otters at play, and the odd alligator or two, without which no visit to Florida would be complete.

Radios Radios is a somewhat nostalgic exhibit of hundreds of antique radios from the 1920s through the 1950s. You think you've seen them all? No way. They were very creative back in those days. All the radios were donated to the park by Webber College, Babson Park, Florida.

Carousel Cove is for small children. Here, playtime has never been more fun. There are lots of interactive games and rides, including an ornate replica of an antique carousel.

Model railway enthusiasts will love **Cypress Junction**, where some 20 high-speed model trains tour tiny replicas of the major United States landmarks: Miami, New Orleans, Mount Rushmore, and so on. They travel over more than 1,100 feet of fully landscaped track.

Island In The Sky, a 153-foot-high revolving platform, provides breathtaking aerial views of Cypress gardens, the surrounding Chain of Lakes and the scenic countryside beyond.

And everywhere the Southern Belles mingle with the visitors. You can have your picture taken arm-in-arm with one or more of these gorgeously costumed young ladies.

If you like to shop, you're in for a whole new experience. More than 10 boutiques and shops feature all sorts of unique items from souvenirs to country antiques, from butterfly jewelry to outdoor apparel.

ADDITIONAL ATTRACTIONS:

If you have extra time, say a couple of hours or so, take highways 665 and 33 north from Winter Haven and drive 24 miles to the junction with Highway 561. From there, **Lake Louisa State Park** is six or seven miles to the northeast.

Lake Louisa offers more than 1,790 acres of outdoor fun and recreational activities for everyone. Situated on only one of a chain of 13 lakes connected by the Palatlakaha River, it offers some of the finest fresh water fishing in Florida. Other than the fishing, you can swim, picnic, canoe, go bird watching, and study the local wildlife. *Open 8–sunset daily.* ☎ *394-3969. Admission $3.25 per vehicle.*

Trip 21

Kissimmee and St. Cloud

Only a century ago, Florida's interior was a vast uncharted wilderness inhabited by a profusion of wildlife and a few Indians. It was a land of boundless cypress swamps and jungle-like vegetation that provided protection to the powerful Seminole chiefs who resisted President Andrew Jackson's campaign to relocate them west of the Mississippi.

It wasn't until after the end of the Civil War that settlement of the area was undertaken in earnest. Steamboats began to carry pioneers and goods into the interior where life was hard and land was cheap. The first settlement was a tiny trading post known as Allendale.

In 1881, Philadelphia businessman Hamilton Disston purchased four million acres of land for 25 cents an acre. He selected Allendale for his headquarters and changed its name to Kissimmee, a Caloosa Indian word meaning "Heaven's Place."

Disston set his men to work draining vast areas of swamp and building sugar plantations and lumber camps, all interconnected by a system of waterways and railroads. He dredged the rivers and lakes, bringing new industry to central Florida. Kissimmee soon became a bustling, boat-building port. With the arrival of the railroad in 1882 it emerged as the commercial center for the entire region.

The first hotel, the Tropical, was built in 1883, with tourism arriving shortly thereafter in the form of such notables as President Chester A. Arthur and Mr. and Mrs. John Jacob Astor. And it was around that time that the livestock industry in central Florida began to take off, peaking around the turn of the century. Ranchers brought cattle into Kissimmee from all over the state for shipment to Cuba. The first hump-back, heat-resistant Brahmas were introduced during the 1930s; the Florida Cattleman's Association was formed in 1934.

Unfortunately, the enterprise that began it all failed. The remnants of Disston's sugar plantation were purchased and the property divided into lots; the old plantation becoming what is now known as St. Cloud.

Today, the area is second only to Orlando as a tourist destination. Both Kissimmee and St. Cloud feature quaint old historic districts that are ideal for walking, browsing, shopping, dining, and sightseeing. Kissimmee is also the location of the main entrance to Walt Disney World, EPCOT and MGM Studios, as well as number of other attractions and theme parks.

GETTING THERE:

The area is just 20 miles south of Orlando and easily accessible via Interstate 4, the Bee Line Express, and the Florida Turnpike.

GETTING AROUND:

Most of your sightseeing will done by driving, but the downtown districts of Kissimmee and St. Cloud are ideal for walking. Parking in both places is plentiful, metered on the downtown streets with garages in strategic locations.

PRACTICALITIES:

The **Area Code** is 407.

A few of the smaller attractions are closed on Sundays, and some are closed Mondays, but this shouldn't be a problem as the main ones are open daily throughout the year, closing only on Christmas Day.

The area close to and around the entrance to Disney World is always busy, with heavy traffic the norm throughout the daylight hours.

TOURIST INFORMATION:

The **Kissimmee-St. Cloud Convention and Visitors Bureau Official Visitor Information Center** is conveniently located in Kissimmee off the Florida Turnpike at Exit 244, and is open daily the year-round; hours vary according to the season.

The **Kissimmee-St. Cloud Convention and Visitors Bureau**, PO Box 422007, Kissimmee, FL 34742-2007, ☎ 800-526-KISS.

FOOD AND DRINK:

As you might expect of a major tourist center, good eating is the rule rather than the exception. Of the dozens of restaurants available, the following establishments can be relied on for tasty food and friendly service, but they are only a place to start. For your evening meal and entertainment, you might try either **Medieval Times** or **Wild Bill's Wild West Dinner Show** at Fort Liberty, or one of the other dinner theaters in the area—all are described later as a part of the tour.

> **Captain Nemo's** (on Highway 192 at 5469 West Irlo Bronson Memorial Highway) is open from 7 until midnight for breakfast, lunch and dinner. Fresh seafood is the mainstay of the dinner menu, and the place is light and airy with a nautical theme. ☎ 396-6911. $–$$.

> **Twin Dragons Restaurant** (on Highway 192 at 4002 West Irlo Bronson Memorial Highway) is open from 11 to 11 for lunch and dinner. If you love Chinese food, this is the place for you. The menu includes both Cantonese and Szechwan dishes, and there's an expansive lunch buffet Monday through Friday. Reservations are advised for dinner. ☎ 846-6161. $$.

SUGGESTED TOUR:

If you want to do it all, you'll have to start early and stay late. Leave Orlando by 9 a.m. at the latest, head down Interstate 4 to exit 25B, and from there drive west on Highway 192 for about two-and-a-half miles to Old Lake Wilson Road. Turn south there and continue one mile to:

A World of Orchids (1). Here, you'll find one of the largest permanent displays of orchids in the world. The park features thousands of flowering orchids, including many rare and unusual varieties in settings, both outdoor and indoor, as well as an enclosed tropical rainforest. Many of the exotic plants have been propagated in the conservatory's own labs and can be purchased in the gift shop. *Open 9:30–5:30 daily except Christmas, New Years Day, July 4, and Thanksgiving.* ☎ *396-1887.* ♿. *Adults $8.95, children under 16 free.*

Return to Highway 192, turn west and drive a half-mile or so to Formosa Garden Boulevard, turning south to **Splendid China** (2). The park offers a glimpse into the somewhat inscrutable world of Chinese culture and history through more than 60 miniature replicas of China's most notable landmarks. These include a half-mile-long reproduction of the Great Wall of China, the Forbidden City, Tibet's Potala Palace, the Stone Forest, and many others. You can enjoy a live show, an authentic Chinese meal, or just wander around at will. *Open 9:30–7 daily.* ☎ *397-8800.* ♿. *Adults $23.55, children 5–11 $13.90.*

From Splendid China, turn east. **Old Town** (3) is just east of the junction with Interstate 4. This famous shopping center is quite unusual, with more than 60 shops and restaurants all set within a re-created 19th-century village. Not just for the grown-ups, the kids, too, will enjoy the experience, especially the antique carousel and the Ferris wheel.

Water Mania (4), just a little farther east on Highway 192 (West Irlo Bronson Memorial Parkway), is not for everyone but, if you like water parks and you've brought along a swimsuit, this is one you won't want to miss. A 36-acre extravaganza of waterslides, playgrounds, bumper boats, and wave pool—you could easily spend an entire day here and many visitors do just that. *Open 9:30–7 through the summer (hours vary the rest of the year).* ☎ *396-2626.* ♿. *Adults $23.95, children 3–12 $17.95.*

From Water Mania, take West Irlo Bronson Highway to Poinciana Boulevard. Turn south there and drive five miles to the **Green Meadows Petting Farm** (5). If you're traveling with children this is one theme park you won't want to miss. There are more than 40 acres of farmland and more than 200 animals where you and the kids can really get acquainted with life on the farm: learn how to actually milk a cow (by hand), ride a pony, and hold a chicken. The petting pen holds all sorts of animals, and you can also take a hayride, which is included in the cost of admission. It's a really neat experience. *Open 9:30 to 5:30 daily; last tour begins 90 minutes before closing time.* ☎ *846-0770.* ♿. *Admission $13.50, children under 3 free.*

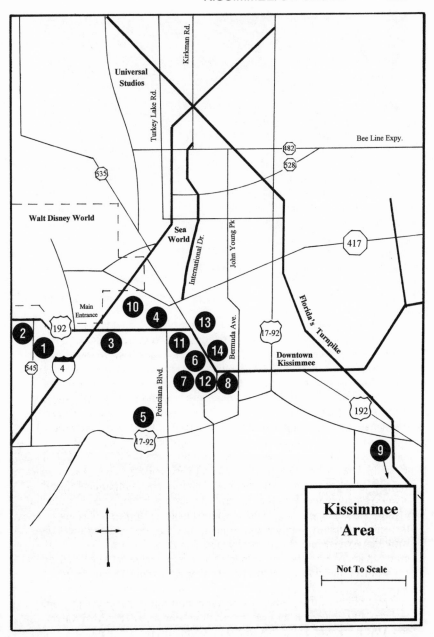

Tournament at Medieval Times

Drive north again and rejoin West Irlo Bronson Highway; **Jungleland** (6), until recently known as the Alligatorland Safari Zoo, is just to the east at 4580 West Irlo Bronson Highway. The zoo/wildlife park is set on seven acres with more than 300 exotic birds, reptiles, and animals in residence. A half-mile trail provides an easy walk through the jungle and lots of encounters with the animals—tigers, bobcats, lions, ostriches, and macaws to name but a few. Here, you can have your picture taken with Radcliffe, alias "Clyde," one of the orangutans that performed with Clint Eastwood in the movie *Every Which Way But Loose,* or even a 12-foot alligator. It's a great experience, and compared to many other theme parks in the area, reasonably priced. *Open 9–5 daily.* ☎ *396-1012.* ♿. *Adults $9.95, children 3–11 $6.95.*

A little farther east at 4510 West Irlo Bronson Highway, **Medieval Life** (7), a part of the Medieval Times complex (more about that later), is a re-creation of an 11th-century village where authentically costumed villagers and tradesmen—potters, blacksmiths, millers and so on—demonstrate the workings of a medieval community. You can also take a tour of a castle dungeon and torture chamber. *Open 4 p.m.–8 p.m. daily.* ☎ *396-1518.* ♿. *Free with Medieval Times Dinner ticket; otherwise, Adults $8, children 3–12 $6.*

From Medieval Life, drive east on West Irlo Bronson Highway to North Hoagland Boulevard where you'll find the **Flying Tigers Warbird Air Museum** (8) at number 231. More than a museum, this is a place of restoration where the old planes that saw service in the wartime skies over Europe and

In the Flying Tigers Warbird Museum

the Pacific are lovingly restored to their original fighting condition. The highlight of your visit is to see, not only such famous aircraft as the P-51 Mustang, B-17 Flying Fortress, and P-38 Lightning, but also to observe restoration work in progress. You can even take a flight over the area in an open-cockpit biplane *Open 9–5:30 daily, 9–5 on Sunday.* ☎ *933-1942.* ♿. *Adults $6, seniors and children under 12 $5. Biplane flights $95–$180.*

Lake Kissimmee State Park (9) is some 40 miles south of Orlando in central Florida on the shores of lakes Kissimmee, Tiger, and Rosalie. It's a bit far but worthy of a mention here. From Orlando, or Kissimmee, take Florida's Turnpike south to its junction with Highway 60. Turn west on 60 and drive on for about 25 miles, then follow the signs. You'll find no crowds here, only the solitude of the countryside. For anglers, the three lakes offer some of the finest sport fishing in Florida. You can spend a quiet afternoon boating, canoeing, or bird watching. The park is home to the white-tailed deer, bald eagle, sandhill cranes, turkeys, and bobcats. Wildlife photographers won't want to miss this opportunity. For hikers, there's more than 13 miles of trails to explore. And if a picnic lunch under the trees in some of Florida's most picturesque countryside is your idea of heaven, then bring your hamper.

In pioneer days, south central Florida was cattle country. The park's interpretive center offers a living history demonstration of what life must have been like for the "cow hunters" at an 1876 Florida cow camp. *Open 8– sundown daily.* ☎ *696-1112.* ♿. *Admission.*

KISSIMMEE/ST. CLOUD AT NIGHT:

There are five grand evening experiences to choose from in Kissimmee, each a great way to end your daytrip. The following should help you pick one. These are extremely popular attractions, so be sure to make a reservation as far in advance as possible.

Arabian Nights (10), just off Interstate 4, Exit 25, at 6225 West Highway 192, is a two-hour dinner show featuring all sorts of equestrian acts, from a Wild West show to a full-blown Roman chariot race. *Performances nightly at 7:30.* ☎ *239-9223.* &. *Adults $36.95, children 3–11 $23.95.*

Capone's Dinner and Show (11), at 4740 West Highway 192, offers a musical evening and dinner based on the Prohibition Era and Al Capone and his gangsters. Lots of fun. *Performances nightly, but schedules vary; call for times.* ☎ *397-2378.* &. *Adults $35.99, children 4–12 $18.*

Medieval Times Dinner and Tournament (12), at 4510 West Highway 192, is held in a replica 11th-century English castle. You'll eat the old-fashioned way, with your fingers. And your table will be only a few feet from the action, as knights on horseback joust and fight with swords and maces. *Performances Sunday through Friday at 8 p.m., Saturday at 8:30.* ☎ *396-1518.* &. *Adults $34.95, seniors $31.56, children 3–12 $22.95.*

American Gladiators Live (13), at 5515 West Highway 192, is the newest of the Kissimmee dinner extravaganzas. It's a 90-minute live competition evening show featuring the American Gladiators battling it out with amateur athletes in the same slam-bang action events we have come to know so well from the weekly TV show. They're all here: Hawk, Laser, Siren, Sky, Ice, Jazz, Turbo, Viper and Sabre. They take on contenders in Assault, Breakthrough & Conquer, Joust, Powerball, the Wall, and Whiplash, and you're close enough to the action to get really involved. Two shows nightly include dinner and popular beverages. The Sunday show includes soft drinks with dinner as an option. *During the peak season: two shows nightly beginning at 6:30 and 9. Off-peak season nightly at 7:30.* ☎ *390-0000.* &. *Adults $34.95, seniors $31.50, children 3–12 $21.50.*

Wild Bill's Wild West Dinner Show (14), at 5260 Highway 192, is set in a complex that includes a museum, frontier fort, and an Indian village. The show is a reproduction of an 1876 traveling Western show, such as those promoted by Buffalo Bill Cody, and features all the trick roping, riding, and Indian dancing you would expect of such a spectacular presentation. The cost of admission includes a four-course meal served as the show unfolds. *Performances 7 p.m. Reservations are required.* ☎ *351-5151.* &. *Adults $33.95, children 3–11 $19.95.*

Section IV

Sunset on the Gulf of Mexico

THE WEST COAST

It's here that the manatees join the hundreds of thousands of tourists in their annual pilgrimage to the warm waters of the Gulf of Mexico, to toast in the sunshine and relax as they wait for warmer weather.

For more than 400 years this area, Florida's West Coast, has been welcoming visitors. The first to arrive were the Spanish conquistadors. They came in search of gold, which they didn't find. More than 300 years later another visitor saw the real potential of the area. Henry Plant brought the railroad to Tampa, and it was he who built the onion-domed hotel that was to become a famous local landmark.

Then came the Greek sponge fishermen who settled in Tarpon Springs and, even today, still harvest the valuable little creatures just as they did a century ago. The Greeks were followed by clansmen from the highlands of Scotland who settled in Dunedin. Next came the Cubans who moved into Tampa and created the Hav-a-Tampa cigar industry. Their warehouses eventually became a trendy gathering place with elegant cafés, artists' studios, fancy ethnic restaurants, and chic specialty shops.

Today, the heart of vacation country on the West Coast encompasses the neighboring cities of Tampa and St. Petersburg—Tampa is skyscrapers, business and industry, while St. Petersburg is sun-soaked beaches and an emerald ocean—supported to the north by a captivating collection of island communities such as Indian Rocks Beach, Madeira Beach, and Treasure Island, and to the south by the likes of Anna Marie Island, Longboat Key, Siesta Key, and many more that offer even more interesting opportunities. And to all that you can add mile after mile of tempting white sand, clear green ocean, and gently waving tropical trees.

GETTING THERE:

By Air: Two airports serve the Greater Tampa-St. Petersburg Area: **Tampa International Airport**, less than 30 minutes from the beaches, is the hub of numerous airlines. **St. Petersburg-Clearwater International Airport** provides a smaller, though no less important, back-up to its larger neighbor. Almost all major domestic airlines offer service into Tampa. St. Pete-Clearwater is served by the smaller carriers such as Air Sunshine, Air Transat, ATA, Canadian Airlines, Seacoast, Sunjet and others.

By Car: The Tampa-St. Petersburg-Clearwater Area is linked to the interstate system and is easily accessible from the north via Interstates 75 and 275, and US Highway 19. From Orlando and the east, access is provided via Interstate 4 and Highway 60.

By Rail: The Amtrak station is at 601 North Nebraska in downtown Tampa. ☎ 800-872-7245, local 221-7601. Bus service from St. Petersburg to the station leaves from Pinellas Square Mall in Pinellas Park at 7200 US 19 North. ☎ 522-9475.

By Bus: The Greyhound/Trailways bus terminals are at 180 9th Street in St. Petersburg, and 610 Polk Street in Tampa. ☎ 800-231-2222.

GETTING AROUND:

Navigating the streets and highways, though time-consuming, is rarely a problem. True, things get a little hectic during rush hours, but if you avoid traveling at peak times—7–9 and 4:30–6—you shouldn't experience problems.

Tampa is laid out on a grid system divided east from west by Florida Avenue, and north from south by Highway 60. You'll need to keep your wits about you while driving in the downtown area as most of the streets are one-way.

St. Petersburg's street system is also grid-form north-south and east-west. All avenues, terraces and places run east-west; streets and ways, north-south. Numbers of north-south streets begin at the bay where they are smallest, and progress westward toward the gulf.

Parking on the streets is limited in the downtown business districts of both Tampa and St. Petersburg. Metered parking lots are plentiful; rates start at 60 cents for the first hour and range upward to between $3.60 and $4.50 for eight hours.

Public transportation is often not as convenient here as in Miami. In Tampa it's provided by Hart Line, which serves the city and its immediate suburbs; ☎ 254-4278 for fares and schedules. **Pinellas Suncoast Transit Authority** handles the St. Petersburg-Clearwater area, ☎ 530-9911.

The Tampa-Ybor Trolley connects downtown shops, restaurants, and attractions with Harbor Island, Ybor City, the Florida Aquarium, Garrison Seaport Center, and other points of interest in between. You can board at any one of 17 stops scattered throughout the business district along Channelside

Drive and Ybor City. The fare is 25¢ per person, and the trolley operates from 7:30 to 5:30 seven days a week, including holidays. ☎ 233-2752.

ACCOMMODATIONS:

With more than 500 motels and hotels in the area, finding somewhere to stay is rarely a problem, but what can you expect to pay? Lodging costs range from $30 to more than $100 per night depending upon location, amenities and season. **Average room rates** during specific seasons are:

September–December: $50
January–April: $65
May–August: $50
September–December: $50

PRACTICALITIES:

The **Area Code** is 813.

The climate is balmy, averaging more sunny days than anywhere else in Florida with 361 days out of 365 per year. If you want to be sure of fine weather, the West Coast is your best choice. The average mean temperature is 73°F, sinking to lows around 70° and highs in July exceeding 90°. Even so, the sun can be unforgiving, so be sure to use adequate sunscreen on those long days out, especially on the beaches.

Opening and Closing Times: Most attractions are open daily the year-round, although one or two do close either on Sunday or Monday.

Admissions: These are generally lower than they are around the great theme parks and attractions in Orlando and to the east. Even so, you'll need to bring along plenty of cash, for there's lots to see and do.

TOURIST INFORMATION:

Tampa/Hillsboro Convention and Visitors Association, 111 Madison Street, Suite 1010, Tampa, FL 33602-4706. ☎ 813-223- 1111, fax 229-6616.

St. Petersburg/Clearwater Area Convention and Visitors Bureau, St. Petersburg ThunderDome, One Stadium Drive, Suite A, St. Petersburg, FL 33705-1706. ☎ 813-582-7892, fax 582-7949.

FOOD AND DRINK:

Believe it or not, there are more than 3,000 restaurants in the greater Tampa-St. Petersburg-Clearwater area, and hundreds more to the north and south in cities such as Naples, Fort Myers, and Sarasota. You can find almost any dining experience you fancy, from the most elegant to the casual, and it's all inexpensive compared to Miami and Orlando. The powers that be state that the average cost of meal is around $3.25 for breakfast, $5 for lunch and, incredibly, $9 for dinner. You'll find examples you can count on for good service, great food and ambiance listed for each daytrip.

Trip 22

Tampa

Tampa owes its commercial success to the Bay, its port, which is now the seventh largest in the nation, the Hillsborough River, and men like Vicente Martínes Ybor who, in 1886, established the first cigar factory in the area, aviation pioneer Tony Jannus and architect D.P. Davis. Today, even though Tampa is the business center of the Bay area, tourism is almost as important here as it is to its sister city across the water. Your reasons for visiting may be tied to commercial interests, but there's no reason why you shouldn't take time out from commerce to enjoy what Tampa has to offer. If you're here on vacation there's plenty to see and do before you venture farther afield.

GETTING THERE:

GETTING AROUND:

PRACTICALITIES:

TOURIST INFORMATION:
See pages 140–141.

FOOD AND DRINK:
There are literally hundreds of restaurants, cafés and bistros in Tampa, and you'll surely find something exciting and new. Seafood is, of course, the staple diet here on Florida's West Coast. It's all caught locally, is just as fresh as can be, comes in all shapes and sizes, and is prepared every way possible: snapper, pompano, scallops, shrimp, lobster and much more. Caribbean cuisine, Cuban, Chinese, Mexican, Italian, French, Japanese, Greek, you name it, you'll find it somewhere in the greater Tampa area. You might like to try one or two of the following:

The Bay Café (just south of I-275 Exit 24 on Kennedy Boulevard at the Embassy Suites) is, as hotel restaurants go, worthy of a mention. Open for breakfast, lunch and dinner from 6:30 a.m. to 2 p.m., and 5–10 p.m. The food is good and reasonably priced. The menu includes fresh seafood and steaks, and there's a daily lunch buffet. Make reservations for dinner if you don't want to wait in line. ☎ 875-1555. $–$$$.

Downtown Tampa waterfront

Café Creole (take I-24 Exit 1 and go to 1330 9th Avenue). If you like authentic Cajun cuisine, this is one restaurant you won't want to miss. Open for lunch and dinner from 11:30. Great gumbo. ☎ 247-6283. $$.

Crawdaddy's (2500 Rocky Point Drive at the east end of the Courtney Campbell Causeway) is open for lunch and dinner from 11–3, and 5–11. Lots of fresh seafood in a Roaring Twenties atmosphere. Noisy—jazz and reggae—busy and popular with locals as well as tourists. You'll need to make a reservation for dinner, ☎ 281-0407. $–$$$.

Morrison's Cafeteria (11810 North Dale Mabury). You can't beat this fast-food chain for a solid lunch or dinner. The menu features real cooking—carved meat, potatoes, gravy, and dessert, etc. ☎ 963-1660. $.

SUGGESTED TOUR AND LOCAL ATTRACTIONS:

Adventure Island (1), at 10001 McKinley Drive adjacent to Busch Gardens, is two miles west of Interstate 75 and two miles east of Interstate 275 in the northern section of the city. Billed as the "Tampa Bay area's ultimate family water-themed park," Adventure Island offers 17 distinct play/recreation areas spread across a 36-acre outdoor complex. Aside from the obvious watery attractions and rides, the park features outdoor restaurants and cafés, picnic and sunbathing areas, gift shops, arcades, dressing rooms, and a volleyball zone. In other words, you don't have to be a water baby to enjoy the park. You could easily spend an entire day here and, of course, that's exactly what its owners had in mind when they designed the place. The adult section—kids can play too, under supervision—is a land of flumes, water rides, swimming areas, and a 17,000 square-foot surfing pool with crashing waves up to five feet high. The children's section, **Fabian's Funport**, has a scaled-down wave pool and an assortment of playtime attractions that will tickle their imaginations: bubbler springs, a colored water play area, a beach, and a funky amphibious spokesperson to greet them. *Open 9:30–6 daily, March through October, with extended hours during the summer months.* ☎ *987-5660.* &. *Adults $20.95, children 3–9 $18.95; admission after 3 p.m.: $13.80 and $11.65.*

The Florida Aquarium (2), 701 Channelside Drive just south of the Crosstown Expressway, is a three-story-high, glass-domed structure that houses an aquarium featuring lots of hands-on and interactive exhibits. These interpret Florida's ecosystem, aquatic habitats, and wetlands. Included is the **Florida Coral Reefs Gallery**, with all the wonders of the colorful world undersea: fish, barracuda, animals, plants, and the reef itself. The **Florida Bays and Beaches Gallery** contains both fresh and saltwater displays, while the **Florida Wetlands Gallery** features a cypress swamp, mangroves and a river with all sorts of fish and wildlife, including otters. There are 101 species of plants and animals native to Florida, including alligators and crocodiles, all shown in their natural habitats. *Open 9–5 daily.* ☎ *273-4020.* &. *Adults $13.95, seniors and children 13–18 $12.55, children 3–12 $6.95.*

Lowry Park Zoo (3), 7530 North Boulevard just west of Interstate 275, is ranked one of the three largest zoos in the United States. The exhibits and state-of-the-art natural habitats include the **Asian Domain, Primate World**, **Florida Wildlife Center**, an **Aviary**, a **Coral Reef** exhibit, a children's **Petting Zoo,** and the **Manatee Aquatic Center** with viewing tanks. There's also a river otter exhibit with an underwater viewing area, pools and habitats for alligators, turtles, and other amphibians, along with aquatic tanks—fresh and saltwater—plus a snake exhibit. *Open 9:30–5 daily.* ☎ *935-8552.* &. *Adults $6.50, seniors $5.50, children 3–11 $4.50.*

The Children's Museum (4), 7550 North Boulevard next to the Lowry Park Zoo, features changing, hands-on exhibits designed as much to enter-

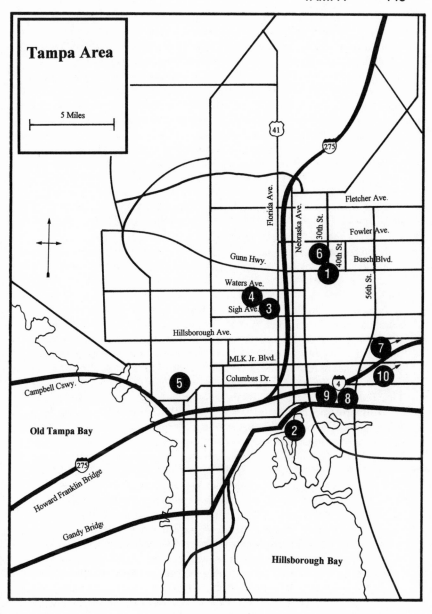

tain as to educate. Here the kids can enjoy the natural wonders of the farmyard, see fruits and vegetables growing, and find how and why they do. They can also enjoy a visit to **Safety Village**, a small town where they'll learn all about safety and security. *Open 9–4:30, Mon.–Thurs.; 9–3 Fri.; 10–5 Sat.; and 1–5 on Sun.* ☎ *935-8441. Ꮠ. Admission $3, children under 2 free.*

The Museum of African-American Art (5), 1308 North Marrion Street off Interstate 275 Exit 26, opened in 1991. It's the first of its kind in Florida and contains one of the most extraordinary collections of African-American art in the nation: the Barnett-Aden Collection features paintings, sculptures, and other works dating from the mid-1800s through the present. The permanent collections are enhanced by visiting exhibits and special events throughout the year. *Open 10–4:30, Tues.–Sat.* ☎ *272-2466. Ꮠ. Adults $3, seniors and children 5–18 $2.*

*The Museum of Science and Industry (6), 4801 East Fowler Avenue three miles east of Interstate 275 Exit 34, or three miles west of Interstate 75 Exit 54, is a huge facility encompassing more than 200,000 square feet filled with interactive displays and exhibits, and an on-going program of workshops, lectures, films, demonstrations, and traveling shows. All these pertain to science, industry, technology, health, aviation, and space flight. Other exhibits include the **Back Woods**, a 40-acre wilderness with three miles of walking trails; a **Butterfly Garden**; the **Gulf Coast Hurricane**, a hurricane simulator that demonstrates the effects of the great winds; and a children's area designed especially for little ones under five. There's also a magnificent planetarium where you can take a trip to the stars, and an IMAX theater with a 10,500-square-foot screen. *Open at 9 daily, closing times vary with the seasons.* ☎ *987-6300. Ꮠ. Admission includes Planetarium and IMAX theater. Adults $11, children 13–18 $9, children 2–12 $7.*

Hillsborough River State Park (7), 12 miles north of Tampa on U.S. Highway 301, is one of the first state parks established in Florida. It was developed by the Civilian Conservation Corps in 1936 and opened to the general public two years later. Of special interest is Fort Foster, a pioneer fort where Park Service personnel run living history programs and act out the everyday lives and duties of the early settlers, much as they might have been in 1837. Facilities include restrooms with hot showers, picnic tables and grills, a concession stand where you can buy gifts, food and drink, and rent a canoe. More than eight miles of nature trails meander through the hammocks, live oaks, sabal palms, magnolias, and hickories along the banks of the Hillsborough River. Popular activities include hiking, bird watching, wildlife photography, swimming, fishing, horseback riding, and picnicking. *Open 8–sunset daily.* ☎ *986-1020. Ꮠ. Admission $3.25 per vehicle.*

Ybor City (8), named for Don Vicente Martinez Ybor, is essentially the historic section of downtown Tampa. Señor Ybor came to the frontier near Tampa Bay and "turned it into a city for thousands of immigrants," and the "Cigar Capital of the World." From the opening of the first cigar factory in

1886 until the 1930s, Ybor City was a thriving community, offering homes and opportunity to one and all. Then, as Florida's early interests began to change Tampa grew, and Ybor City was slowly but surely absorbed into the urban sprawl that became the Tampa Bay area we know today. The story of how and why this happened is related through the exhibits, tools, utensils, and artifacts housed in the **Ybor City State Museum** (9) at 1818 9th Avenue in Tampa, and you can take a free, escorted walking tour of the historic district—*contact Bill Morris at 634-6505 or the* **Ybor City Chamber of Commerce** *for a map at 1800 East Ninth Street,* ☎ *248-3712.* The museum is in a building that once housed the Ferlita Bakery. *Open 9–noon and 1–5, Tues.–Sat.* ☎ *247-6323.* &. *Admission includes a visit to La Casita. Adults $2, children under 6 free.*

La Casita, in Preservation Park next to the museum, is a one-time cigar worker's home. It has been extensively restored and furnished with period pieces, circa 1895, typical of a cigar worker's cottage. *Open 10–noon and 1–3, Tues.–Sat.* ☎ *247-6323.* &.

ADDITIONAL ATTRACTIONS:

Set in the midst of an extensive system of lakes to the northeast of Lakeland, the **Tenoroc State Recreation Area** (10), located northeast of Lakeland on State Route 659, was once the site of an extensive and, so many say, destructive phosphate mining operation. The site has since been reclaimed, repaired, and transformed into what is arguably one of Florida's finest outdoor recreation areas. Certainly its designation and reputation as one of Florida's "Best Fishing" locations is well earned, as the fishing is as good as can be found anywhere. There's an abundance of bass, bluegill, and crappie, all ripe for the taking.

Other popular activities include primitive camping, horseback riding, nature study and bird watching, picnicking and hiking (Tenoroc is one of Florida's "Best Hiking" parks, too).

Facilities at the park include trails, boat ramps, and a large picnic pavilion. Due to special boating regulations it's best to check with the Park Service before launching your boat. The types of boats permitted on the water vary from lake to lake. *Open 8–sunset daily.* ☎ *499-2421. Admission $3.25 per vehicle.*

Busch Gardens

The Gardens are Tampa Bay's answer to the great theme parks to the east. Growing steadily larger and ever more popular, Busch Gardens is a complete daytrip in its own right. It's located at the corner of Busch Boulevard and 40th Street, eight miles northeast of downtown Tampa. For more 30 years, the 335-acre park has given visitors and residents of the Tampa Bay area more pleasure and entertainment than could ever be accounted for. The overall theme is one of the great African continent. Although it's an eclectic mixture of thrilling rides, side shows, live entertainment, restaurants, games, and other special attractions, Busch Gardens is actually one of the nation's premier zoos with more than 2,800 exotic animals in residence, all of which provides something special for everyone. There are nine themed areas within the park boundaries, of which Egypt is the latest addition.

GETTING THERE:

The park is two miles east of Interstate 275 at the Busch Boulevard exit, or two miles west of Interstate 75 at Exit 54.

PRACTICALITIES:

Park hours are 9:30–6 the year round, except during summer and selected holiday periods when hours are extended.

Admission: Adults $36.15 plus tax, children 3–9 $29.75 plus tax.

Parking: Cars $4, motorcycles $3, trucks and campers $5.

The weather is almost always hot, and the paved areas of the park only enhance the situation. Most of your time will be spent outdoors—at least six hours—so adequate sunscreen is a must.

TOURIST INFORMATION:

Busch Gardens, PO Box 9158, Tampa, FL 33674-9158, ☎ 813-987-5000.

Tigers at Claw Island

FOOD AND DRINK:

Take your pick. There are more than 20 cafés, ice-cream parlors, soft drink stands, and restaurants inside the park, serving everything from a four-course meal to sandwiches and sundaes. It's kind of tough, if you're watching the old waistline.

SUGGESTED TOUR AND ATTRACTIONS:

As always, the best-kept secret to enjoying a daytrip to the park is how to make the most of your time there. And, as always, that secret is to start at the end and work your way back to the beginning.

When you enter the park, first get your bearings. Then go quickly—don't stop along the way to see the sights, you'll do that later—through Morocco, close to the main entrance, and turn right. From there it's a short walk to the Alligator Pond where you'll turn right again, then left past the fountain, through the Myombe Reserve into Nairobi; the Nairobi Train Station will be just in front of you. At the station, take the first train out and ride it all the way to the Congo and disembark. You'll really enjoy the train ride through and around the Serengeti Plain and, at some later time during your visit, you should try to do the train ride again in its entirety. When disembarking in the Congo, the River Rapids and Kumba will be just to your right, past the Ubanga-Banga Bumper Cars. You can get a quick snack at the Vivi Restaurant or proceed straight to the Python for the ride of your life; well, not quite the ride of your life, the Montu inverted roller coaster in Egypt will provide that. For now, though, begin with the **Congo** (1); if you came early you should have it pretty much to yourself.

Similar to the depth of the African jungle, this area presents a number of exciting attractions highlighted by **Kumba**, a world-class roller coaster with mighty loops and drops that will almost turn you inside-out. The nearby **Congo River Rapids** and the **Python** roller coaster only add to the thrills. In the midst of all this, **Claw Island** and its white and yellow tiger inhabitants seems tame by comparison, but you should take time to see the great cats, they photograph well.

Following the plan to proceed from rear to front, the next stop is **Stanleyville** (2). This is a fun place, very much the African village where you can get acquainted with the orangutans, warthogs, and snakes. **Orchid Canyon** is a sweet-scented diversion just across the way from the **Tanganyika Tidal Wave Lagoon**, and **Stanley Falls** offers another roller coaster ride—a log flume this time, with a water splash.

From Stanleyville, it's onward into the **Land Of The Dragons** (3). This is one for the kids; but since there's a little kid in every grown-up this section of the park should appeal to one and all. Surrounded by brilliant colors, you'll enter a magical dreamland that's just as limitless as your imagination. Accompanied by **Dumphrey**, a friendly dragon, the youngsters enjoy a number of attractions, including a three-story tree house complete with towers and stairways; the big kids will enjoy the experience, too.

Next, it's the **Bird Gardens** (4). Here among the intertwining greenery you'll see all sorts of exotic birds, some in aviaries, some flying free. The highlights include the **World of Birds**, a live show, and **Eagle Canyon**, which features bald and golden eagles. There's also a koala bear habitat that houses a number of the cuddly little animals from "down under." Before you leave the Bird Gardens, be sure to take time out and visit the **Hospitality House** for a free beer and moment or two of relaxation.

From the Bird Gardens, it's the road to **Morocco** (5) near the main entrance. Very much akin to the Middle Eastern souk you've come to know in the movies, the area is a shopping bazaar where authentic, hand-crafted items are sold. Snacks or meals are available at the **Boujad Bakery** and **Zagora Café**. It's also an area where you can see a live show in either the **Palace Theater**, the **Marrakech Theater**, or the **Tangiers Theater**.

Just beyond Morocco, to the right, the **Crown Colony** (6) is where you'll find the park's main restaurant, from which there's a stunning view over the Serengeti Plain. It's also the location of **Clydesdale Hamlet**, home of the famous Budweiser Horses, and it's here that you can board the **Monorail** or **Skyride** for an aerial trip over the park.

Beyond the Crown Colony, **Egypt** (7) is the newest addition to Busch Gardens. This seven-acre section, the ninth themed area within the park, recreates the sights and sounds of Egypt's culture from the earliest times to the

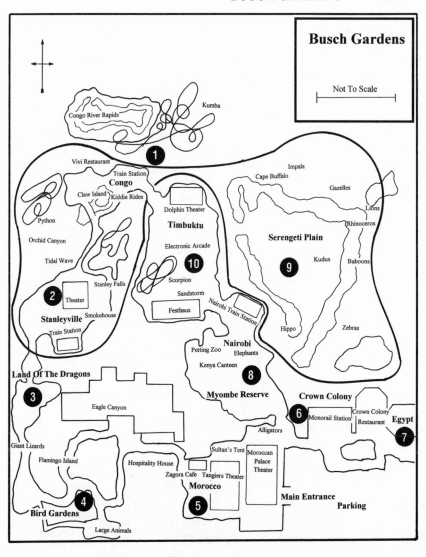

Busch Gardens

Not To Scale

present. Once inside you can visit **Tut's Tomb**, a replica of the young king's burial place as it was being excavated by Howard Carter during the 1920s. The **Sand Dig** gives youngsters the opportunity to discover Egyptian antiquities buried in the sand. The **Golden Scarab: Treasures of the Nile** is a shopping bazaar featuring goods for sale handcrafted by on-site artisans. Finally there's **Montu.** Billed as the world's longest and tallest inverted roller coaster, the monster slings its riders through four first-of-a-kind elements over a track more than 3,500 feet long at speeds exceeding 60 miles an hour.

Now it's time to retrace your footsteps to **Nairobi** (8). This time, however, you'll be able to enjoy some atmosphere along the way. Be sure to stop by the **Sultan's Tent** as you leave Morocco and see the **Snake Charmer**, a lovely lady who does unbelievable things with snakes. Also be sure to get some pictures of the alligators and the gorilla in the **Myombe Reserve.**

The great apes in the Myombe Reserve are claimed to be the highlight of the Nairobi section, but the elephants are just as spectacular. Their habitat is one of rocks and sand. There's also a petting zoo, an animal nursery, and giant tortoises to visit. And **Nocturnal Mountain** offers a look at the more obscure creatures of the African twilight. If you like, you can take advantage of where you are, head for the station and take the full train ride around the **Serengeti Plain** (9), a 60-acre natural grass veldt that illustrates the characteristics of nearly 500 animals, including giraffes, hippos, impala, gazelles, baboons, zebras, and many more. The Plain is off limits to pedestrians, so the train and the monorail are the only ways you can see it. From the Serengeti, the train runs on around the park, stopping at the Congo and Stanleyville before returning to the Nairobi station.

The final stop on your tour is **Timbuktu** (10), right at the center of the park. Here, in a replica of that most remote of ancient desert trading posts, you can ride the **Scorpion**, a steel roller coaster, as well as the **Phoenix** and the **Sandstorm**, two more thrilling rides. The **Dolphin Theater** is the highlight of Timbuktu. Check for show times, you won't want to miss this treat.

St. Petersburg

As much a resort as it is a business community, St. Petersburg is Tampa's sister city to the west. While Tampa is all skyscrapers and office blocks, here you'll find few buildings rising above four stories. It's a place that for more years than recorded history reflects has been attractive to visitors. Some historians believe Ponce de León visited Mullet Key on the southernmost tip of the Pinellas Suncoast in 1513, and evidence confirms that both Pánfilo de Narváez and Hernando de Soto visited the area: Narváez in 1528 and de Soto in 1539. It was they who gave Pinellas its name, derived from the Spanish words for "Point of Pines," punta pinal. Centuries before the Spanish arrived, however, the St. Petersburg area was home to the Tocobaga Indians. Pirates came to Tampa Bay in the early 1830s, followed in 1842 by James Stevenson who established a homestead and became known as the "Father of Clearwater." In 1875, General John C. Williams of Detroit, Michigan, purchased the 1,600 acres that were to become downtown St. Petersburg. Today, more than ever before, the trend continues. Almost four million people visited St. Petersburg and Clearwater in 1995 and the number continues to grow.

GETTING THERE:
See page 140.

PRACTICALITIES:
The **Area Code** is 813.

Most attractions are open daily, with a few exceptions that close either Sunday or Monday, sometimes both. Those that operate seven days a week may open late or close early on Sunday.

Sunscreen is a must.

TOURIST INFORMATION:
St. Petersburg/Clearwater Area Convention & Visitors Bureau, St. Petersburg ThunderDome, One Stadium Drive, Suite A, St. Petersburg, FL 33705-1706, ☎ 582-7892, fax 582-7949.

St. Petersburg Chamber of Commerce, 100 2nd Avenue North, St. Petersburg, FL 33701, ☎ 821-4069.

The Pier Information Center, ☎ 821-6164.

FOOD AND DRINK:

Apropos (300 2nd Avenue at the corner of Bayshore Drive) is open for breakfast, lunch, and dinner from 7:30–9. Harborside with a great view. The menu includes healthy foods as well traditional American fare. ☎ 823-8934. $–$$.

Leverocks Waterfront Steakhouse (800 Bay Pines Boulevard) serves great steaks and prime rib, as well as fresh seafood. Open for lunch and dinner from 11:30–10. Overlooks Boca Ciega Bay. ☎ 345-5335. $–$$.

Piccalilli Cafeteria (1900 34th Street) serves all sorts of goodies from snacks to salads, poultry, fresh seafood, beef, and a great selection of desserts. ☎ 326-1501. $.

The Terrace Room (in the Stouffer Renaissance Vinoy Resort at 501 Fifth Avenue NE) is the place to go if you enjoy fine dining. The setting is elegant and the food—beef and fresh seafood—is excellent. You'll need to make a reservation and gentlemen must wear a jacket. ☎ 894-1000. $$$.

SUGGESTED TOURS AND LOCAL ATTRACTIONS:

There's lots to see and do in St. Petersburg, more than can be done in a single day, so you'll have to pick and choose.

The best place to start your daytrip is in the downtown section of St. Petersburg, on the shores of Tampa Bay. Begin at the **Sunken Gardens** (1) by taking Interstate 275 to Exit 12, and from there to 1825 4th Street. Here you'll see a collection of more than 50,000 exotic tropical plants and flowers set in a five-acre garden with a walk-through aviary full of tropical birds of every shape, size and color. You can also enjoy an alligator wrestling show, visit a biblical wax exhibit, and get some refreshment in the restaurant. *Open 10–5 daily.* ☎ 896-3186. ♿. *Adults $14, children $8.*

Next, take 4th Street south to 2nd Avenue and turn east. The **Florida International Museum** (2) is at 261 Second Avenue North, on the south side of the street. This is a large museum, more than 300,000 square feet, that presents major traveling international exhibitions, such as the "*The Splendors of Ancient Egypt*" held in January, 1996, which exhibited more than 70 objects from the magnificent collection of the Egyptian Museum of Cairo. There are no permanent exhibits, but you can always expect something special. ☎ 822-3693 for details. *Open 9 a.m.– 10 p.m. daily January through June.* ♿. *Adults $12, seniors $10.75, children 5–16 $5.*

From the Florida International Museum go east to Beach Drive. The **Museum of Fine Arts** (3) is just to the north at number 255. Here, you can view the works of notable American artists and photographers, an outstanding collection of European, pre-Columbian and Far Eastern art, and special exhibits on loan from other metropolitan museums. The period rooms are furnished with antiques and pieces of local historical significance. *Open 10–*

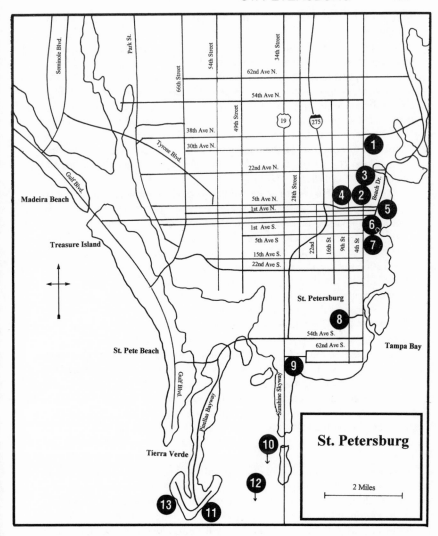

5 Tues.–Sat., and 1–5 on Sun. ☎ *896-2667.* ♿. *Adults $5, seniors $3, children $2.*

Just a little farther to the west, at 335 Second Avenue, the **St. Petersburg Museum of History** (4) features five themed areas depicting regional history and development. These include a prehistoric coastal area with displays of primitive tools and fossils, an 1880s general store, a replica of the Orange Belt Railroad Depot, and a re-creation of Victorian Florida. The museum also features a section devoted to the history of commercial aviation, beginning in 1914 when Tony Jannus made his historic 21-mile flight in a Model B Benoist 43 Airboat from St. Petersburg to Tampa; you can see a replica of the plane. *Open 10–5 Mon.–Sat., and 1–5 on Sun.* ☎ *894-1052.* ♿. *Adults $4, seniors $3.50, children 7–17 $1.50.*

*The Pier (5). No visit to St. Petersburg would be complete without a visit to the great inverted pyramid at the eastern end of Second Avenue. The famous landmark was re-opened in 1988 after extensive renovations. Extending some 2,400 feet into Tampa Bay, the pier is a microcosm of covered shelters, specialty shops and stores, a farmer's market, a dining court, an observation deck, catwalks for anglers and, of course, the five-story inverted pyramid itself, the Pier's signature. The view from the observation deck is nothing short of spectacular, with downtown St. Pete laid out before you to the west, and the great waters of Tampa Bay to the east. *Open daily.* ☎ *821-6164.* ♿. *Free trolley service from the parking area. Admission free, parking $3.*

From the Pier, return to 2nd Avenue and drive west to 4th Avenue. Turn south there and go to Third Street South where you'll find the **Salvador Dali Museum** (6), featuring the works of one of the world's most famous and controversial Spanish masters. Valued at more than $125 million, the collection includes 94 oil paintings, 200 water colors and drawings, and 1,000 graphics, sculptures and other objets d'art. *Open 9:30–5:30 daily, noon–5:30 on Sun.* ☎ *823-3767.* ♿. *Adults $8, seniors $7, students $4, children under 10 free.*

Great Explorations (7) is not far away at 1120 Fourth Street South. This is very much a hands-on experience where you touch, move and interact with exhibits designed to both educate and entertain. The exhibition areas include **Phenomenal Arts, Explore Galore, Exchange, Think Tank, Touch Tunnel**, and **Body Shop**. There is also a gift shop. *Open 10–5 daily, noon–5 on Sun.* ☎ *821- 8992.* ♿. *Adults $6, seniors $5.50, children 4–17 $5.*

Next, take Interstate 275 to Exit 4 and then drive east on 54th Avenue South for almost two miles to M.L. King Street and turn north. From there it's a short drive to Country Club Way where you'll turn west to **Boyd Hill Nature Park** (8). The park features more than 216 acres of woodland and areas of great natural beauty. Photographers won't want to miss this opportunity. Lots of wildlife can be seen along the six nature trails that meander through the various ecosystems. Take a guided tour or just go off on your own. *Open 9–5 daily.* ☎ *893-7326.* ♿. *Adults $1, children 50¢.*

The Pier

The **Sunshine Skyway** (9), a 15-mile bridge that soars more than 175 feet into the sky, connects Pinellas and Manatee counties south of St. Petersburg across Tampa Bay. Its designers were inspired by the Bretonne Bridge spanning the River Seine in France. The Sunshine Skyway and three smaller bridges provide the link with Interstate 275 and the south. Picnic, swimming, and fishing areas are provided just off the highway. *Toll $1.*

ADDITIONAL ATTRACTIONS:

The **Weedon Island State Preserve** (10) off Gandy Boulevard, just south of Gandy Bridge at 1500 Weedon Island Drive, to the north of the downtown area, is one of the few remaining mangrove swamps in the densely-populated Tampa Bay area. The island has an interesting, though somewhat turbulent, history. Over the years, as Florida's interests changed, so did the 1,000-acre park. In the early days there were citrus groves on the island, then, as Florida's fledgling tourist industry began to grow, came a Roaring Twenties nightclub, a motion picture studio, one of Florida's first airports, and one of the most significant archaeological discoveries in the southeast. Today, the Weedon Island State Preserve is one of Tampa Bay's more popular outdoor recreation areas. You have to travel only a mile or two to leave the great cities of Tampa and St. Petersburg far behind, or so it seems.

The nightclub, the old airport, and the movie studio are long gone, as is the gay life of the 1920s. Visitors to the preserve, instead of drinking and dancing, now enjoy the great outdoors: hiking, canoeing, swimming, fishing, picnicking, nature study, bird watching, or simply relaxing under the hot Florida sunshine. *Open 8–sundown daily.* &. *Admission $3.25 per vehicle.*

Fort De Soto National Monument and Park (11) is on the far side (south) of the entrance to Tampa Bay. Take the Sunshine Skyway and Interstate 275 south across the bay to Mullet Key and the historic fort built during the Spanish-American War. Mullet Key is the largest of the five islands that make up this unusual park system of more than 900 unspoiled acres, seven miles of pristine beaches, two fishing piers, a picnic area with a concession stand, and covered picnic shelters. As for the fort itself, it wasn't completed by the end of the war that made it necessary, and its guns were never fired in anger. Today, you can wander around the old stronghold via a series of walkways. It's possible to spend an entire day here, and many people do. *Open dawn to dusk daily.* ☎ *866-2484.* ♿. *Tolls on access roads 80¢, Sunshine Skyway $1.*

Also, just south of St. Petersburg, across Tampa Bay, via Interstate 275 and the Sunshine Skyway, is the **Gamble Plantation State Historic Site** (12). Located at 3708 Patten Avenue in Ellenton, the mansion was once the home of Major Robert Gamble and the nucleus of an extensive sugar plantation of more than 3,500 acres. It is the only surviving plantation house in southern Florida.

The mansion with its signature white columns and beautifully landscaped gardens represent a bygone era, a way of life, an economic system, and a southern Florida that vanished at the end of the Civil War. When you visit, you'll also see the Judah P. Benjamin Confederate Memorial, dedicated to the Confederate Secretary of State. He was forced to take refuge at the Gamble Plantation while awaiting safe passage to England after the collapse of the Confederate government in Richmond.

In 1925, the mansion and 16 acres were saved by the United Daughters of the Confederacy, and donated to the State of Florida. The mansion and gardens have been renovated, refurnished, and returned to a semblance of the glory it enjoyed in the mid-19th century. *Open 9–5 Mon.–Thurs.* ☎ *723-4536.* ♿. *Admission $1.*

Egmont Key State Park (13) is a tiny 440-acre island near the Fort De Soto National Monument at the mouth of Tampa Bay. The little island has a colorful history. First it was a prison camp for captured Seminole Indians during the Third Seminole War, then a Union naval base during the Civil War, and today it's the location of the only fully-manned lighthouse in the United States. Egmont Key is a joint venture operated by the Florida Department of Natural Resources, the U.S. Fish and Wildlife Service, and the U.S. Coast Guard. It's a lonely place, accessible only by private boat, where it's easy to find a secluded spot to spend a few quiet hours and enjoy the sea, sand, and sunshine. Popular activities at the park include swimming, boating, and fishing. If you are traveling with your own boat, or if you can rent one, or even persuade some kind soul to ferry you there and back, it's a stop you won't want to miss. *Open daily.* ☎ *893-2627. Admission $2.*

Clearwater, Clearwater Beach, Dunedin, Indian Rocks Beach, and Indian Shores

The following is a fairly long driving tour of one of Florida's most spectacular sections of Gulf Coast shoreline. If you decide to try it, you're in for a long and perhaps exhausting day, but one you're sure to remember.

GETTING THERE:

Clearwater Beach Park, Big Pier 60, and Clearwater Island Beach are all easy to reach via the Highway 60 bridge across Clearwater Harbor. Once across the water, Highway 699 runs north and south, giving access to mile after mile of pristine beach from Passe-a-Grille Beach Park at the entrance to Tampa Bay in the south, all the way north through Indian Shores and Indian Rocks, and then onward to Dunedin. Although the beaches on the Gulf shore are rarely deserted, there's always plenty of room, lots of places where you can find a quiet spot for an afternoon in the sunshine, swimming or fishing the surf.

PRACTICALITIES:

With the exception of one or two, most of the attractions are open daily.

TOURIST INFORMATION:

Greater Clearwater Chamber of Commerce, 128 North Osceola Avenue, PO Box 2457, Clearwater, FL 34617, ☎ 461-0011.

Dunedin Chamber of Commerce, 301-Main Street, Dunedin, FL 34698, ☎ 733-3197.

The Gulf Beaches Chamber of Commerce, 105 5th Avenue, Indian Rocks Beach, FL 34635, ☎ 595-4575 or 800-944-1847.

FOOD AND DRINK:

Of the many eating opportunities along the way, the two that follow are among the better choices. The food, service and surroundings are exceptional at both, but you should not hesitate to explore and try something new. Who knows what's just around the next corner?

Jesse's Seafood House (20 Island Way, just north of Highway 60 off the causeway between Clearwater and Clearwater Beach) is open for lunch and dinner from 11:30–9 Monday through Thursday, and 11:30–10 Friday and Saturday. The seafood here is exceptional and the menu includes a number of items for the health conscious. The view from the dining room over the water borders on the spectacular. ☎ 443-6210. $–$$.

Sabals (at 315 Main Street, Dunedin) might be just the place to enjoy an elegant dinner after a long daytrip. Open 6–10 Tuesday through Saturday, the menu is basic American with steaks and prime rib, but the atmosphere is elegant and intimate. ☎ 734-3463. $$$.

SUGGESTED TOUR AND LOCAL ATTRACTIONS:

Starting at the southern end of the tour, the **Suncoast Seabird Sanctuary** (1), at 18328 Gulf Boulevard in Indian Shores, is a refuge and rehabilitation center for as many as 500 injured and permanently crippled seabirds. The center is known world-wide for its efforts to preserve wild birds, and you can see the results of its programs in the cormorants, herons, pelicans, birds of prey, and the many other species now resident there. *Open 9–dusk daily.* ☎ *391-6211.* ♿. *Free.*

A little farther to the north in Indian Rocks Beach you'll find **Hamlin's Landing** (2), at 401 Second Street East, a new waterfront shopping and dining complex on the Intracoastal Waterway. It's a rambling Victorian structure with specialty shops, restaurants, and neat little cafés where you can stop for an early lunch or late breakfast. *Open daily.*

From Indian Rocks Beach, continue northward along Highway 699 to **Clearwater** and **Clearwater Beach** where, at 16100 Fairchild Drive, you might stop at **Boatyard Village** (3), a re-created, 1890s-period fishing village nestled in a small cove on Tampa Bay. This neat little shopping center features all sorts of specialty shops, boutiques, galleries, entertainment, and even a playhouse. And there always seems to be something going on: special events and entertainment are scheduled regularly. *Open 10–6 daily, 10–5 on Sun. Free.*

The **Florida Military Aviation Museum** (4) is at 16055 Fairchild Drive, opposite Boatyard Village. A collection of restored military aircraft is on display in an outdoor museum. If you have a military or Air Force background, this is one of those stops you won't want to miss. *Open 10–4 Tues., Thurs., and Sat.; 1–5 on Sun.* ☎ *535-9007.* ♿. *Adults $2, children 6–12 $1.*

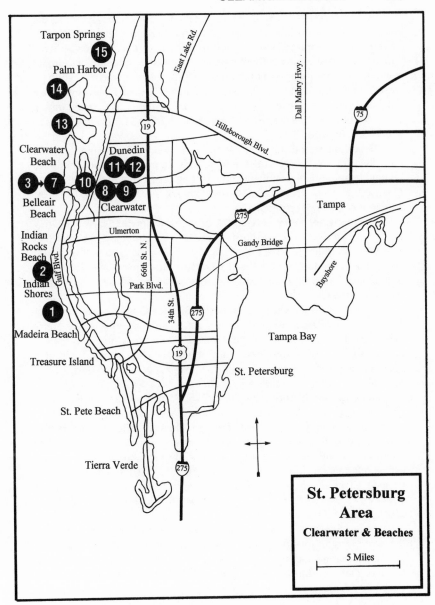

Tarpon Springs

Palm Harbor

Clearwater
Beach

Dunedin

Belleair
Beach

Clearwater

Ulmerton

Indian
Rocks
Beach

Indian
Shores

Madeira Beach

Treasure Island

St. Pete Beach

Tierra Verde

East Lake Rd.

Hillsborough Blvd.

Dall Mabry Hwy.

Tampa

Gulf Blvd.

66th St. N.

Park Blvd.

34th St.

Gandy Bridge

Bayshore

Tampa Bay

St. Petersburg

**St. Petersburg
Area**

Clearwater & Beaches

5 Miles

You'll find one of Clearwater's most celebrated attractions just across the water via Highway 60 at 25 Causeway Boulevard in Clearwater Beach. **Captain Memo's Pirate Cruise** (5) offers several two-hour cruises daily on the Gulf of Mexico in a fairly authentic reproduction of a pirate ship. It's fun, it's exciting, and you'll enjoy some of the most spectacular coastal scenery in west Florida. Best of all is the Sunset Champagne Cruise that leaves the dock daily at 7 p.m. Free beverages are served during the cruise. *Seven days a week.* ☎ *446-2587. Day cruises: Adults $25, children $15. Evening cruises: Adults $28, children $18.*

Celebration Station (6) is at 24546 US-19 North. This family-oriented mini theme park features rides for the kids, large and small. There are bumper boats, go-karts, miniature golf, batting cages, shows, and lots to eat. *Open 10–11 Sun.–Thurs., and 10–midnight Fri. and Sat.* ☎ *791-1799.* &. *Different pricing options apply.*

The **Clearwater Ferry Service** (7), at the downtown Clearwater Drew Dock, offers three cruising excursions including a Dolphin Encounter that provides opportunities to see the dolphins and seabirds, a half-hour trip across the water for the Caladesi Island Adventure (more about Caladesi Island later), and a six-hour Tarpon Springs excursion. ☎ *442-7433. Rates and schedules vary, so call for details.*

The next stop is the **Clearwater Marine Science Center Aquarium** (8) at 249 Windward Passage. Here you can get a close- up look at the area's ocean life. Live and model displays include tanks containing a variety of exotic fish, baby sea turtles, and "Sam" the bottlenose dolphin. It's quite a special place, and well worth a visit. *Open 9–5 Mon.–Fri., 9–4 Sat., 11–4 Sun.* ☎ *447-0980.* &. *Adults $5.75, children 3–12 $3.75.*

Moccasin Lake Nature Park (9), at 2750 Park Trail Lane, is a 50-acre nature center with a large lake, upland forest, wetlands, and many species of animals and birds indigenous to the area. There's a mile-long nature trail that meanders through the park and offers an easy, relaxing stroll. The Interpretive Center features wildlife exhibits, displays, and all sorts of interesting information. The park is also unusual in that the sun and ocean provide all its energy—electrical power and water supply. *Open 10–5 Tues.–Fri., 10–6 Sat. and Sun., closed Mon.* ☎ *462-6024.* &. *Adults $2, children 3–11 $1.*

*The Sea Screamer (10) is one ride you won't want to miss. You'll board the world's largest speedboat—it's 73 feet long—at Slip 10 at the Clearwater Municipal Marina and head out to sea on a fast, thrilling ride in the Gulf of Mexico. *Daily, call for schedules.* ☎ *447-7200.* &. *Adults $10, children under 12 $7, four and under ride free.*

From Clearwater it's northward on Highway 19 to Dunedin where, apart from the beaches and a couple of great museums, three state parks and recreation areas offer sea and shore, recreation or relaxation, and you could easily spend and entire day at any one of them. You won't be able to visit all three in a single day—they are located on barrier islands—but each is unusual and has something special to offer. Take your pick and try to visit at least one.

Dunedin Fine Arts Center (11), at 1143 Michigan Boulevard, has a fine permanent collection of paintings and sculpture, and is host to visiting collections. *Open 9–5 Mon.–Fri., and 1–4 Sun., closed Sat.* ☎ *738-1892.* ♿. *Free.*

Dunedin has its roots set deep in the Highlands of Scotland and, so they say, gets its name from the same Gaelic word from which Edinburgh is derived. The **Dunedin Historical Museum** (12) at 341 Main Street, housed in what once was the station for the Orange Belt Railroad system, a building that dates to 1889, has a fine collection of artifacts, photographs, drawings, and other memorabilia that trace and interpret the Scottish community's past. *Open 10–1 Tues.–Sat.* ☎ *736-1176.* ♿. *Free.*

Caladesi Island (13) is the first of three state parks located in the Dunedin area. Accessible only by ferry or private boat, the park is located on a large, yet essentially undeveloped, Gulf Coast barrier island just west of Dunedin. Its beach was rated in 1995 as the second best in the United States. This is a fairly remote area, one of Florida's last great romantic hideaways. You can walk for miles along the beaches, or escape to secret places along one of the island's deserted nature trails. Those coming by private boat can tie up at one of the 99 slips at the bay-side marina, or simply drop anchor in the clear emerald waters and swim ashore for an afternoon of picnicking and romance. If you came by ferry, you can head for the beach to swim, fish, or sunbathe the hours away, or you can enjoy a quiet picnic and cookout. There are tables and grills at the picnic area, as well as a concession stand and freshwater showers at the beach.

Hiking is popular too, and the extensive system of nature trails provides unique opportunities for nature study, bird watching, and wildlife photography. For the angler, there's plenty of sport: bluefish, redfish, flounder, mullet, sheephead, and whiting abound. *Open 8–sundown daily. A scheduled passenger ferry runs from nearby Honeymoon Island State Recreation Area, and from the city of Clearwater.* ☎ *734-5263, or 442-7433 in Clearwater, for ferry information. Boat docks: adults $4; children $2.50.*

Honeymoon Island (14), a little father north at the extreme west end of Highway 586, is next. The name conjures up all sorts of romantic images: deserted tropical islands, sugar-white beaches, sea breezes blowing gently in from the ocean, waving palms, and endless days of perfect weather. For the most part, Honeymoon Island is all this and more. It's a place for those who want to find a perfect little hideaway. The sun-drenched miles of snow-white beaches are an open invitation to laze away the hours far away from the hustle and bustle of the regular honeymoon establishments. But Honeymoon Island is not just for lovers. It's a place where the entire family can enjoy swimming or fishing in the ocean or simply lounging in the sunshine. There's even a "Pet Beach" where you and your small friend can enjoy a stroll together.

For nature lovers there are two bird observatories. Naturalists will find plenty to interest them, including osprey nests and a wide variety of shore-birds and marine life. Along the island's northern loop trail, hikers can enjoy one of Florida's few remaining stands of virgin slash pine.

The fishing is great, the swimming even better—there are freshwater showers on the beach—and the clear green waters of the Gulf of Mexico are safe and inviting. There's also a picnic area where you can enjoy a snack in the sunshine. *Open 8–sunset daily.* ☎ *469-5942.* ♿. *Admission $3.25 per vehicle.*

Unless you are trailing a private boat, or can find one to rent, **Ancelote Key State Preserve** (15), located three miles out to sea west of Tarpon Springs, is beyond your reach.

The six distinct biological communities at Ancelote Key provide habitats for a wide variety of plant life, wild animals and birds including the bald eagle and the piping plover. It's a remote place where tall pines provide a nesting place for the osprey, and where the federal lighthouse at the southern end of the island still stands, a lonely, though nowadays obsolete link with the past. It's a place where the waters of the Gulf of Mexico lap gently upon more than four miles of pristine beaches populated only by the crabs and birds that spend their days endlessly fishing and foraging for food. It's no small wonder, then, that Ancelote Key is one of those places where the air is clear, the breeze fresh, and you can spend a quiet afternoon relaxing in the sunshine.

There are no facilities at Ancelote Key. That means no fresh water and no concessions, so be sure to plan your visit and bring all you need along with you.

Once on the island you can swim, fish, sunbathe, or spend your time bird watching, chasing the crabs, or collecting shells. You can even take a tent and camp out on the beach, if you like. *Open daily.* ☎ *469-5942 at Caladesi Island for information.*

Sarasota

Sarasota County is just south of Tampa and St. Petersburg, and is brimming with things to see and do. Perhaps John Ringling was the first to realize the potential of the area, perhaps it was Hernando de Soto several hundred years earlier; no matter, since their arrival the tourist industry for the city and its Gulf Coast Islands has boomed.

GETTING THERE:

From Tampa, take Interstate 75 south to its junction with State Route 780 (Fruitville Road). Turn right onto 780; from there it's a straight run in. Sarasota is about 60 miles south of Tampa.

From St. Petersburg, drive south over the Sunshine Skyway on Interstate 275 to its junction with Highway 41 and turn south into downtown Sarasota. The total distance is about 42 miles.

GETTING AROUND:

Some of the attractions are within walking distance of one another, others are a short drive away. A combination of foot and horsepower will take you around.

PRACTICALITIES:

The **Area Code** is 941.

Most attractions in the Sarasota area stay open the year-round, but some do close on either Sunday or Monday, and a few close early and open late. Not to worry. If you miss something you'd really like to see, Sarasota is close to Tampa Bay and you can always return another day.

Many of the attractions listed demand that you spend at least some time in the great outdoors. That being the case, you'll be substantially exposed to the sun. Be sure to use sunscreen and wear a hat. Stay out of the sun for long periods during the hours 11–3, the hottest time of the day.

TOURIST INFORMATION:

Sarasota Visitor Information Center, 655 North Tamiami Trail, Sarasota, FL 34236, ☎ 957-1887 or 800-522-9799, fax 951-2956.

FOOD AND DRINK:

Sarasota is a gourmet's delight. If it's available anywhere, you'll find it here. There are dozens, hundreds, of restaurants, cafés, deli's, ice cream parlors, snack stands, seafood shacks, and fast food eateries in the city and on the Gulf Coast Islands. Here's a few to get you started, but be sure to explore for yourself. What you'll find just around the next corner might be a culinary experience beyond compare; let us know about it.

Snapper's (3634 Webber Street) is open for lunch and dinner from 11–9. The menu features all sorts of English-style seafood dishes, as well as an assortment of specialties. Best make a reservation for dinner. ☎ 923-8933. $–$$

Walt's Raw Oyster Bar & Restaurant (560 North Washington Boulevard) is also open for lunch and dinner from 11–10. The name says it all: lots of fresh seafood in a nautical setting; excellent chowders, great sandwiches and, of course, oysters on the half-shell. ☎ 365-1735. $–$$.

LOCAL ATTRACTIONS:

Visitors to Sarasota can pick and choose from a wide variety of attractions, the best of which are:

Bellm Cars and Music of Yesterday (1), 5500 North Tamiami Trail (Highway 41), is a unique museum featuring antique and classic cars, as well as old juke boxes (more than 1,200 of them!), arcade games, and nickel flicks. Enjoy it all on the guided tour that starts every half-hour. The penny arcade is a favorite; you get to play the games for a few extra coins. Allow at least 90 minutes. *Open 9:30–5:30 daily.* ☎ *355-6228.* ♿. *Adults $8, children 6–12 $4.*

Gulf Coast World of Science (2), 8251 15th Street East, is another of those hands-on science museums, perfect for kids, small and grown-up alike, where you can get involved and play with the exhibits. These include an echo chamber, frozen shadow, static electricity, and a host of small animal and reptile exhibits. There's also a "take apart" section where all sorts of mechanical bits and pieces and gizmos are stripped down and dissected for your inspection. *Open 10–5 Tue.–Sat., 1–5 on Sun. Allow at least 90 minutes.* ☎ *957-4969.* ♿. *Adults $3, children $1.50.*

***John and Mable Ringling Museum of Art** (3), 5401 Bay Shore Road just west of Highway 41 at the airport, is a magnificent Italian Renaissance villa-turned-art museum that houses a superb collection of Old Master paintings and 17th-century tapestries, all put together over many years by the great circus magnate and his wife. Next door, the **Ringling Residence**, Ca' d'Zan, a 30-room mansion set on the shores of Sarasota Bay, is an architectural marvel, a replica of a Venetian palace. The **Circus Museum** contains memorabilia from Ringling's "Big Top." The exhibits include all sorts of circus equipment and paraphernalia: costumes, posters, wagons, photographs, etc.

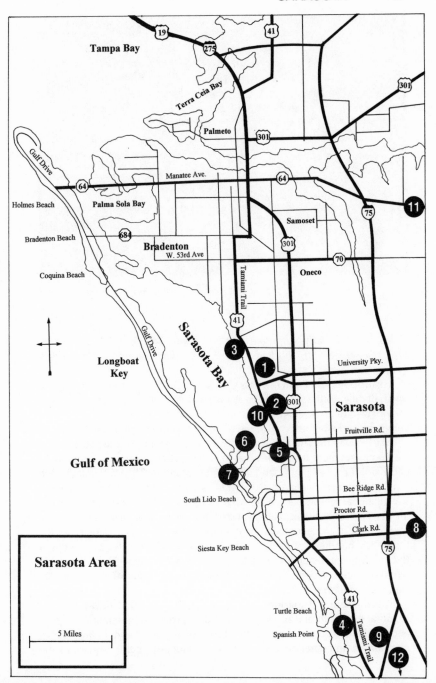

The John and Mable Ringling Museum of Art

Open 10–5:30 daily. Allow at least two hours. ☎ *359-5700.* ♿. *Adults $8.50, seniors $7.50, children under 13 free. Admission to the grounds is free.*

Historic Spanish Point (4). This section of Little Sarasota Bay is in Osprey, one half mile north of Blackburn Point Road. Spanish Point contains a late Victorian-style homestead, an Indian burial mound, a 19th-century chapel, cemetery, and what once must have been a beautiful formal garden.

Marie Selby Botanical Gardens (5), 811 South Palm Avenue at Highway 41, comprises more than nine acres of lush vegetation, orchids, bromeliads, carnivorous pitcher plants, and other exotic plantlife. The Waterfall Garden is a profusion of hibiscus, cacti, water lilies, palms, and dozens of varieties of succulents, as well as bamboo and banyan trees. The Baywalk Sanctuary has an elevated boardwalk that meanders through a mangrove swamp and provides an unprecedented view over the gardens. And then there are the butterflies, hundreds of them, maybe thousands. There's also a Museum of Botany with hands-on exhibits that provide a close-up glimpse into the world of nature. *Open 10–5 daily. Allow at least an hour.* ☎ *366-5730.* ♿. *Adults $6, children 6–11 $3.*

*Mote Marine Aquarium (6), 1600 Ken Thompson Parkway on City Island at the south end of New Pass Bridge, provides a fascinating experience and close-up encounter with all sorts of marine life, including sharks, rays, turtles, and other denizens of the deep. Not just a public aquarium, the

The Ringling Residence

Mote is also one of the few research facilities of its kind. Perhaps the highlight of your visit will be the 30-foot "touch tank" where you can handle rays, crabs, guitar fish, sea urchins, and starfish, to mention just a few. *Open 10–5 daily. Allow at least 90 minutes.* ☎ *388-2451.* ♿. *Adults $8, children 4–17 $6.*

Pelican Man's Bird Sanctuary (7), 1708 Ken Thompson Parkway, is just a short walk away from the Mote Aquarium. If you like birds, you'll want to visit the Pelican Man. Home to more than 200 distressed birds, the sanctuary is manned by volunteers who help to rescue and rehabilitate thousands of pelicans and other birds. A boardwalk takes you through the aviary where you can see many of the injured birds close up: ospreys, cormorants, sandhill cranes, seagulls of every sort and size and, of course, pelicans. *Open 10–5 daily. Allow an hour.* ☎ *388-4444.* ♿. *Donations.*

The **Myakka River State Park** (8) is located 12 miles east of Sarasota on State Route 72. From Highway 41, take Clark Road and travel east and then follow the signs.

Myakka River, one of the largest parks in the Florida system, covers an area of some 28,875 acres. It's a vast, diverse world of wild and scenic beauty featuring an abundance of natural plant communities, lakes, river marshes, hammocks and prairies. The Myakka River flows for more than twelve miles through the park on its journey to the Gulf of Mexico. The main road winds through oak and palm hammocks, opening views across the grassy mashes, sloughs, and the Upper Myakka Lake, where you can see deer, raccoon, and many species of wild birds, either from the park drive or from the wooden bird walk. Beyond the paved drive, across the large, open expanses of pine flatwoods, prairies, and wetlands, you may see cottontails, red-shouldered hawks, deer, and bobcats at home in their natural environment.

For those who like to get out and about, there's a boat basin and dock on the Upper Myakka Lake where you can rent a canoe or bicycle, launch your own boat, and buy a snack and soft drink at the concession stand, which means there's also a picnic area with tables and grills; it's the ideal spot for a quiet lunch in the great outdoors. Anglers will find the Myakka River and Upper Myakka Lake well stocked with bass, bream, and catfish; while photographers can take advantage of all the park has to offer. *Open 8–sunset daily. Allow at least three hours.* ☎ *361-6511.* ♿. *Admission $3.25 per vehicle.*

If you're looking for a little peace and quiet, far away from the hustle of the resort areas, the **Oscar Scherer State Recreation Area** (9), on Highway 41 between Sarasota and Venice, may be just the place. Drive south from downtown Sarasota for 12 miles.

Oscar Sherer is an extensive tract of scrubby and pine flatwoods, largely undiscovered by the vacationing public. The scrubby flatwoods are vital to Florida's diminishing population of rare and endangered birds and animals, offering a natural and protected habitat for several of the state's most endangered species, including the Florida scrub jay, gopher tortoise, gopher frog, and indigo snake. Bald eagles, bobcats, river otters, and alligators can often be seen in the park during the winter months.

The pine flatwoods, the second major plant community in the park, offer homes to a wide variety of songbirds and woodpeckers, as well as the gopher tortoise.

The park is an ideal swimming spot, and the fishing here is beyond compare. You can cast a line in freshwater above the dam, and saltwater fishing below it—a rare and unusual treat. Canoes may be rented by the hour or the day at the ranger station. *Open 8–sunset daily. Allow at least three hours.* ☎ *483-5956.* ♿. *Admission $3.25 per vehicle.*

Sarasota Jungle Gardens (10), 3701 Bayshore Road off Highway 41 via Myrtle Street, is a 10-acre jungle where narrow, well-beaten paths wind their way through the lush tropical vegetation and exotic gardens. Wandering the trails and pathways, you'll see flamingoes, swans, leopards, alligators, otters, monkeys, cockatoos, macaws, and many other colorful birds and animals, all living in as natural an environment as possible. There's also a petting zoo for the kids, and the Gardens of Christ contain eight religious exhibits portraying moments from the life of Jesus. *Open 9–5 daily. Allow at least 90 minutes.* ☎ *355-5305.* ♿. *Adults $9, seniors $7, children 3–12 $5.*

Lake Manatee State Recreation Area (11), 15 miles east of Bradenton on State Route 64, is a 556-acre tract that extends for more than three miles along the south shore of Lake Manatee, a large reservoir that provides water for Manatee and Sarasota counties. The park, a land of pine flatwoods, sand pine scrubs, marshes, and hammock also provides natural habitats for a variety of animal and plant life. It's a quiet area and somewhat remote. It's also a good place to spend a few hours in the great outdoors, fishing, swimming, boating, canoeing, and picnicking. There's a hiking trail, campfire circle, a boat ramp, a shady picnic area with tables and grills, public rest rooms, and plenty of parking. *Open 8–sunset daily. Allow at least three hours.* ☎ *741-3028. Admission $3.25 per vehicle.*

Situated on one of the great chains of barrier islands that protect the Gulf Coast, south of Sarasota via Highways 41, 775 and the Boca Grande Causeway (private toll), **Gasparilla Island State Recreation Area** (12) is a romantic place where legends of pirate treasure and beautiful captives are rife. The island was allegedly named for the infamous pirate Captain Jose Gaspar, who settled here in the 1700s with his band of roughnecks. For years the pirates used the island as base for raids against the mainland until, after a concerted effort by the United States government, they were driven from the waters of the Gulf of Mexico.

Today, the park is a refuge, not for corsairs, but for people like you with a will to escape to quiet beaches and the deep, green waters of the Gulf. It's a place for sunbathing, swimming, fishing, gathering shells, and generally taking things easy. *Open 8-sunset daily. Allow at least three hours.* ☎ *964-0375. Admission $3.25 per vehicle.*

The **Don Pedro Island State Recreation Area** (13) also lies on one of an extensive chain of barrier islands off the Gulf coast, and it too is reached via Highways 41 and 775. Unfortunately, you'll need a private boat to get across the water. If you don't have one, you always take the ferry out of Placida. Don Pedro Island lies offshore in Charlotte County between Knight Island and Little Gasparilla Island. It's a secluded, romantic spot, far away from the tourist traps farther north. Its natural features include a wide, white sandy beach with an extensive system of sand dunes covered with the protected sea oats and mangroves. Shelling is popular on the mile-long beach. So is surf fishing, swimming, and sunbathing. Facilities are a little sparse, but there are public restrooms, a boat dock, and a picnic pavilion with tables and grills. *Open 8–sunset daily.* ☎ *964-0375. Adults $2, children $1.*

Lee Island Coast and Fort Myers

Even though he never visited the area, Confederate General Robert E. Lee provided the name for both this coast and the county it's in, founded in 1887. Back then the population was a mere 1,400 souls. Today, more than 300,000 people make their homes in and around Fort Myers, and more than 1.6 million visitors arrive each year via every imaginable mode of transportation. It's an historic place, the one-time winter home of Thomas Edison, Henry Ford, and other notables. This is a land where the sea meets the sky above more than 50 miles of pristine sandy beaches, of botanical gardens, tiny off-shore islands and vast wildlife reserves and state parks. In Fort Myers itself, majestic royal palms line the streets. More than 70 varieties of palms and a profusion of exotic plants and flowers add color to an already delightful downtown district. In short, it's a great place for a daytrip with a difference.

GETTING THERE:

From Tampa and St. Petersburg, take either Interstate 75 or Highway 41 and drive south for about 125 miles, you can't miss it.

GETTING AROUND:

This daytrip is offered in the form of a driving tour of the Lee Island Coast. It includes some stops in Fort Myers, and more along the way, so you can get out and take walks.

PRACTICALITIES:

The **Area Code** for the Fort Myers area is 941.

As always, the best time to make a daytrip is when the sun is shining. True, there are some stops that will take you indoors, but there's nothing quite so drab or depressing as a rainy day and a misty coastline.

Some of the attractions close on Sundays or Mondays, and some of those that do open start late and close early; be sure to take that into account when making your plans.

TOURIST INFORMATION:

Lee County Visitor & Convention Bureau, 2180 West First Street, Suite 100, Fort Myers, FL 33901, ☎ 800-237-6444 or 941-338-3500, fax 941-334-1106.

The Greater Fort Myers Chamber of Commerce, 2310 Edwards Drive, Fort Myers, FL 33902, ☎ 800-366-3622 or 941-332-3624.

FOOD AND DRINK:

Of all the great restaurants and cafés you'll find in the Fort Myers area, these are just a beginning:

Ballenger's, at 11390 Summerlin Square Drive—it's on the corner of San Carlos Boulevard—serves lunch and dinner from 11–10 weekdays, dinner from 4 on Saturday, and lunch and dinner on Sunday from 10:30 until 8. The staple is seafood, fried or broiled, and you'll surely find the prime rib and chicken dishes to your liking. ☎ 466-2626. $–$$.

Skipper's Galley, 3040 Estero Boulevard, is also a seafood restaurant, but with a wide range of red meat dishes as well as a number of Italian veal specials. The dining room overlooks the beach; the early evening skies are always a treat. Open for dinner from 4 until 10. ☎ 463-6139. $$$.

SUGGESTED TOUR AND LOCAL ATTRACTIONS:

As you drive south from Tampa/St. Petersburg, either on US-41 or Interstate 75 (the following assumes US-41), you'll arrive first in North Fort Myers, and that's as good a place as any to begin your tour. It was in North Fort Myers that the southernmost battle of the Civil War was fought. Here, you can visit the **Shell Factory** (1), just off Highway 41 at 2787 North Tamiami Trail, for a free tour of the processing facility and world's largest collection of shells and coral. The factory shop offers unusual souvenirs, outdoor wear, and other items. *Open 9–6 daily.* ☎ 995-2141. &. *Free.*

From the Shell factory, return to Highway 41 and continue south to the junction with Highway 78 (Pine Island Road) where you can turn east or west. If you turn west, it's a drive of some 12 miles to the **Matlacha Pass Aquatic Preserve** (2), a wide strip of water that separates **Pine Island** (3) from the mainland. The Preserve is best explored by sea kayak—you can rent one at any of the nearby marinas. On Pine Island itself, a remote place where time seems to stand still, you'll discover a fruit farm, learn all about the history of the Calusa Indians at the **Museum of the Island** (4), and visit **Bokeelia Island Seaport Pier** (5) at the northern tip of the island. You can also charter a boat and go deep-sea fishing for snook, mackerel, or the mighty tarpon in the waters of Pine Island Sound. Pine Island is a neat place, a bit wild and woolly in spots, but definitely a place to see if you have the time.

If at the junction of Highways 41 and 78 you turn east instead of heading for Pine Island, you'll find **Babcock Wilderness Adventures** (6) just off the highway at 8000 State Route 31 in Punta Gorda. There, you can take a swamp buggy tour through the Telegraph Cypress Swamp. The 90-minute ride provides a fascinating educational experience, as well as a comfortable sidebar to your daytrip. *Two tours daily at 9 and 11 May–Oct.; four tours daily at 9, 11, 1, and 3 Jan.–Apr.; tours every 30 minutes Nov.–Dec. All seats by reservation. Adults $17.95, under 12 $9.95.* ☎ *338-6367 or 800-500-5583.*

Return to Highway 41, continue south across the Caloosahatchee River, and enter the Fort Myers Historic District. Turn right on Highway 867 (McGregor Boulevard) and proceed to the **Edison/Ford Winter Homes Complex** (7) at number 2350. Seminole Lodge is where the great inventor Thomas A. Edison spent most of his winters for 45 years from 1886 until his death in 1931. It was here he perfected some of his most famous inventions. He was also an avid gardener to which the grounds around the estate will attest. Tours include the Edison home, his workshop and laboratory, and a museum containing a vast amount of memorabilia. The **Henry Ford Winter Home**, (8) "Mangoes," is adjacent to the Edison Home. Purchased by Ford in 1916 so that he could spend time with his good friend Edison, the old house has been restored to the condition it was in when the magnate lived there. You'll tour the house and grounds and visit the garage where you can see three of Ford's tin lizzies, all in running condition. *The complex is open 9–3:30 Mon.–Sat., noon–3:30 Sun.* ☎ *334-3614. Adults $10, children 6–12 $5; includes both homes.*

Continue south on McGregor (Highway 867) all the way to the Sanibel Causeway ($3 toll), and across the San Carlos Bay to **Sanibel Island** (9). You'll find a slower pace on Sanibel. There are no traffic lights and, while you'll need your car to get from place to place, you will want to get out and walk, for Sanibel is known for its pristine beaches, wonderful shelling opportunities and, of course, the **J.N. "Ding" Darling National Wildlife Refuge** (10) that covers about a third of the island. Here, you can walk the nature trails, see many species of wildlife in the raw, and visit the nature center. Just across the road from "Ding" Darling is the **Sanibel/Captiva Conservation Foundation** (11) where you can hike over miles of nature trail, or visit the observation tower for a fine view over the island. At opposite ends of the island are two of Sanibel's best beaches, **Lighthouse** (12) and **Bowman's** (13); try to visit one of them. If you decide to go all the way north to **Captiva Island** (14), you'll first have to cross the bridge—don't blink or you'll miss it—then visit **Turner Beach** (15) and **Blind Pass** (16). From there it's on through the canopy of Australian pines for six miles, passing along the way some of the most beautiful scenery in the entire Fort Myers area: pristine beaches and an emerald ocean shoreline. If you have the time, you can take a boat ride out to the islands via **Captiva Cruises**: Cabbage Key, Useppa, Cayo Costa (more

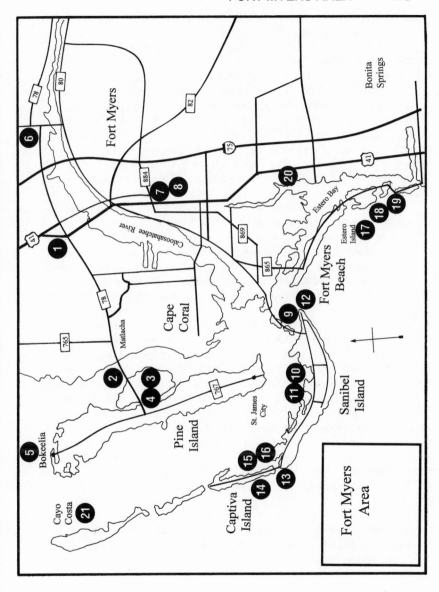

about Cayo later), and Boca Grande on Gasparilla Island. *Captive Cruises operates daily from 9–9.* ☎ *472-5300. Rates vary with the cruise, call for details.* You can even rent a boat and sally forth on your own. Check at any of the marinas on the island.

From Sanibel Island, you can drive south via San Carlos Boulevard to **Estero Island** (17), better known as Fort Myers Beach. This is the place where fun-seekers go board sailing, parasailing, water skiing, swimming, sunbathing, sailing, and fishing. The gently sloping shores and beaches are perfect for a family outing, safe for the little ones to run, splash, and dig the hours away. Continue south on San Carlos, hugging the coast as you go and, just south of Big Carlos Pass, you'll find the **Carl E. Johnson Park** (18), a wonderful, quiet public park seemingly far away from the crowded beaches to north.

*Lovers Key State Recreation Area (19) is a little farther south between Carl E. Johnson and Bonita Beach. Why a "must visit" stop? The Key is a quiet romantic backwater, remote and secluded; not many such unspoiled places remain in Florida. The park comprises parts of Black Island, Lovers Key, and Inner Key. It's a 434-acre hinterland of canals and tidal lagoons, bordered by mangroves, which supports an almost infinite variety of fish and marine animals. The remains of the maritime hammock on Black Island provides a home to several species of woodpeckers, owls, hawks, and songbirds. It's also a popular nesting ground for the osprey, a refuge for the wild marsh rabbit, the raccoon, and the squirrel. In the lagoons it's often possible to observe roseate spoonbills and reddish egrets feeding. Off-shore, you can see visiting bottle-nosed dolphins playing in the sunshine, and perhaps the endangered West Indian manatee closer in, in the shallows.

For recreation, Lovers Key is hard to beat. Some of the best onshore and offshore fishing grounds are on and around the park. Trout, redfish, snook, and tarpon can be caught according to the season. Castnetting for mullet, too, is a an activity unique to this out-of-the-way park. Other popular pastimes might include hiking, shelling, canoeing, and other beach-related activities. Swimming, however, because of the strong currents, is not recommended. *Open 8–sunset daily.* ☎ *597-6196.* ♿. *Admission $3.25 per vehicle.*

From Lover's Key, it's back to Fort Myers via Highway 41. You'll need to go a little farther south, beyond Bonita Springs, to Bonita Beach Road and turn east to the junction with 41. Turn north there and it's a straight run into Tampa and St. Pete.

ADDITIONAL ATTRACTIONS:

There are a couple more sites in the Fort Myers area that you might like to visit. The first you can pick up on your way back to Tampa at the junction of Highway 41 and Corkscrew Road north of Bonita Springs Park.

The **Koreshan Historic Site** (20) preserves the remains of a somewhat bizarre, and certainly unusual, settlement on the banks of the Estero River. It was in 1869 that a New York-born doctor by the name of Cyrus Teed claimed to have received a "divine illumination," a vision of a spiritual life as revealed to Teed by a divine deity. Teed began to preach his new religion, Koresh, and eventually, with a group of dedicated followers, moved southward from Chicago to establish his "New Jerusalem" in Florida in Estero. For a while the new religion seemed to flourish, but after Teed died in 1908 at the age of 69, the membership of the group declined until, in 1961, the four remaining members of the group deeded the 305 acres of their land to the State of Florida in Teed's memory.

It's an interesting place. Aside from historical significance, there's also a hiking trail, campfire circle, boat ramp, a picnic area, and public rest rooms. Canoe rentals are available, too, and the Park Service offers guided walks and a series of campfire programs according to seasonal demand. The park is also a great fishing location, and there are boundless opportunities for bird watching and wildlife photography. *Open 8–sunset daily.* ☎ *992-0311. Admission $3.25 per vehicle.*

The other "additional attraction" is **Cayo Costa State Park** (21), located just to the south of Boca Grande on one of a chain of barrier islands. The islands themselves are important in that they are the first line of defense against the storms that otherwise would batter Charlotte Harbor and Pine Island.

Although the island is accessible only by private boat, passenger ferry, or Captiva Cruises (472-5300), Cayo Costa, and all it has to offer, presents a stunning mixture of nature preserve and vacation destination. The natural features of the island include pine forests, oak palm hammocks, mangrove swamps, and mile after mile of pristine beach and snowy white sand. It's one of those romantic spots where you can enjoy an evening on the beach with a well-filled picnic basket, a little good company, and watch the setting sun turn the western sky and the emerald-green sea into a spectacular symphony of gold and silver.

If you like to fish, you won't find a better place that Cayo Costa. In fact, whatever the outdoor activity you prefer—boating, swimming, sun bathing, nature study and bird watching, wildlife photography, hiking the miles of sandy beach and, during the winter months, shelling—you'll find nowhere better to enjoy it than here, out where the sea meets the sky, and solitude is more than just a feeling. *Open 8–sunset daily.* ☎ *964-0375. Admission $2, children $1.*

Trip 28

Naples

Naples is something of an enigma. With a population of less than 20,000, it's not a very big place. Although easily accessible—just a few miles down the road from Fort Myers—Naples is all too often ignored by the vacationing public, which is a pity because the city is a mine of treasures waiting to be explored. Naples boasts of more than 41 miles of public beaches, all pristine and almost all quiet, with plenty of room to spread out and enjoy the pale green waters of the Gulf, the wide expanses of sand and a variety of attractions unique to the area.

GETTING THERE:

By Road: From Tampa, Naples is about 165 miles to the south via Interstate 75, or you can take the scenic route at a much more leisurely pace following the coast on Highway 41, which parallels I-75 for most of the way.

GETTING AROUND:

You'll be able to walk almost everywhere in the downtown areas, but driving is the way to get from one stop to the next. Parking is no problem. You'll find plenty of room on the streets downtown and at the beaches.

PRACTICALITIES:

The **Area Code** is 914.

As always, a few of the attractions close on Sundays or Mondays, perhaps both, and some open late and close early on Sundays. Be sure to take precautions against sunburn: use sunscreen, wear a hat, etc.

TOURIST INFORMATION:

Naples Visitors Center, 1075 5th Avenue South, Naples, FL 33940, ☎ 643-1919.

Naples Area Chamber of Commerce, 3620 Tamiami Trail North, Naples, FL 22940, ☎ 262-6141.

FOOD AND DRINK:

Naples is blessed with many good restaurants, with even more in the outlying areas and close to the beaches. Some choices include:

> **Chardonnay** (at the Best Western Naples Inn, 2331 Tamiami Trail North) offers fine dining, country French cuisine and an elegant atmosphere. Reservations are a must, and gentlemen need to wear a jacket. Open for dinner 5:50–10. ☎ 261-1744. $$$.

The Grill Room (at Vanderbilt Beach, in the Ritz Carlton, 280 Vanderbilt Beach Road) also offers fine dining and an elegant, club-like atmosphere. The menu features top-of-the-line American cuisine. Dress well and reserve. ☎ 598-3300. $$$.

The English Pub (2408 Linwood Avenue) is open for lunch and dinner, serving authentic English pub food in a mock-Tudor dining room. The menu includes such British staples as fish & chips, steak & kidney pie, bangers & mash, and shepherd's pie. ☎ 774-2408. $-$$.

The Grouper House (396 Goodlette) is open for dinner from 4:30. The specialty is the Captain's buffet with lots of fresh seafood, poultry and meat dishes. ☎ 263- 4900. $$.

The Chef's Garden & Truffles (1300 3rd Street South) serves lunch and dinner from 11:30–2; 6–9:30. The menu is American and the prices can be a little stiff, but the food is excellent. ☎ 262-5500. $$–$$$.

The Fifth Avenue Deli & Bakery (467 5th Avenue) offers only a small stand-up counter where you can eat from a selection of sandwiches, soups and other gourmet deli items. Open for breakfast, lunch, and into the late afternoon from 8–5:30; closed on Sunday. ☎ 262-4106. $.

SUGGESTED TOUR AND LOCAL ATTRACTIONS:

Naples Trolley Tours: Once you arrive in Naples a trolley might be your best way to see the historic sites, shopping areas, and residential sites in and around the city. The driver provides a commentary that covers Naples' history in great detail and in an interesting and sometimes humorous way. *Tours run daily between 10:30 and 5:30; call for a list of pick-up sites.* ☎ *262-7300.* ♿. *Fare includes an all-day boarding pass. Adults $10, children 3–12 $5.*

The Coastland Center (1), at 1900 North Tamiami Trail, is a major shopping mall with all the stores, outlets, restaurants, and cafés we've come to associate with such a complex.

The Third Street South Shopping Area (2) in the **Old Naples** historic district offers all sorts of opportunities for browsing, souvenir hunting, and dining. Here, you'll find Gulf Shore charm and historic significance. It's a quaint old shopping area with specialty shops that offer everything from hand-crafted toys and gourmet goodies to fine art and heirloom jewelry.

Frannie's Teddy Bear Museum (3), 2511 Pine Ridge Road, one mile west of Interstate 75 Exit 16, is one for the kids. They can wander around and see all sorts of the furry little stuffed animals, some not so little, too. All of their playtime friends are here, including Smokey Bear, Paddington, and others, as well as many antique and rare limited editions of the cuddle toy named for President Teddy Roosevelt. *Open 10–5 Mon.–Sat., 1–5 on Sun. Closed Mon. And Tues, from May-Nov.* ☎ *598-2711 or 800-681-2327.* ♿. *Adults $6, seniors $4, children 4–12 $2.*

Jungle Larry's Zoological Gardens at Caribbean Gardens (4), at 1590 Goodlette Road, is set among 52 acres of wildlife preserve and botanical gardens where wild birds and animals live together, free to go where they like, in a jungle setting. You can wander around as you please, walk a self-guided nature trail, take a 30-minute boat ride to see monkeys roaming around their island habitat, visit a petting zoo where the kids can get to know all sorts of domesticated animals, and enjoy an animal show at either 11:30 or 3. There's also a picnic area. *Open 9:30–5:30 daily.* ☎ *262-5409.* ♿. *Adults $12.95, children 4–15 $7.95.*

Collier County Museum (5), in the County Government Center at the junction of Highway 41 East and Airport Road, offers a peek at what it must have been like in the early days of Naples. Exhibits trace the city's history from the time when this was home to the Calusa Indians right up to the present. You can visit a re-created Indian village, a historic steam locomotive used long ago in the logging industry, and browse the exhibits of old photographs, papers, artifacts, and memorabilia. It's not a big museum, but one worth visiting. *Open 9–5 Mon.–Fri., closed holidays.* ☎ *774-8476. Free.*

The Conservancy (6), at 1440 Merrihue Drive just off Goodlette-Frank Road, is a wildlife rehabilitation and nature center that features nature trails, an outdoor aviary, and a Nature Discovery Center where you can get know a little about some of the creatures you may have heard about but are not really familiar with. These include the loggerhead turtle, snakes, and other such elusive creatures. It also offers a marine aquarium and an opportunity to touch and feel some of the animals and reptiles. The highlight of your visit will be a 45-minute boat ride with a knowledgeable guide through the mangrove forest and lagoon. You can also rent a canoe or kayak and try your hand on the water by yourself. *Open 9–4:30 Mon.–Sat., 1–4:30 on Sun. Closed Sun. From Apr.–Dec., also Sat. From July–Sept.* ☎ *262-0304.* ♿. *Admission to the center $4, children 7–18 $2, admission to the grounds free.*

Naples Fishing Pier (7) is one of Naples' best known landmarks. It extends more than 1,000 feet into the Gulf of Mexico at 12th Avenue South and is a favorite place for romantic, sunset strolls. The pier is also the place where serious anglers pursue snook, grouper, red snapper, and other regional species. Facilities include a bait shack, snack bar, restrooms, and showers. Parking is metered, but admission to the pier is free. *Open 24 hours daily; concession 7–6:30 daily.*

The Beaches: No matter where you happen to be in Naples there's always a beach nearby. City, state, and county parks offer plenty of public parking, picnic facilities, boat ramps if you happen to be trailing your own craft, playgrounds, freshwater showers, restrooms, and almost anything else you might need to make your daytrip to the beach a memorable experience. The sand is soft and white, the ocean safe and inviting with colors that range from the palest green to the deepest blue. You can spend your hours on the sands shelling, fishing in the surf, swimming, sunbathing, or sleeping under

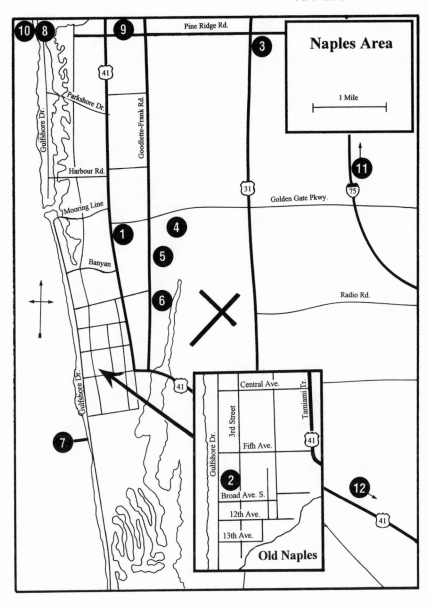

Naples Area

1 Mile

the shade of a waving palm or beach umbrella. Return in the early evening and you'll enjoy a spectacular sunset; stay until after dark and you might see a loggerhead turtle struggle ashore to lay its eggs in the sand. But where to go? With so many miles of shoreline available, that's a good question. Here are few suggestions:

Just off Vanderbilt Drive at 11100 Gulf Shore Drive North in North Naples, **Delnor-Wiggins State Recreation Area** (8) is a popular spot with both locals and visitors. Situated on a barrier island, separated from the mainland by tidal creeks and mangrove swamps, with its miles of pristine shoreline with protected sea oats, sea grapes, cabbage palms, and mangroves, the park provides habitats for a wide variety of marine and bird life. A pass at the north end of the island provides a natural outlet into the Cocohatchee River. The backwaters of the park, which occupy more than 80% of its area, are covered with lush green vegetation and provide a well-protected refuge and a major source of nutrition for the abundance of marine animals that begins life here before heading out into the Gulf.

You'll find the natural coastal system of the parkland area, and the shallow waters of the Gulf, home to all sorts of shore and wading birds, small mammals, and reptiles, and to countless forms of small marine life: soft corals, mollusks, crustaceans, fish, sea turtles and, during the winter months, even the endangered West Indian manatee. For recreation you can go fishing, swimming, shelling, sun bathing, and bird watching. It's also a great spot for wildlife photography, and you can hike for miles along the beach.

You'll also find that the facilities provided by the Park Service are extensive. These include five parking lots with a system of boardwalks, each providing easy access to the beaches; several picnic sites with tables, grills, bicycle racks, and public telephones; public bathhouses with changing stalls and fresh water showers; and an observation tower that provides a spectacular panoramic view over the entire recreation area. There's also a boat ramp giving access to the Cocohatchee River and the Gulf of Mexico. *Open 8– sunset daily.* ☎ *597-6196.* ♿. *Admission $3.25 per vehicle.*

Also in North Naples, off Vanderbilt Drive, **Cocohatchee River Park** (9) is a new public area with lots of facilities as well as some of the best sand and sea in the region. These include ample parking for cars, campers, and trailers; picnic shelters, restrooms, a recreation pavilion, and a children's playground. *Open 7–dusk daily.* ♿. *Parking and admission is free.*

Barefoot Beach State Recreation Area (10), just to the north of Wiggins Pass, is another sanctuary-like state park. It's a reserve for purists, a practically untouched stretch of sand and sea where you can really get away by yourself. There are no facilities or lifeguards, but there's also no admission fee. *Open 8–sundown.*

The entrance to the **Corkscrew Swamp Sanctuary** (11) is 20 miles north of Naples off Immokalee Road. A famous winter nesting place for the North American wood stork, this 11,000-acre preserve falls under the protection of the National Audubon Society. The sanctuary is also home to all sorts of exotic wildlife, including alligators, otters, and bobcats, as well as being the location of one of largest of the few remaining stands of virgin bald cypress in the nation. The giant bald cypress are hundreds of years old and form a natural cathedral through which a boardwalk winds its way, offering a wonderful opportunity to observe the swamp and its creatures close-up. *Open daily 7–5.* ☎ *657-3771.* ♿. *Adults $6.50, children 6–18 $3.*

Located on the fringe of the Florida Everglades, **Collier-Seminole State Park** (12), some 17 miles south of Naples on Highway 41, presents a rare glimpse of what the region must have looked like before the arrival of the first European explorers. The 6,400-acre park features a vast hinterland of vegetation and wildlife so typical of the Everglades. It was during the early 1940s that Barron Collier, a wealthy entrepreneur and property developer, decided to give something back to the state. He purchased the land, designed the park and, in 1947, turned it over to the State of Florida.

Most of the park is dominated by a dense system of swamplands: mangroves, salt marshes, and cypress swamps, along with pine flatwoods and the rare Florida royal palm. One rather special feature is a tropical hammock of trees characteristic of the Yucatan and the West Indies. As you might imagine, such a lush, steamy environment is home to a plethora of wildlife, including several of the state's threatened and endangered species. The brown pelican calls the park home, as does the wood stork, bald eagle, red-cockaded woodpecker, the rare American crocodile, Florida black bear, and the mangrove fox-squirrel. Sometimes, with a great deal of patience, it's possible to observe two of Florida's official state animals: the rare Florida panther and the West Indian manatee.

Facilities at the park are extensive and include an interpretive center, a 6½-mile hiking trail, an extensive system of boardwalks, and an observation platform overlooking the salt marsh. There's also a campfire circle, a boat ramp and a dock—just the spot for those trailing their own boat—a picnic area with tables and grills, public rest rooms, lots of parking, and a concession facility where you can purchase snacks, drinks, and fishing supplies. You can also rent a canoe.

If you like to fish, canoe, or boat, the Black Water River and the Ten Thousand Islands of the Gulf of Mexico offer unlimited opportunities. You can hike in almost perfect seclusion along the trail through the pine flatwoods and the cypress swamp, or you can stroll the nature trail and boardwalk system and get closer to nature, bird watching, and the like. Did you bring a packed lunch? The picnic area is the ideal spot to enjoy it. Just settle down at a table under the trees and spread the cloth. Finally, you can take a guided pontoon boat ride out on the Black Water River. Knowledgeable guides provide commentary as you go; they tell the story of the early settlers and explain the plant and animal life in and around the park. *Open 8–sunset daily; boat tours 9–5; the last boat leaves at 4.* ☎ *394-3397.* ♿. *Admission $3.25 per vehicle; boat fare: adults $8.50, children 6–12 $5.50.*

Trip 29

Everglades City

Almost at the end of the world, and just about as far south as you can go from the Tampa-St. Petersburg area, Everglades City is a tiny town, remote, but often busy with more than its fair share of tourists. This is, of course, because it's the western port of entry into the Everglades National Park, and the departure point for airboat tours and fishing trips therein.

GETTING THERE:

Take Interstate 75 south from Tampa to Exit 15, then FL-951 to US-41. Continue southeast to FL-29, taking that south into Everglades City. The entire drive is about 190 miles, depending upon your starting point.

GETTING AROUND:

If you really want to see the Everglades, you'll park your car and take to the waters in an airboat.

PRACTICALITIES:

The **Area Code** is 941.

Tours operate daily the year round, so your only consideration is the weather. The sun is extremely hot, making an adequate sunscreen essential. Don't stay out, unprotected, for long periods; you'll blister for sure. Insect repellent is also a good idea.

TOURIST INFORMATION:

The Everglades Area Chamber of Commerce, PO Box 130, Everglades City, FL 33929, ☎ 695-2800 or 800-543-3367.

FOOD AND DRINK:

Most hotels will prepare a packed lunch. Be sure to ask at the desk the night before you make your trip. Take along a cooler and plenty to drink. There are a couple of restaurants in Everglades City, but this trip is an outdoor experience and once you leave the city there's nothing but blue skies, water, and wilderness.

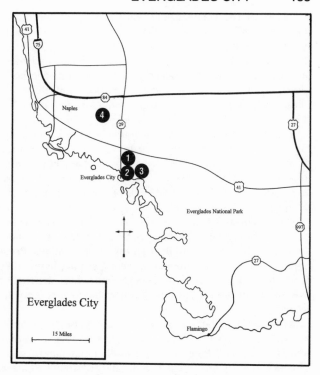

Everglades City

15 Miles

The Oyster House (three miles south of the city on Highway 29, the Chokoloskee Causeway) could be considered a daytrip stop in its own right. The Causeway is an exciting ride out from Everglades City and the view is spectacular. The restaurant is open for lunch and dinner 11–10. The menu, of course, is almost all fresh seafood caught locally, with a few diversions such as frog legs, stone crab claws, and alligator. ☎ 695-2073. $–$$.

SUGGESTED TOUR:

Be sure to stop by the **E.J. Hamilton Observation Tower,** (1) it's off Highway 29 and you can't miss it—just follow the signs. The wooden tower is 80 feet high and offers a spectacular panoramic view of the Everglades to the east and the 10,000 Islands to the west. The climb up the 180 steps to the top is quite a pull, the more so because of the heat, so you'll need to be in good physical shape. Be sure to take your camera. There's also a wooden boardwalk on which you can take a stroll through the mangrove beds to a waterway where you can see all sorts of birds and other wildlife. *The tower is open 24 hours daily. Admission $1.*

*Eden Of The Everglades (2), on Highway 29 two miles south of the junction with Highway 41, offers 45-minute pontoon boat tours of the waterways around the 10,000 Islands. It's a relaxing sidebar after the long drive down, and the scenery is spectacular. If the pontoon tour seems a little tame, you can opt for an airboat ride: not quite as relaxing, but an unforgettable experience nonetheless. There's also a boardwalk through the mangrove forest, a land almost beyond imagination. *Open 9–5 daily.* ☎ *695-2800 or 800-543-3367.* ♿. *Adults $12, children 3–10 $9.*

Everglades National Park Boat Tours (3), at the park's ranger station one mile south of Everglades City, offers the opportunity to see the Everglades in relative comfort. The guides are knowledgeable and provide commentary, information, and local folklore. *Boat tours leave the station daily between 8 and 5.* ☎ *695-2591 or 800-445-7724 for reservations.* ♿. *Adult fare $11, children 6–12 $5.50.*

Take Highway 29 northeast from its junction with Highway 41 and drive about four miles to the **Fakahatchee Strand State Preserve** (4), which lies at the western edge of the vast **Big Cypress Swamp National Preserve**. The Big Cypress is a seemingly boundless, gently sloping limestone plain where, during the rainy season (June through September), the water flows slowly over the plain, southward through the mangrove swamps to the Gulf of Mexico.

In many places the flow of water has cut channels into the soft limestone which, over the countless years, have gathered deep tracts of fertile organic soil. The channels, long, narrow, densely populated by swamp forests of cypress and mangrove, are known locally as "strands." One such strand is the Fakahatchee Strand State Preserve. More than 20 miles long, and varying in width from three to five miles, it's the largest and most unusual of the strands, and the major drainage channel of the southwestern Big Cypress Swamp. Over the years Big Cypress has suffered from the ravages of human exploitation—logging and land drainage—but even so has managed to survive and even thrive. The great stands of bald cypress, royal palms, and epiphytic orchids, along with many other species of rare and wonderful plants, make the Fakahatchee Strand State Preserve unique in the Florida park system.

Activities include nature study, bird watching, and wildlife photography from the 2,000-foot-long boardwalk that meanders through the virgin cypress swamps and offers a delightful opportunity to observe nature at its very best. *The preserve headquarters are on Janes Memorial Scenic Drive, just west of Copeland on Highway 29. Open 8–sunset daily.* ☎ *695-4593. Admission $3.25 per vehicle.*

The Everglades and Flamingo (see page 43) can be reached by taking Highway 41 to its junction with Highway 997, almost to Miami, and proceeding south from there. It's a long drive, and you may decide you can see all you need of the Everglades by taking the tour out of Everglades City.

The Northwest Coast

Although less visited than destinations to the south, the coastal area north of Tampa and St. Petersburg abounds with delightful discoveries far removed from the tourist hordes. The best of these are explored on both this and the following daytrips, which could be combined into a mini vacation by staying overnight.

GETTING THERE:

From Tampa, take FL-60 west to its junction with US-19 and turn north for about 63 miles to Homosassa Springs. All of the attractions are within a few miles of this.

PRACTICALITIES:

The **Area Code** is 352.

All of the sites are open daily, but you will need good weather for this largely outdoor trip.

TOURIST INFORMATION:

Crystal River Chamber of Commerce, 28 N.W. Highway 19, Crystal River, FL 34428, ☎ 795-3149.

FOOD AND DRINK:

All of the listed state parks and recreation areas have picnic facilities, some with tables and grills, so you might prefer to bring lunch with you. Otherwise, why not try:

    K.C. Crump's, in Homosassa Springs, at 11210 W. Halls River Rd., reached via local road 490A 3½ miles west of FL-19. Open for lunch and dinner, 11:30–10. American cuisine with local seafood, served in an old fishing lodge, on the patio, or even on an offshore island. ☎ 628-1500. $$-$$$.

LOCAL ATTRACTIONS:

Begin by driving north on Highway 19 from St. Petersburg and go for about 63 miles until you reach Homosassa Springs. The **Yulee Sugar Mill Ruins State Historic Site** (1) is just to the west on Route 490.

The Yulee Sugar Mill Ruins were once part of a thriving, 5,100-acre sugar plantation owned by David Levy Yulee. Yulee was a member of the Territorial Legislative Council and served in the U.S. Congress after Florida joined the Union. The great plantation was operated for 13 years by more than 1,000 slaves, and was a major supplier of sugar products for southern troops during the Civil War. There's a picnic area and restrooms. *Open 8–sunset daily.* ☎ *795-3817. Admission free.*

From the Yulee Sugar Mill Ruins, rejoin Highway 19 and drive north, following the signs for the **Homosassa Springs State Wildlife Park** (2). Homosassa Springs is one of those extraordinary places in the world where you can experience something very special. The rare and gentle Florida manatee is hardly ever seen by the vacationing public, but here, at Homosassa Springs State Wildlife Park, it's an everyday occurrence. You can walk "underwater" to view, not only the manatee, but many of Florida's other aquatic species in the Spring of 10,000 Fish.

Besides the manatee, there are many wildlife exhibits, including a Florida black bear, bobcats, alligators, and an extensive collection of wild birds. A series of educational and interpretive programs provided by the Park Service focus on Florida's manatees, alligators, and other wildlife. The Animal Encounters Arena features Florida's snakes and many other species of Florida wildlife. Be sure to say hello to Lucifer the Hippo. If you're a hiker, you should try out the nature trail that winds its way through wetlands and woods, or you can opt for a guided boat tour. A shuttle boat will ferry you from Highway 19 to the park. *Open 9–5:30 daily; the last shuttle leaves the dock 90 minutes before closing.* ☎ *628-2311.* ♿. *Adults $7.95, children 3– 12 $4.95.*

Fort Cooper State Park (3), at Inverness, is a bit out of the way, but well worth a visit if you have the time. Take Highway 490 northeast out of Homosassa Springs to the junction with Highway 44. From there it's a drive east of 10 miles into Inverness, and couple of miles more to the park at 3100 South Old Floral City Road.

Fort Cooper and beautiful Lake Holathikaha have not yet been discovered by the vacationing public, and it remains something of a gem. The swamps, marshlands, hardwood hammock, and the sandhills around the lake provide habitats for a variety of Florida's abundant wildlife. It's an area of wild and scenic beauty where the trees are festooned with moss, and more than ten miles of self-guided nature and hiking trails thread their way through the undergrowth. Nature still rules here, and the hand of man has been laid only lightly on the natural order of life in the park.

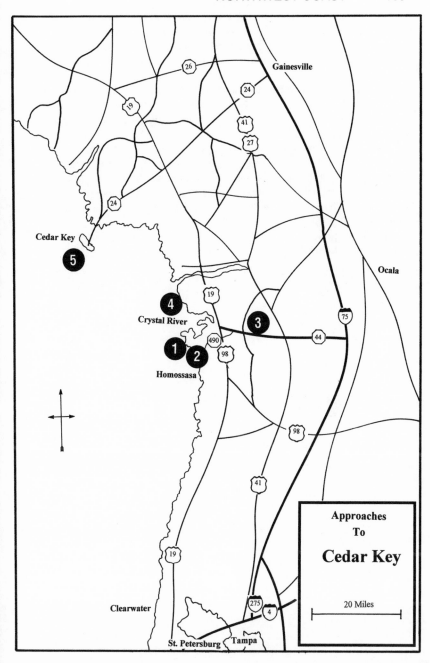

Approaches
To

Cedar Key

20 Miles

For you outdoorsy types, there's hiking, bird watching, swimming in the crystal clear waters of the spring-fed lake, fishing, horseback riding, and picnicking. It's also a great place for wildlife photography, and you can rent a canoe or paddleboat. There are pavilions, tables, and grills in the picnic area. *Open 8–sunset daily.* ☎ *726-0315.* &. *Admission $3.25 per vehicle.*

The **Crystal River State Archaeological Site** (4) is 2.5 miles west of Highway 19 at 3400 N. Museum Point. For over 1,600 years this 14-acre site was home to more than 7,500 Indians and is thought to be the longest continuously occupied site in Florida. The six-mound complex was built by a cultural group that archaeologists call pre-Columbian mound builders. At its conception, the Crystal River complex was an important religious and ceremonial center. Indians traveled great distances to bring their dead here for burial, to join in the ceremonies, and to trade with local Indians. Crystal River State Archaeological Site is a National Historic Landmark. *Open 9–5 daily.* ☎ *795- 3817. Admission $3.25 per vehicle.*

At this point you could elect to continue on to the Cedar Key trip, beginning on the next page.

Cedar Key

The focus of this trip is Cedar Key, a tiny community on the Gulf of Mexico some 125 miles north of St. Petersburg. It's a rather remote spot on the map, but popular and often quite busy. If time permits, why not stay overnight and combine this daytrip with the previous one?

GETTING THERE:

From Tampa, take Highway 60 west to its junction with US-19 in St. Petersburg and turn north. From there it's a straight run until you reach the junction with Highway 24, where you'll turn southwest and drive the remaining 20 miles into Cedar Key.

GETTING AROUND:

Your main mode of transportation, other than your car, will be your own two feet. Cedar Key is a tightly-knit community where everything is close together and easily accessible on foot.

PRACTICALITIES:

The **Area Code** for Cedar Key is 352.

The Historical Society Museum is open daily except on Thanksgiving, Christmas, and New Year's Day, but note that the State Museum is closed on Tuesdays and Wednesdays.

TOURIST INFORMATION:

Cedar Key Chamber of Commerce, PO Box 610, Cedar Key, FL 32625, ☎ 543-5600.

FOOD AND DRINK:

Cedar Key offers a number of nice places to eat, including:

The Fabulous Island Room, at the Cedar Cove Beach and Yacht Club, is open for lunch and dinner from 11:30–2, and 5–10. As you might expect of a restaurant on a tiny Gulf Coast key, the cuisine is almost exclusively seafood, with some pasta dishes and healthy choices for good measure. It's a popular dining spot, so reservations are a good idea. ☎ 543-6520. $–$$$.

LOCAL ATTRACTIONS:

See map on page 189. **Cedar Key** (5) is one of a series of Keys in the Gulf of Mexico: Atsena Otie, Seahorse Key, Snake Key, North Key, and Dead Man's Key, all of which can easily be reached by boat.

It was the steamboat business that first brought prosperity to the tiny island. Business grew in the area all through the 1850s, with steamboats stopping regularly at Depot Key, which became known as Atsena Otie Key in 1858. Soon new industries came to the area. Timber, in particular, became a thriving concern with a cedar mill owned and operated by pencil magnate Eberhard Faber. In 1860 a railroad link between the east and west coasts was completed, but it wasn't until 1861 that the first train arrived in Cedar Key from Fernandina north of Jacksonville, and so Cedar Key became a thriving seaport. During the Civil War it was a strategic point from which blockade runners supplied the Confederacy with food, guns, ammunition, and other essentials, while exporting cotton and lumber overseas to England and Europe. The Civil War left Depot Key in ruins, but work soon began to re-establish the sawmills and timber industry. The efforts were successful. By September 1868, seven steamship lines operated out of Cedar Key to Galveston, New Orleans, and Mobile. Unfortunately, as the newer ships grew in size and draft, they created a need for deep-water ports more able to handle them. And so, Cedar Key slowly lost its sea-going traffic until finally it became a sleepy, but picturesque, little backwater retreat.

Today, Cedar Key is an enticing little town. Its tiny downtown area is filled with historic buildings, gift shops, restaurants, and cafés. The railroads no longer run into Cedar Key, and the steamships are long gone, so the city is quiet most of the time, a dot on the map, a place where time really does seem to stand still. Drop in at the Cedar Key Chamber of Commerce on 2nd Street for more information, maps, and brochures, or call 352-543-5600.

The **Cedar Key Historical Society Museum** (6), at 2nd and State Road 24, features displays and exhibits including artifacts, photographs, and memorabilia that interpret Cedar Key's history from when it all began in the 1850s. Other exhibits include Seminole and Timucuan Indian relics and tools. They will also supply you with all you need for a **self-guided walking tour** of the Key. *Open 11–5 Mon.–Sat. 2–5 on Sun.* ☎ *543-5549.* ♿. *Adults $1, children 12–18 50¢.*

While you're in town, be sure to visit the **Cedar Key State Museum** (7), 1710 Museum Drive just off Highway 24, where much of Cedar Key's history has been preserved and remains for you to discover. The exhibits in the museum tell a colorful and interesting story of times gone by, of the Key's importance to Florida's burgeoning industries, early and modern, and they include many of the tools, utensils, and artifacts of an age that otherwise might have been forgotten. The museum is a tiny window into the past when the Key was a bustling seaport. *Open 9–5 Thurs.–Mon.* ☎ *543-5350.* ♿. *Admission $1, children under 6 free.*

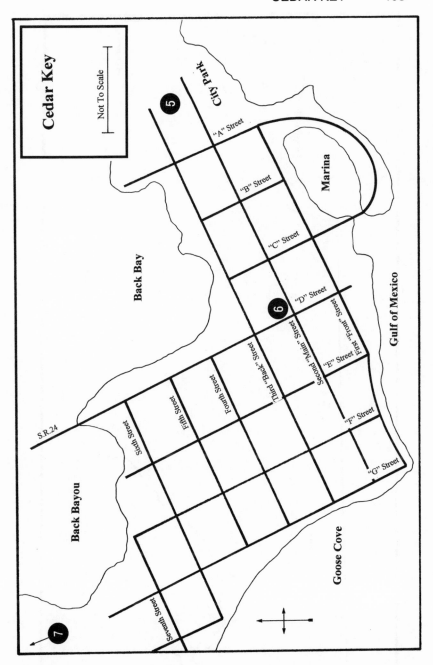

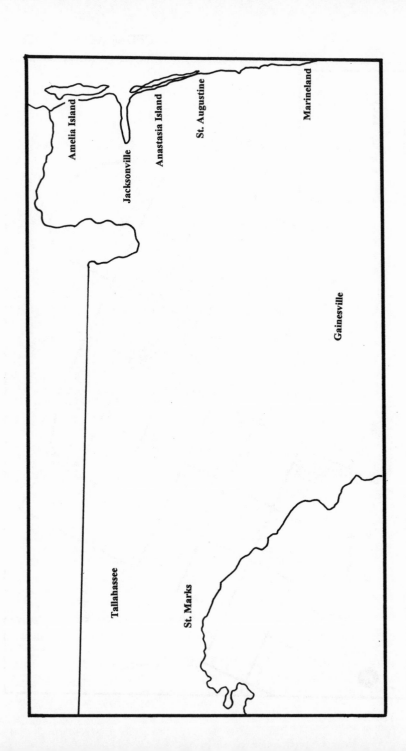

Section V

The Jacksonville area is rich in unspoiled beaches

JACKSONVILLE AND THE NORTHEAST

Jacksonville, a sprawling metropolis on the northeast coast, is the heart of Florida's historic region and the largest city by area in the United States. It's also the commercial center for Northeast Florida. The city's 12-mile River-walk, just across the St. Johns River from the downtown area, is a contemporary diversion of restaurants, shops, and stores. Likewise, Jacksonville Landing is a waterfront marketplace with more than 120 retail outlets and restaurants, and is the site of many local festivals and concerts.

St. Augustine, 25 miles south of Jacksonville Beach, is the oldest city in the nation, and the first permanent European settlement on the American mainland.

The coastal area of the region is a quiet, virtually unexplored outdoor destination of unspoiled beaches, secluded resorts, nature trails, bridleways, golf courses, lakes, and rivers where you can fish, hike, and relax; never too far away from the attractions and comforts of the big city.

Jacksonville offers plenty to see and do, from pristine Jacksonville Beach to the Kingsley Plantation, home of a one-time slave trader who married an African princess, to the Anheuser-Busch brewery, Jacksonville Zoo, and a whole world of museums, art centers, and historical sites.

GETTING THERE:

By Air: Downtown Jacksonville is 15 minutes by car or cab from Jacksonville International Airport, and is served by 13 large and regional airlines with 250 flights daily to and from most major cities in the country. The flight from New York takes about two hours; from Atlanta one hour; and from Orlando about 45 minutes.

By Car: Three major interstate highways serve Jacksonville: I-95, I-295 and I-10. Interstate 75 bypasses Jacksonville 30 miles to the west, but connects to the city via I-10. As well as the Interstates, four major highways converge on the city: US-1, US-17, US-90 and US-301. Because Jacksonville lies on both sides of the St. Johns River, there are seven major bridges and the Mayport Ferry to get you across the water. Jacksonville is six hours by car from Atlanta, two and a half hours from Orlando, two and a half hours from Tallahassee, and about two hours from Savannah, Georgia.

By Bus: the city is served by Greyhound/Trailways bus lines, with a station at 10 Pearl Street. ☎ 800-231-2222.

By Train: Passenger train service is provided by Amtrak at 3570 Clifford Lane. ☎ 800-872-7245, local 904-766-5110.

GETTING AROUND:

The driving directions for each trip assume that you're leaving from Jacksonville. Chances are, however, that you might be staying (or living) elsewhere in the Greater Jacksonville Area—St. Augustine, etc.—so you'll need to modify the routes a bit.

The Jacksonville Transportation Authority (JTA, ☎ 630-3100) provides local bus service on 50 routes throughout the city seven days a week. JTA also operates the Automated Skyway Express, a monorail system serving the downtown area.

Driving in the city is a hectic experience. Traffic is always busy, and parking, plentiful in some places, is at a premium in others. It's best to park in one of the outlying areas or at your hotel, and take the bus downtown. If you must drive there are several commercial parking lots.

ACCOMMODATIONS:

There are plenty of hotels in the downtown area, but unless you like the noise, hustle and bustle, it's best to stay in the outlying areas and either drive into town or hop on a bus. Those staying at one of the beach hotels can expect to pay more for the privilege. Make reservations well in advance as they are almost always heavily booked throughout the summer season. What can you expect to pay? In the lower range at one of the chain motels on Jacksonville's outer loop, from $30 to $50; in the medium range, $50 to $80; and for such motels as the Residence Inn by Marriott, you can pay as much $160 per night for a suite. Hotel rooms run from a low of $50 per night at the Best Western Bradbury to as much as $375 at the Marina Hotel & Conference Center. If you stay on Jacksonville Beach expect to pay upward of $160 per night. For more information, call the Jacksonville and the Beaches Convention & Visitors Bureau at 798-9148.

PRACTICALITIES:

The **Area Code** for Jacksonville and Northeast Florida is 904.

Weather: Northeast Florida is a land of mild winters, cool in spring and fall, and warm summers with lots of sunshine—ideal for indoor and outdoor activities. The average temperatures range from an evening low of about 42°F (it can get below freezing in January and February) to a daytime high of around 66° in winter; in spring and fall the range is 55 to 79; and in summer 71 to 90. Northeast Florida can be a little moist at times, especially in spring and fall.

Opening Times: Most of Jacksonville's attractions are open daily. On Sunday, however, you're certain to find one or two closed. Still others open late and close early, so it's best if you do your sightseeing on Mondays through Saturdays.

TOURIST INFORMATION:

Jacksonville and the Beaches Convention & Visitors Bureau, 3 Independent Drive, Jacksonville, FL 32202, ☎ 800-733-2668 or 798-9148, fax 798-9103.

Downtown Walk and Jacksonville Landing

By most standards, Jacksonville is a modern city. When a great fire destroyed most of its downtown area in 1901, only the shells of a few old structures were saved to be incorporated into the new center. So while Jacksonville's past is a story of its origins that weathered the Civil War and the ravaging fire of 1901, its modern architecture and attractive layout make it very appealing. Billed as "The Winter City in a Summer Land," it's a great place for walking the streets. The partial tour of the downtown area that follows covers only four blocks and makes 12 stops, and is followed by a visit to the waterfront. Jacksonville is, by area, the largest city in the United States, so walking is not the best way to see the remaining sights.

GETTING THERE:

PRACTICALITIES:
See pages 196–197.

FOOD AND DRINK:
While its cuisine is decidedly southern in nature, Jacksonville offers menus to suit every taste and budget. Local restaurants serve anything from southern-fried chicken with biscuits and gravy to sushi or steak. There are plenty of eateries and cafés in the downtown area and on the Riverwalk, and more on the beaches. Some you might enjoy are:
   Downtown:
      Jenkins' Quality Bar-B-Que (830 Pearl Street) is something of a Jacksonville institution. The menu includes barbecued beef, pork, and chicken smothered in homemade sauce. ☎ 353-6388. $.
   Baymeadows:
      Venny's (9862 Baymeadows Road) is a family operated restaurant with an Italian menu that includes homemade pizza, fettuccine, lasagna, chicken, and veal. ☎ 642- 1161. $.

The Jacksonville skyline

Jacksonville Beach:
Maker 32 (14549 Beach Boulevard) serves American regional cuisine, including domestic lamb, Atlantic salmon, game birds, fresh pasta, and in-house baked foods. The wine list is extensive. ☎ 223-1534. $$.

The Cove Restaurant (2600 Beach Boulevard) specializes in Key West dolphin (the fish), macadamia salmon, scampi, and steak. Reservations accepted. ☎ 249-7777. $$.

Orange Park:
Whitey's Fish Camp (2032 CR 220 Orange Park) is the place to go for something a little different. There's a full-service bar, and you can dine outside on the water front. Specialties include fresh catfish, gator tail, and shrimp, as well as a variety of fresh seafood. Reservations accepted. ☎ 269-4198. $$.

Southbank:
Filling Station Café (1004 Hendricks Avenue) is a sophisticated, art deco café with an extensive and interesting menu. You might like to try the cashew-encrusted grouper in a champagne cream sauce, pan-seared tuna, or even a New York strip. Reservations accepted. ☎ 398-3663. $$.

SUGGESTED TOUR:

Park your car on Duval Street, just off the 300 block of North Main Street, and walk west across Main to the **Rhodes-Futch Building** (1). Built in 1904 to replace the one destroyed in the great fire in 1901, this was the home of A.G. Rhodes' furniture company, which he originally started in Atlanta in the 1870s. So successful was his business here that he expanded and built a much larger store next door in 1914. That building was the last tall, reinforced-concrete structure built in Jacksonville prior to the 1920s.

Turn north on Main, walk to the corner of Duval Street, turn left and walk to the end of the block where you'll find the **Western Union Telegraph Company Building** (2) on the left. Built in 1931 for just $500,000, it is decorated with terra-cotta and the winged globe symbols of the Western Union logo.

Look north across Duval Street and you'll see the **Old YMCA Building** (3). In its time it was considered something of a pioneer because of its use of the Prairie School style, the first truly American type of architecture that was later made famous by the likes of Frank Lloyd Wright and Louis Sullivan.

Head west across Laura Street to **Hemming Plaza** (4)—it's the block bounded by Laura, Duval, Monroe, and Hogan Streets. This historic town square, once the site of the famous Windsor and St. James hotels, was originally built in 1866. Here you can see the Confederate Memorial donated in 1899 by Charles C. Hemming, a Civil War veteran, and the old St. James building of 1912.

To the south, at the corner of Monroe and Laura Streets, stands the **Snyder Memorial Methodist Church** (5), a product of what is now known as the "Rebuilding Era." After the 1901 fire, hundreds of craftsmen and artisans came to Jacksonville to reconstruct the ravaged downtown area; this old structure was a part of that effort. Built in 1903 and originally known as the Trinity Methodist Church, it remains virtually unchanged.

Continue south on Laura to the corner of Adams Street and the **Greenleaf and Crosby Building and Clock** (6). Standing over 15 feet tall, the famous Crosby Clock was erected after the fire to lend sophistication to the new downtown area. Unfortunately, it was hit by a bus in 1974 and destroyed. Restoration of the clock was a tedious and time-consuming job. Thousands of tiny pieces had to be identified and cemented together, but the effort was well worth it. Today, the historic timepiece looks just as good as the day it was installed almost 100 years ago. The Greenleaf and Crosby building was completed in 1927, and was the home of a jewelry company established in 1880. It is extensively decorated with terra-cotta panels with pictures of eagles, griffins, flowers, and urns.

Across the street at the corner of Adams and Laura is the **Barnett National Bank Building** (7), built in 1926. At 18 stories, it's the tallest building in Jacksonville and home to Barnett Banks, established in 1877. Between the third and fourth stories you can see a series of stone lion heads. Next door,

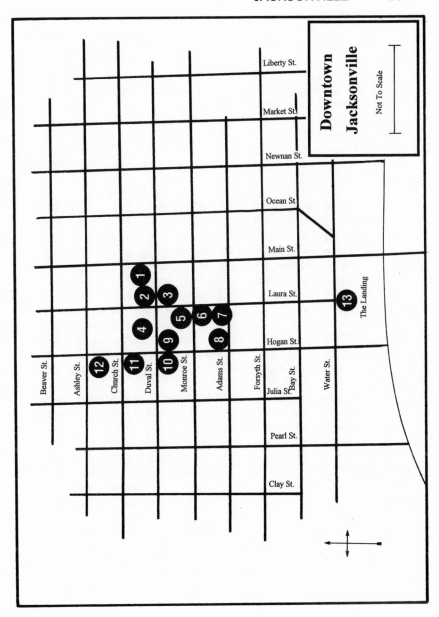

the Atlantic National Bank Annex was also built in 1926, and decorated with white glazed terra-cotta.

Turn west and walk to the corner of Adams and Hogan Streets and the **Levy Building** (8). Completed in 1927, the terra-cotta- clad structure was one of four commercial buildings in the downtown area designed by March and Saxelby, and was originally a department store. Today it houses the offices of architects Saxelby, Powell, Roberts and Ponder.

Turn left at the corner and walk north on Hogan to Hemming Plaza and the site of **The Kings Road** (9). This is the original location of Florida's first highway. The road was built by the British during their 20 years of occupation in Florida (1763-1783). It extended from here south to New Smyrna, and north to St. Marys, Georgia.

Continue walking north on Hogan and look west across the street where you'll see the **Seminole Club** (10), the city's oldest social club built in the Colonial Revival style. Established in 1887, it has twice been destroyed by fire. Teddy Roosevelt once made a campaign speech from the front porch.

A little farther north, on the west corner of Hogan and Church Streets, you'll see the **Old Federal Reserve Bank** (11). It's an imposing structure, featuring a Neo-Classical Revival design.

The final stop on your walk is the **Old First Baptist Church and Sunday School** (12) at 133 West Church Street. Continue north on Hogan to the corner of Hogan and Church, looking north across the street to see the church. Built in 1903 in the Romanesque Style, it replaced an earlier church that stood on the same site. Its design was inspired by the famous Trinity Church in Boston. The Church Sunday School was at one time the second largest Baptist Sunday School in the world.

Return to your car and drive west on Duval for one block, turn left on Laura and drive south to the waterfront and **Jacksonville Landing** (13); there's a large parking area adjoining it to the east.

The Landing is quite special. If you like to shop, this is the place for you. The Landing is an attractive microcosm of riverfront boardwalks, shops, restaurants, an open-air courtyard, and an amusement center; a place that the whole family can enjoy. You'll find all your favorite specialty stores here, and you can dine on a level to suit the occasion, anything from fast food to the freshest catch of the day. For the kids, large and small, TILT's Ostrich Landing is a 10,000-square-foot amusement center with lots of high-tech games, a riverboat shooting gallery, a family boardwalk, and plenty of other fun things to do. There's always something going on in the courtyard, with free year-round musical entertainment from country to classical. *Open Mon.–Thurs. 10–8; Fri.–Sat. 10–9; Sun. noon–5:30. Many restaurants stay open later. Independent Drive.* ☎ *353-1188. Free.* ♿.

Timucuan Ecological & Historic Preserve and Fort Caroline National Monument

The 46,000-acre Timucuan Ecological and Historic Preserve, nested between the Nassau river to the north and the St. Johns to the south, incorporates a great tract of wetland and several interesting and significant historic sites. Mostly wild and desolate, the preserve is named for the people who populated the area prior to the arrival of the first European explorers. Sadly, the Timucuan Indians, who lived in northeast Florida for thousands of years, all but disappeared by the turn of the 18th century.

Four historic sites represent several important chapters in America's past. Fort Caroline was the earliest European settlement within the preserve, while the Kingsley Plantation offers a glimpse of the ante-bellum South, slavery and all.

Timucuan also encompasses significant natural resources, the most important of which is its 30,000 acres of wetlands. These provide a habitat for many threatened and endangered species, such as the bald eagle, sea turtle, manatee, wood stork, and various kinds of waterfowl. The wetlands also store water, help to control the effects of erosion and flooding, and serve as a natural filter for water pollution. Best of all, they offer urban dwellers a chance to see the great outdoors as it really is, or at least as it once was, far from the smog, dirt, noise, pollution, and other human beings. This daytrip will provide you with a memorable escape into Florida's backcountry, a chance to look back in time to the dawn of American history. It can easily be completed in an afternoon, but allow a full day to do it properly.

GETTING THERE:

The farthest point on this trip, the Kingsley Plantation, is about 30 miles northeast of Jacksonville. You'll need a car to get around; just follow the directions in the "Suggested Tour" section.

PRACTICALITIES:

The Preserve and its four historic sites are open daily, so come any time. Guided tours and walks, however, are offered only on weekends at Fort Caroline and Theodore Roosevelt, and on Thursdays through Mondays at the Kingsley Plantation. Restrooms are available at all four sites, but there's no drinking water at Theodore Roosevelt.

FOOD AND DRINK:

There's not much food available along the way, so it's best to pack a picnic lunch. Some nice spots to enjoy it are at Fort Caroline and at the Theodore Roosevelt Area. You can make the outdoor eating experience just as memorable as you like by packing an interesting lunch; try something special instead of the usual sandwich and soda.

SUGGESTED TOUR:

From Jacksonville, go east on Highway 10 to Monument Road (FL-9A). Turn north there and drive on until you cross Fort Caroline Road, and then the St. Johns River; the **Yellow Bluff State Historic Site** (1) will be just beyond on the right; it's not well marked, so you'll need to keep your wits about you. The fort, now a part of the Talbot Islands State Park System, was constructed by Confederate troops in 1862. It was designed to defend the river approaches into Jacksonville against the advance of Federal gunboats from the Atlantic ocean just to the east. Although it was garrisoned alternatively by both Confederate and Union forces, it never saw much action. Today, only a few remnants of the old earthworks and a couple of cannon remain to mark the location of the one-time redoubt, and there's a plaque that gives a fairly detailed description of its history. Still, it's a significant site that you're very likely to have all to yourself, and one that's well worth a visit. *Open daily during daylight hours.* ☎ *251-2320. Free.*

Return to Monument Drive, head south to Fort Caroline Road, and turn east. **Fort Caroline** (2), once an important part of the Spanish defensive line along Florida's east coast, is just a short distance down the road. The site was originally established during France's ill-fated attempts at colonization. In 1564, 300 French men and women arrived with René de Laudonnière to establish a somewhat tentative foothold. By 1565, famine had driven the colonists to the point where they were ready to abandon their outpost. Fortunately, or unfortunately as things turned out, reinforcements and food arrived from France and plans to leave were cancelled. Farther south, Spanish Captain General Pedro Menéndez de Avilés, under orders from his sovereign to colonize Florida in its entirety, was preparing to move against the French. His first attempt to destroy Fort Caroline was unsuccessful, and he was forced to retire his fleet southward. The French retaliated and sailed after him, only to lose their fleet in a storm. Avilés now marched overland with some 500 men and attacked the fort again. This time he was successful.

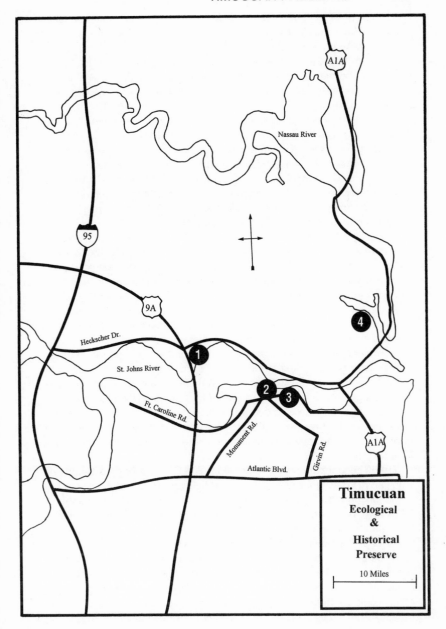

A1A

Nassau River

95

9A

Heckscher Dr.

St. Johns River

1

Ft. Caroline Rd.

2 3

Monument Rd.

Girvin Rd.

Atlantic Blvd.

A1A

4

Timucuan
Ecological
&
Historical
Preserve

10 Miles

More than 140 Frenchmen were killed, and 70 women and children taken prisoner. Three hundred more shipwrecked Frenchmen were massacred south of St. Augustine on the Matanzas Inlet.

In 1658, Fort Caroline, now defended by a Spanish garrison, was attacked and burned by another French colonizing expedition. While their attack on the fort was successful, French colonial aspirations were not; Florida remained under Spanish rule for more than 250 years. Gun batteries were established on the site during both the U.S. Civil War and the Spanish-American War, but the great triangular, wood-and-earth fort of the 1500s is no more. You can see what it must have been like, however, as a scale model has been constructed along 280 feet of the riverfront. This was made possible by first-hand descriptions of the fort and sketches by Jacques Le Moyne, a French cartographer who survived both of Avilés' attacks. *Open daily 9–5 except Christmas. 12713 Fort Carolina Road.* ☎ *641-7155. Free.* & *with cart service to the fort for physically disabled persons.*

Just a little farther to the west along Fort Caroline Road you'll find the **Theodore Roosevelt Area** (3). Here, on the southern banks of the St. Johns River, the more than 600 acres of preserve that bear the great president's name have been set aside for the more casual outdoors men and women to enjoy. This rather remote wetland area, once a part of a vast wilderness that lined the lower St. Johns, is now a beautiful getaway with more than four miles of hiking trails and nature walks. For those traveling with bicycles on board, there are some limited biking trails that wind through several ecological communities—coastal hammocks, hardwood forests, and salt marshes, as well as 35 acres of shell mounds left behind by the Timucuan Indians—and offer the opportunity to view many varieties of rare plants and animals. The best time to visit is either on a Saturday or Sunday when National Park Service Rangers offer free guided walks through Theodore Roosevelt. This is absolutely the best way to see the preserve and to understand it. *Open daily during daylight hours. Picnic areas and restrooms, but no drinking water.* ☎ *641-7155.*

From Theodore Roosevelt, return along Fort Caroline Road to its junction with Girvin Road, turn south and drive to Highway 10. Turn east there and go to the junction of Highway A1A and turn north. Follow A1A across the St. Johns River onto Fort George Island, following signs to the **Kingsley Plantation** (4) in the heart of the Timucuan Preserve.

Perhaps Zephaniah Kingsley was the first to fall for the age-old pitch and "buy some swamp land in Florida." Buy it he did, and he managed to make a success of it, albeit using the labor of slaves. Kingsley moved to Fort George Island in 1814. He brought with him a wife and three small children; a fourth child would be born on the plantation. His wife was a former slave and princess from Senegal that he once owned, but freed in 1811. At first, his operation was a fairly small one, producing Sea Island cotton, citrus, sugar cane, and corn on land worked by a force of 60 slaves, but as the years went by his enterprise grew until he eventually owned more than 32,000 acres and 200 slaves. Though a slave owner, he was a fair man and treated his human possessions well. When the United States purchased Florida from Spain in 1821, American territorial law brought about some changes as to the ownership of slaves. At a time when other slaveholders, less benevolent than Kingsley, lived in fear of rebellion, oppressive new laws were enacted and conditions for the black labor force in Florida deteriorated. Kingsley was opposed to the new restrictive regulations, arguing that humane treatment would ensure, not only peace among the slaves, but the perpetuation of slavery itself. In 1829 he published his opinions in a *Treatise on The Patriarchal, or Co-operative System of Society As It Exists in Some Governments Under the Name of Slavery.*

By 1837, however, Kingsley had enough. He packed his bags, sold the plantation to a nephew, and moved his family and some of his former slaves to Haiti.

Today, the old plantation symbolizes dramatic times in American history. Legends of its former owners and the enslaved men and women live on, but only the Planter's Residence, the Kitchen House, Barn, and 23 of the original 32 slave cabins remain of what must have a small city among the swamps and hammocks of northeast Florida. To visit the Kingsley Plantation is to take a walk back through time. *Open daily 9–5 with guided tours available Thurs.–Mon.* ♿. ☎ *251-3527. Free.*

Trip 34

Amelia Island

Amelia Island is Florida's most northerly barrier island. Its pristine beaches, historic sites, and state parks make it a pleasure for the entire family. The sun shines most of the time, and the kids can enjoy fun in the sand.

For more than four centuries Amelia Island has played a significant role in the shaping of Florida's history. Though small, it's the only territory in the United States to have seen rule under eight flags. Named for the daughter of England's King George II, Amelia, with its captivating beauty, agreeable climate, and neat little harbor has, over the years, attracted all sorts of adventurers, aristocrats, entrepreneurs, and ne'er-do-wells. Situated at the northeasternmost tip of Florida, it's history can be summed up as follows: "the French visited the island, the Spanish developed it, the English named it, and the Americans tamed it."

It was on May 3, 1562, when Frenchman Jean Ribault first stepped ashore that Amelia's modern history began. Before then, the island had been inhabited for more than 4,000 years by the Timucuan Indians. The Spanish soon followed Ribault, then the English who gave the island its name. Its most colorful period began with Jefferson's Embargo Act of 1807 and the closure of all American ports to foreign shipping. It was then that Fernandina, Amelia's Spanish harbor, came into its own as a haven for smugglers and buccaneers as well as a center for the slave trade. What is known today as Old Town was a bustling little seaport populated by adventurers and a host of ruthless opportunists. The bluff, now occupied by the bed-and-breakfast inn Posada San Carlos, was lined with bordellos; Fernandina was a "festering fleshpot." All this came to an end, however, when Spain ceded its Floridian possessions to the United States in 1821.

The present site of Fernandina Beach is the result of a dream of U.S. Senator David Yulee, who promised to make it "the spotlight of the Western World." He persuaded the town to resettle a half-mile down river where he built the first cross-state railroad, which connected the island to the bustling Gulf coast port of Cedar Key. Today, the old railroad depot and a replica caboose serve as the island's visitor center.

During the dark days preceding the Civil War, Confederate authorities began building a fort off the northern tip of the island. But Union soldiers took it before it was completed without a shot being fired. Work on the fort continued under the First New York Volunteer engineers, but by war's end the massive structure was far from finished, and it never was. Fort Clinch is now a magnificent state park and recreation area.

Tourism came to Amelia Island as early as 1875 when northerners voyaged from New York to the island aboard ships of the Mallory Steamship Line, thus creating the dawn of Amelia's "Golden Age." By 1896 it was being hailed as "The Queen of Summer Resorts."

The Golden Age promoted a building boom in Fernandina Beach. Historic Centre Street is now a historic site in its own right, with all sorts of fine homes, old shops and stores, and Florida's oldest watering hole, the famous Palace Saloon.

In the 1890s, Amelia fell victim to the progress of modern transportation; Henry Flagler's new railroad took wealthy tourists far to the south. Thus, modernization by-passed the island—a catastrophe at the time but a blessing for today, for Amelia Island retains its identity as an authentic Victorian seaport and village.

GETTING THERE:

From Jacksonville, take Highway 105 east to Little Talbot Island, and then on to its junction with A1A. Continue north on 105/A1A to Amelia Island; it's a drive of about 35 miles.

GETTING AROUND:

For the most part, you'll need to use your car. Only in Fernandina Beach will you be able to park it and walk.

PRACTICALITIES:

You can take this trip any day of the week when the weather is good. One or two places open late and close early on Sunday. The local **Area Code** is 904.

FOOD AND DRINK:

There are lots of great restaurants on Amelia Island, most of them in Fernandina Beach. This being one of the shrimping centers in Florida, the emphasis is on fresh seafood. Some choices are:

> **Brett's Waterway Café** is on the water and overlooks the Fernandina Harbor Marina at the foot of Centre Street. It's an upscale eatery where the food is good, and the menu includes such specialties as aged beef and fresh seafood. Open daily for lunch and dinner. ☎ 261-2660. $–$$.

> **The Crab Trap** features nautical decor and a casual, relaxed atmosphere. Specialties include boiled crab and shrimp. Open daily for dinner from 5 p.m. 31 North 2nd Street. ☎ 261-4749. $$.

Florida House Inn, the state's oldest hotel, is another not-to-be-missed lunch opportunity. Home cooking is served boarding-house style and it's always "all you can eat." Open for lunch Monday through Saturday. 22 South 3rd Street. ☎ 261-0013. $$.

Horizons, rated one of Florida's Top 25 restaurants by *Jacksonville Magazine*, is a great place to eat dinner. The menu features fine continental cuisine, including veal, rack of lamb, beef, pasta, and fresh fish. Open for dinner from 6 p.m. Corner of 8th and Ash Streets. ☎ 321-2430. $$$.

The Palace Saloon on Centre Street in Fernandina is a must; no visit to the island would be complete without a stop at the old watering hole. Lunch there is a real treat. Specialties include fresh seafood, sandwiches, and soups. Open 11–2 a.m. 117 Centre Street. ☎ 261-6320. $$.

TOURIST INFORMATION:

Amelia Island Chamber of Commerce, The Depot, Centre Street, Fernandina Beach, FL 32035, ☎ 800-2-AMELIA.

SUGGESTED TOUR:

This daytrip takes in most of the sights on Amelia Island and some on those adjacent to it. It's best that you drive out on Highway 105, then A1A to the northernmost point on the island, and work your way back to Jacksonville.

Fort Clinch State Park (1) incorporates some 1,121 acres at the north end of Florida's most northerly barrier island. It is separated from Georgia by the Cumberland Sound, and has more than 8,400 feet of shoreline on the sound itself. There's another 4,000 feet of shoreline on the Atlantic coast, while the west is bounded by an extensive estuarine marsh system. Construction of the fort, which was named for General Duncan L. Clinch, an important figure in the Seminole War of the 1830s, began in 1847 and continued through the Civil War. When war broke out in 1861, it was occupied by a Confederate garrison, but was taken by Federal forces in 1862 following General Robert E. Lee's order to withdraw. No great battles were fought here, not even a good-sized skirmish. After the war, the Federal garrison was greatly reduced and the fort eventually abandoned. In 1898 it again saw service for a few months during the Spanish-American war, then deserted. The state purchased the property and 256 acres in 1935 as part of a program to acquire adjacent lands for one of the first of Florida's state parks. In the 1930s the Civilian Conservation Corps moved in and went to work developing the new park, formally opened to the public in 1938.

Today, the fort remains in remarkably good condition. Its history is brought to life by Park Service rangers dressed in Civil War era Federal uniforms as they carry out the daily chores of a soldier of the times: cooking,

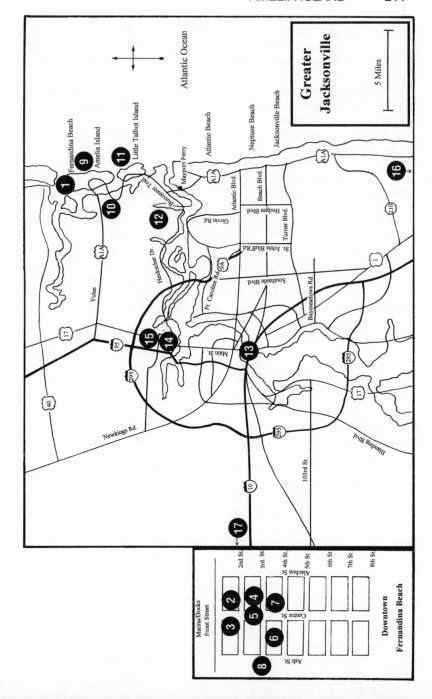

sentry duty, and so forth. You can watch special full-garrison reenactments in May and October, and you can take a guided candlelight tour any evening when the weather is good. Be sure to make a reservation. The visitor center contains exhibits that interpret the history of the fort: tools, utensils, and artifacts.

The are restrooms at the visitor center, fresh water showers at the beach, and several hiking trails. There's also a picnic area near the beach, a great place for an outdoor lunch.

If you have some spare time, you can go fishing from the beach or the pier. The Amelia River, Cumberland Sound, and the Atlantic Ocean are full of speckled trout, striped bass, redfish, bluefish, drum, sheephead, flounder, whiting, and pompano. Or you might enjoy a quiet walk along the nature trail or the beach. There's always swimming in the Atlantic Ocean, or you might just sunbathe. If you're a nature lover, the west side of the park is a wonderful place to observe the wading birds and other species of marine life that make their homes in the hammocks and dunes. *Fort Clinch State Park, 2601 Atlantic Avenue, Fernandina Beach, FL 32034,* ☎ *261-4212. Open daily 8 until sunset. $3.25 per vehicle (up to eight people).* ♿.

Rejoin Highway A1A, turn east and drive to **Fernandina Beach**, parking on or near the waterfront. From there, you can begin a walking tour of historic **Centre Street**, the once-bustling downtown area of the old Victorian seaport. Today, it's a picturesque shopping center full of history, lined with quaint old buildings, cobbled walks, and gas lanterns.

Just east of the docks at the foot of Centre Street, you'll find the **Depot** (2) of Florida's first cross-state railroad. Though not the original one, it was opened in 1899. Train service was discontinued in the mid-1930s. Today, it houses the Chamber of Commerce and also serves as Fernandina Beach's Visitor Information Center.

Just across the street is the **Duryee Building** (3). Built in 1882 by Major W.B.C. Duryee, the Collector of Customs during those times, it housed not only his office, but also a bar, a bank, and a newspaper.

The ***Palace** (4), on the corner of Centre and 2nd Street, is Florida's oldest saloon. To give you even a short history of the old tavern would fill a book; thousands of words have already been written about it. It has an atmosphere that comes only with age, dark and heavy with red velvet drapes; paddle fans turn slowly below an embossed tin ceiling; half-naked, hand-carved mahogany female figures gaze out across the 40-foot bar upon which is set a great brass cash register of indeterminate age. Built in 1878, it's the place where sea captains, some reputable, some of questionable morality, and some downright crooked, came to socialize and drink. Today, you can still take a drink, eat a meal, and enjoy a rollicking good time, but gone are the characters who gave it its reputation and identity. *Open 11 a.m. until 2 a.m. 117 Centre Street.* ☎ *261-6320.*

The Three Star Saloon (5) was built by William Marston in 1877 and opened as a bar. Since then it has gone through a series of owners and businesses, including a clothing store and a jeweler's. Its facade remains much the same as it was when it first opened.

A little farther east, near Centre on South Third Street, is the **Florida House** (6), the state's oldest hotel. Built by the railroad in 1857, it's now a bed-and-breakfast inn. The Florida House is open for lunch and dinner, a neat experience.

Back on Centre the elegant **Post Office Building** (7) was completed in 1812. Postcards to send? This is the place.

The Historic District of Fernandina Beach is listed on the National Register of Historic Places, and covers some 50 blocks, of which Centre Street is the heart. To learn more, you can take a guided walking tour offered by the **Amelia Island Museum of History** (8). Once Nassau County's jail house, abandoned and derelict for many years, the old building now houses an award-winning museum. Here, from the days of the Timucuan Indians through occupations by the French, Spanish, English, and finally American governments, you can learn the story of Amelia Island's long and sometimes colorful history. And, if you really want to see Fernandina Beach, you can take the full tour. Bookings must be made 24 hours ahead, and there must be a minimum of four people. *Open daily 10–5; closed Sunday. 233 South 3rd Street.* ☎ *261-7378. Admission free. Guided tours of the museum twice daily at 11 and 2, $2.50 per person. Guided walking tours of the Historic district begin at $5 per person.*

From Fernandina Beach, rejoin Highway A1A and travel south, back toward Jacksonville, for about eight miles to **Amelia Island State Recreation Area** (9). Here, more than 200 acres of undeveloped sea island offer almost unlimited recreational opportunities. The beaches, though seemingly remote, are not beyond the bounds of civilization. The golden sand is clean, the sea crystal clear, the fishing superb and, most important, the sun almost always shines. And there's lots to do if you have the time. The Seahorse Stable—☎ 261-4878—offers guided horseback rides along the beaches; you can hike for miles along the sands; watch the sea birds wheel and dive over the ocean; sunbathe and swim; or do a little fishing from the beach. You can take along your own picnic lunch or buy a snack and soft drink at the concession stand. In short, this is a great place to spend a few quiet hours away from the fast pace of the cities and resorts. *Amelia Island State Recreation Area, C/O the Talbot Islands GEOpark, 11435 Fort George Road East, Fort George, FL 32226.* ☎ *251-2320.*

Back on Highway A1A, heading south to Jacksonville, you'll cross South Amelia River onto Talbot Island where, on one of those unique sea islands so typical of northeastern Florida, you'll find **Big Talbot Island State Park** (10). The park seems very remote, a picturesque series of hammocks, sand dunes, and troughs covered with sea oats, morning glories, and a wide range of other ground-covering plant life and wildflowers, grasses, sedges, willows, slash pines, and red cedars. During the fall and spring months, a variety of migrating birds stop off to enjoy these isolated, and often wild, sea island plant communities.

At the southwestern end of the island is the river mouth at Fort George; to the east the Atlantic Ocean with its magnificent beaches that remain largely undiscovered and certainly unspoiled. Canoe routes interlace the salt marshes, and hikers can spend hours wandering the historic trails. Then there's the wildlife; if you love nature, this is the place for bird watching and nature study. Fishermen will find plenty of sport here. You can cast into the surf, river, and creeks, for striped bass, speckled trout, bluefish, redfish, flounder, mullet, sheephead, and whiting. *Open 8–sunset. Big Talbot Island State Park, C/O the Talbot Islands GEOpark, 11435 Fort George Road East, Fort George, FL 32226. ☎ 251-2320. $3.25 per vehicle (up to eight people).*

From Big Talbot, rejoin Highway A1A and head south across Nassau Sound to **Little Talbot Island State Park** (11), yet another of northeast Florida's unique sea islands. This is a large park encompassing 2,500 acres of barrier island, and more than five miles of glistening, sandy beaches. The island is a wild and woolly area, picturesque, an undisturbed hammock of rolling sand dunes and troughs covered with live oak, red cedars, southern magnolia, American holly, sea oats, and morning glories. Here you can wander through the dunes and forests. You'll see river otters, marsh rabbits, perhaps even a bobcat, as well as a wide variety of sea and shore birds that inhabit the island.

The beach at Little Talbot is listed as one of the nation's "Top 20 Best Beaches," so it's no surprise that the island offers superb swimming, surfing, and sunbathing. *Little Talbot Island State Park, C/O the Talbot Islands GEOpark, 11435 Fort George Road East, Fort George, FL 32226. ☎ 251-2320. $3.25 per vehicle (up to eight people).*

Back on A1A, or Highway 105 as it has once again become, you'll continue southward, and then southwest toward Jacksonville. As you reach the southern tip of Fort George Island, about three miles south of Little Talbot Island State Park, you'll come to the **Fort George State Cultural Site** (12), the final stop on this trip. Moss-draped laurel and live oaks provide a lush canopy over Fort George Island, which has been continuously occupied for more than 5,000 years. Yet another member of Florida's Talbot Islands GEOpark complex, it includes Mount Cornelia—the highest point on the Atlantic coast south of Sandy Hook, New Jersey. Fort George is an interesting and educational experience, well worth stopping by if you have time. *Fort George Island State Cultural Site, C/O the Talbot Islands GEOpark, 11435 Fort George Road East, Fort George, FL 32226. ☎ 251-2320. $3.25 per vehicle (up to eight people).*

More Jacksonville Attractions

Jacksonville offers several other attractions that didn't quite fit into any of the previous daytrips, but which are too good to miss. While you can't do them all in a single day, you can pick and choose the combination of sites that best suits your interests and create your own daytrip.

The whole family will enjoy the downtown Museum of Science and History, as they will the Jacksonville Zoo, just a few miles to the north. Nearby, the Anheuser-Busch Brewery offers their Budweiser Tour of the brewing process, including free samples. Nature lovers can drive south to the wild and remote Guana River State Park, while Civil War buffs may prefer the Olustee Battlefield State Historic Site to the west.

GETTING THERE:

You'll need a car for all of these sites, except possibly the downtown Museum of Science and History. Specific driving instructions are given for each location. See the map on page 211.

PRACTICALITIES:

FOOD AND DRINK:

See the appropriate entries on pages 198–199.

LOCAL ATTRACTIONS:

MUSEUM OF SCIENCE AND HISTORY (13): Located in the downtown district on the Southbank Riverwalk, just across the river from Jacksonville Landing, this museum is one of the city's premier attractions for family entertainment. Take Interstate 95, cross the St. Johns River, then take the San Marco Boulevard exit and head north back toward the river to Museum Circle.

As much a regional history and science center as it is a museum, this is an exciting, hands-on experience for the curious, young and old alike. Inside you'll find all sorts of interesting exhibits, including the **Alexander Brest Planetarium** where you can ride a comet through our solar system, or be transported vast distances through space into the swirling center of a distant galaxy without ever leaving your seat. It's a cosmic journey that begins beneath a 60-foot-diameter dome illuminated by almost 9,000 stars, and ends beyond the farthest reaches of your imagination. The sound system, some 18,000 watts, provides the final touch; you can feel the awesome power of a shuttle launch or hear a whisper in space.

Currents of Time is where the history of Jacksonville and Northeast Florida comes alive in a series of exhibits that center on the St. Johns River. It's a tableau that begins beyond the mists of recorded time with the Timucuan Indians who first populated the region, then carries you forward through the occupations by the French, Spanish, and English, the turmoil of the Civil War, the devastating fire of 1901, and on into the present.

Maple Leaf: Port at Last is a unique exhibit that features artifacts recovered from the more than 400 tons of cargo aboard the Maple Leaf, a Union Civil War steamship that disappeared beneath the dark waters of the St. Johns River more than 125 years ago. The mud and silt provided an oxygen-free environment in which the personal belongings and equipment of three Federal regiments lay undisturbed and beautifully preserved—musical instruments, surgeon's tools, shoes, military hardware, swords, buttons, bottles, game pieces, and even paper. The exhibit interprets the story of how the ship was located and how the artifacts were recovered from under 10 to 20 feet of mud.

Ribbon of Life is the story of the St. Johns river and the manatee. Here, you'll explore a diorama of the history and ecology of one of the few northward flowing rivers in the United States. A special section of the exhibit is devoted to Florida's most endangered species, the manatees.

The **Bryan Science Theater** offers a hair-raising experience that's not to be missed, including Super Science shows and natural history programs with live animal demonstrations.

The Museum also features fun and hands-on action; you'll find it in the 2nd floor Exhibition Hall, home to the Science PODS (Personally Operated Discovery Stations). Interactive exhibits offer a new way to learn all about sound, electricity, vision, health, physics, and motion.

Other attractions include a 1,200-gallon marine aquarium, a freshwater pond full of fish and reptiles, an aviary, and a terrarium. *Open Mon.–Fri. 10–5, Sat. 10–6, Sun. 1–6. Closed Thanksgiving, Christmas, and New Year's.* ☎ *396-7062. Adults $5, seniors $4, children 3–12 $3; fees include all exhibits.* ♿.

JACKSONVILLE ZOO (14): Take Interstate 95 north a few miles to Exit 124A (Heckscher Drive) and follow the signs.

Jacksonville Zoo, like most of its kind, is dedicated not only to its collection of wild and exotic animals, but also to its visitors. Far from being simply a community of cages, it's a wild kingdom constantly evolving and changing to meet new needs. The public, no longer willing to make do with the traditional zoo concept, wants much more—and here they get it. It all begins under the authentic thatched roof of the Main Camp Safari Lodge, which only hints at the exciting adventures yet to come. Your excursion visits the 17-acre "Plains of Africa," featuring rhinoceros, Cape buffalo, leopards, elephants, giraffes, and zebras. Take a train ride on The General for a great view of the complex, shop at the Zulu Trading Post, see the babies close up at the Animal Nursery, and stroll along the Boardwalk through the Wetlands. From there, you can take the kids to meet the animals in the Children's Zoo, or take in a lively animal show, "Let's Talk Animals," where experts give demonstrations and discuss habits and habitats; "Raptor Rap" is a weekly program about birds of prey. The "Elephant Encounter" is also a neat experience. Held daily at the elephant exhibit, this is your chance to ask an expert everything you ever wanted to know about pachyderms. *Open daily 9–5. Closed New Year's Day, Thanksgiving and Christmas. 8605 Zoo Road.* ☎ *757-4462. Adults $6.50, seniors $4.50, children 3–12 $4.* ♿*, wheelchair and stroller rental available.*

THE ANHEUSER-BUSCH BREWERY TOUR (15): If you're looking for something really different, you should try the Jacksonville Anheuser-Busch Brewery Tour. You'll see exactly how Budweiser is made, a process that, from start to finish, takes some 30 days.

Take Interstate 95 to Exit 125, Busch Drive, south of the Jacksonville Airport. The tour starts with an orientation talk and then you're taken around the plant, following the brewing procedure from the mashing through the straining, brew kettle, cooling, and fermentation processes to the beechwood aging tanks, and then on to the final stages of finishing and packing. From there, it's off to the Hospitality Room for a snack and, of course, a sample of the product. Even if you don't drink, the learning experience is fascinating; if you do, the fresh brew will taste all the better for knowing how it's made. *Open Monday through Saturday 10–5. 111 Busch Drive.* ☎ *751-8116. Free.* ♿.

GUANA RIVER STATE PARK (16): From Jacksonville take U.S. Highway 90 east to its junction with Highway A1A and turn south for about 10 miles. The park is off A1A, north of St. Augustine.

Guana River is a wild and remote 2,400-acre region of coastal river channels, salt water creeks and marshes, tidewater pools, undulating sand dunes, and tide water forests. The park is home to a vast range of plant life, seabirds, and mammals. Huge sand dunes, some more than 40 feet high, rise above a shoreline that stretches away like a great yellow ribbon between the deep blue of the Atlantic Ocean and the grassy hillocks of the dunes that act as a natural barrier against the sometimes furious action of the ocean. Tidal waters infiltrate the surrounding countryside in the form of hundreds of tiny saltwater creeks, streams, pools, and the Guana River itself. In 1957 a dam was built across the river to flood the marshes and river channel, forming the half-mile-wide, ten-mile-long Guana Lake. It is thought that Guana River might have been Ponce de León's first landing place, but that is only speculation. Today, the park is a haven for nature lovers from around the world, but even more so for its local inhabitants. These, though often difficult to find, include alligators, otters, deer, foxes, flying squirrels, and bobcats.

For daytrippers, there's plenty to see and do. If you like to hike, there are several easy trails and many miles of beach to enjoy. If fishing is your pleasure, you'll find that the Atlantic surf literally teems with redfish, bluefish, drum, sheephead, flounder, whiting, and pompano. You can also try Guana Lake, or either the Guana or Tolomato Rivers for sea trout, flounder, or croaker. For swimming or sunbathing, no place is more pristine than this unspoiled state park. Finally, you can take a picnic lunch and enjoy the experience of an outdoor meal, either on the beach or beside the lake. *Open daily 8 a.m. to sunset. 2690 South Ponte Vedra Blvd., Ponte Vedra Beach, FL 32082.* ☎ *825-5071.* ♿. *$3.50 per vehicle up to eight people.*

OLUSTEE BATTLEFIELD (17): Drive west from Jacksonville on either Interstate 10 or US-90 for about 32 miles to the junction between the two highways. From there take US-90 west for five miles; the site is two miles east of Olustee on US-90.

This State Historic Site commemorates the largest battle fought in Florida during the Civil War. On February 7th, 1864, a large force of Union soldiers under the command of General Truman A. Seymore landed at Jacksonville with an objective of occupying the city and disrupting the Confederate line of supply.

Union scouts and raiders moved westward, meeting little resistance. By February 19, Seymore's troops, a force of 5,500 men and 16 pieces of artillery, reached Macclenny, some 40 miles east of Lake City and 20 miles west of Jacksonville. To this point they had encountered little opposition.

In the meantime the fortunes of the Confederate State of Florida had been placed in the capable hands of Brigadier Generals Joseph Finegan and Alfred Colquit. On hearing that Federal forces were on the move Finegan began looking for a defensible position. He found it at Olustee. With a large lake, Ocean Pond, to the left and heavy, almost impenetrable swampland to the right, only a narrow passage remained open. Finegan called out for reinforcements and Colquit responded bringing fresh troops from Savannah, Georgia. By the time the two opposing armies met they were almost equal in numbers.

On February 20, Seymore's army moved out of Macclenny and marched westward. Finegan sent skirmishers eastward to draw the Union forces into his trap at Olustee, where contact was made in the early afternoon. In line of battle, infantry in the center supported by cavalry on either flank, Finegan's forces waited. The battle was joined in an open forest of virgin pines, free of underbrush and other entanglements. There were no earthworks, and the fighting raged back and forth among the trees, sometimes hand-to-hand, all through the afternoon and on into the early evening. It lasted for more than five hours before the Union forces withdrew. They left behind 1,861 casualties, one third of their entire force. Confederate casualties were 946. The Olustee was an unqualified victory for the Confederacy.

Today, the park's interpretive center has a variety of exhibits that tell the story of the battle. A seven-minute recorded presentation describes the conflict from a Confederate soldier's point of view. The battlefield itself is marked by a trail with interpretive signs along the line of battle. A reenactment of the battle is staged once each year, in February. *Open Thurs.–Mon. 9–5. Closed Tues.–Wed. Olustee Battlefield State Historic Site, PO Box 2, Olustee, FL 32072.* ☎ *758-0400. Free.* ♿.

Trip 36

Saint Augustine

The Spanish explorer Juan Ponce de León, in his quest for the Fountain of Youth, in 1513 landed on the site that we know today as St. Augustine. He claimed it for Spain, but it wasn't until 1565 that Pedro Menéndez de Avilés established a settlement here. This was some 42 years before the first permanent English colony at Jamestown, Virginia. From the earliest days, the settlement came under almost constant attack by the English. Sir Francis Drake looted and burned the city in 1586, but the fortified town remained under Spanish rule until 1763 when Florida was ceded to England. In 1783 Florida was returned to Spain, then ceded to the United States in 1819. Florida became a territory three years later, and a state in 1845.

St. Augustine has retained many features of its long and colorful history. Old Spanish houses with wrought-iron grilles and balconies line the narrow streets. San Augustin Antiguo, or Old St. Augustine, is a re-creation of the 18th-century Spanish colonial village and, just outside the city gates, the Spanish fortress Castillo de San Marcos faces the bay. Construction of the magnificent old fort began in 1672, making it the oldest existing masonry fort in the United States.

The city boasts an historic district of 144 blocks on the National Register of Historic Places, and it's here that you'll find the oldest examples in the United States of almost everything: the oldest house, wooden schoolhouse, store, jail, and so on. Add a large number of cultural and historic attractions, several state recreation areas, 24 miles of the finest beaches in Northern Florida, even an alligator farm, and you have a destination like no other. Its many facets are covered on both this and the following four daytrips, described on pages 229-244.

GETTING THERE:

By car: leave Jacksonville either via **Interstate 95** or **US-1** and head south for about 40 miles. If you take the Interstate you'll drive to its junction with Highway 16 and turn left. From there, it's a drive of about five miles to the center of town. US-1 will take you there directly.

GETTING AROUND:

You'll do most of your local sightseeing on foot, but keep your car handy.

Carriage tours are a great way to see the sights. Several companies offer pickups on the bayfront south of the fort. From there the horse-drawn carriages tour the main historic area and drivers give running commentaries on all the points of interest. Try Colee's Sightseeing Carriages (☎ 829-2818), and Gamsey Carriage Company (☎ 829-2391).

St. Augustine Sightseeing Trains, 170 San Marco Avenue. The first tour begins at 8:30 a.m., the last at 5 p.m. Departures are every 20 minutes, with a narrated tour of more than 400 years of the city's historic sites, including shops, restaurants, and other points of interest. Tours last about an hour and the ticket includes stop-off privileges at all major points. Look for the red and blue train. (☎ 800-226-6545).

Matanzas Queen, 8635 A1A, is a free shuttle ferry across the Intracoastal Waterway to Fort Matanzas, the southern watchtower of the Castillo. (☎ 471-0116).

Scenic Cruises—*Victory II & III*—depart from Municipal Marina, one block south of the Bridge of Lions, for an hour and a half of sightseeing along the Matanzas Bay. This is a great way to spend part of your day. For schedule, ☎ 800-542-8316 or 824-1806.

PRACTICALITIES:

St. Augustine will provide you with several daytrips, described both here and on pages 229–244. One day you may decide to do the Historic District, another the beaches and Anastasia Island. The trips can be taken on any day of the week, but some of the historic sites open late and close early on Sundays. St. Augustine is always busy, especially so during the winter months, and parking can be a problem. There are parking areas near the Visitor Information Center on San Marco Avenue, off Hypolita Street in the town center, and Cordova Street near Flagler College. There's also a free parking lot on St. Francis Street near the Oldest House. Metered parking is available on Treasury Street, St. George Street, and Granada Street.

The **Area Code** for St. Augustine and the Beaches is 904.

FOOD AND DRINK:

There's a wonderful selection of restaurants in St. Augustine itself, at the beaches, and on Anastasia Island. Some of the better choices are:

Downtown:

Le Pavillon, 45 San Marco Avenue, is a nice Old World home. Specialties include rack of lamb, home-made soups, and desserts. Reservations accepted, ☎ 824-6202. $$.

Raintree: 102 San Marco Avenue, offers casual dining in an historic house with an atrium, courtyard, and garden. Specialties include poultry, seafood, pasta, and game in a traditional menu that changes daily. Reservations accepted, ☎ 824-7221. $$.

Matanzas Bay Cafe, 12 Avenida Menendez (just across from the Fort), also offers casual dining along with creative cuisine featuring fresh seafood, steaks, chicken, and pasta. Reservations accepted, ☎ 829-8141. $$.

St. Augustine Beach:

Aruanno's, 2705 Highway A1A, features an Italian menu with specialties that include fresh seafood, beef, and pasta. Reservations accepted, ☎ 471-9373. $$.

TOURIST INFORMATION:

St. Augustine/St. Johns County Chamber of Commerce, One Riberia Street, St. Augustine, FL 32084, ☎ 829-5681.

St. Augustine Visitor Information Center, 10 Castillo Drive, St. Augustine, FL 32084, ☎ 825-1000

South Beaches Information Center, St. Johns County Pier, St. Augustine, FL 32084, ☎ 471-1596.

SUGGESTED TOUR:

Park your car and begin at the Visitor Information Center on St. George Street, north of the City Gate, where you'll find the **Zero Milestone** (1). This marks the eastern end of the Old Spanish Trail from St. Augustine to San Diego, in front of the Center.

Cross and walk down the road to **Castle Warden/Ripley's Museum** (2). This vast old pile was built in 1887 as a residence for William Warden. The architecture is Moorish Revival and the construction is of poured concrete. For a while, in 1941, the house was opened as a hotel. Then, in 1951, it became the Ripley's Believe-it-or-Not Museum. *Open daily 9 a.m.–10 p.m. Adults $7.50, seniors $5.50, children 5–12 $4.25.* ☎ *824-1606.*

Cross the road again and walk a short distance to the **Old Protestant Cemetery** (3), a burial ground opened during the yellow fever epidemic in 1821 for non-Catholics.

The **City Gate** (4) is just a little farther on. Built in 1739 by the Spanish, it provided the only access to the north side of the city. The coquina stone pillars were added in 1808 to strengthen the wall.

Stay on the right-hand side of the road and continue on through the City Gate to the **Oldest Wooden Schoolhouse** (5), constructed during the Second Spanish Period. Inside you'll see a classroom with life-size figures of the students and teacher, rare school books, slates and slate pencils, and old maps. *Open daily 9–5. Adults $2, seniors $1.50, children 6-12 $1.* ☎ *824-0192.*

Stay on the right-hand side of the street and walk a short distance to the **Ribera House** (6), a reconstructed First Spanish Period residence. Built on the original site of Juan Ribera's home, it illustrates the pure Spanish architecture of the period.

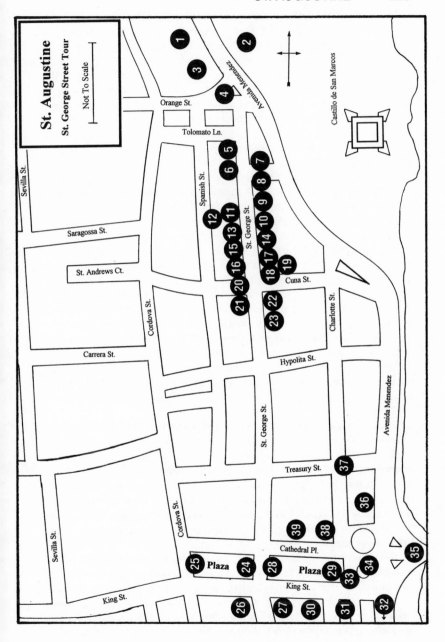

Cross the street and proceed to the **Gallegos House** (7). It, too, is a reconstructed dwelling of the First Spanish Period. Built on its original foundation using Spanish colonial construction techniques, it represents a military dwelling for an NCO stationed at the fort.

Continue on to the **Gomez House** (8), a reconstructed timber house of the First Spanish Period that represents the home of one Lorenzo Gomez, a Spanish foot soldier. The post-and-beam framework is made from native yellow pine joined together in the manner of the old Spanish builders, and is typical of a dwelling allocated to a soldier of a Spanish Colonial garrison.

You are now entering an area where you can catch a glimpse of what life was like for the soldiers and settlers in St. Augustine during Spanish Colonial times. The *Old Spanish Quarter is a living history museum village, a collection of restored historic houses and gardens where guides and craftspeople re-create the atmosphere and lifestyle of the 1740s. Here you can see the workings of a blacksmith's shop, an outdoor kitchen, a weaver's, and a carpenter's, along with dwellings and furniture as they would have been more than 250 years ago. *The Spanish Quarter is open daily 9–5. Adults $5, seniors $3.75, children 6–18 $2.50, families $10; admission includes all public buildings and exhibits.* ☎ 825-6830.

Continue south on the left-hand side of the street to the **Maria Triay House** (9), another reconstructed home of the First Spanish period. Records show that the property once belonged to Maria and Francisco Triay. The masonry building has a sleeping loft and a gabled shingle roof. Today it does service as the **Spanish Quarter Museum Orientation Center** and entrance.

From the Triay House continue on a few yards to the **Bernardo González House** (10). González served in the Spanish cavalry. Here you can watch as weavers demonstrate the art of spinning and cloth making as it was done in the 1700s.

Just across the street stands the **Joseph Salcedo House** (11). Salcedo was an artillery officer, a captain in the Spanish army. The lovingly reconstructed house that was his home is built on the original foundations and is a classic example of early 18th-century St. Augustine architecture.

Across the street, the **Spanish Bakery** (12), located behind the Salcedo House, once was the family kitchen. In the 17th and 18th centuries, kitchens were usually detached from the main house as a safety precaution against fire. Today, it's a bake shop where you can buy goodies all made to old Colonial recipes.

Next door to the Salcedo House, the **Arrivas House** (13) is an original Spanish Colonial home. It is significant for its mixture of Spanish, English, and American characteristics, added during the 18th and 19th centuries.

Back on the left-hand side of the road, you'll want to visit the **Avero House** (14), now St. Photios Shrine. This is one of St. Augustine's few remaining buildings constructed during the First Spanish Period, and now survives as the oldest house of worship in the nation. It was in 1768 that the first Greek immigrants arrived in America and founded the colony of New Smyrna. The colony failed in 1777 and the Greeks moved north to St. Augustine. They held their first religious service in this building, restored in the 1970s by the Greek Orthodox Church of North America. Today, you can visit the shrine and see exhibits that depict the early lives and times of the Greeks, and the development of their church. *Open daily 9–5. Free.*

Back across the street, next to the Avero House, the **Rodriguez-Avero-Sánchez House** (15) is an original home that evolved from a simple one-room structure. Built in 1753 from coquina stone taken from quarries that are now part of the Anastasia State Recreation Area, it is another of the few surviving structures of the First Spanish Period. The wooden second story was added just prior to the outbreak of the Civil War. Today, the old building is a retail store. *Open 9–5. Free.*

Next door, the **Juan Paredes-Dodge House** (16) is an original Second Spanish Period coquina stone home built between 1808 and 1813, a Colonial structure that shares a common wall and chimney with the Rodriguez-Avero-Sánchez house. The old house is now a gift shop owned by the Historic St. Augustine Preservation Board. *Open 9–5 daily. Free.*

Back on the other side of the street, the **De Mesa-Sánchez House** (17) is another original construction. It began in 1760 as a two-room structure, with a second story being added by Juan Sánchez during the Second Spanish Period. The old home is furnished and reflects the lifestyle of a middle-class Spanish family toward the end of the Spanish occupation.

A few yards farther along on the same side of the road you'll see the **Peso de Burgo-Pellicer House** (18). This reconstructed frame duplex was originally built during the British Period in 1787. It had a common dividing wall and separate outdoor kitchens.

Next, the **Oliveros House** (19) is another reconstruction of a building that once stood on the same spot. The original house, built in 1798, was still standing in 1908. The new building is a cigar factory.

On the other side of the street, the **Sánchez de Ortigosa House** (20) is a reconstructed stone house of the First Spanish Period. The roof is made with tile laid over hand-cut rafters with an over-layer of concrete to seal them. The house is now a gift shop.

Continue southward and cross Hypolita Street, the **Benet Store** (21) is on the corner of St. George and Hypolita. This reconstruction of a store was originally built during the Second Spanish Period and is now used as a gift shop. Pedro Benet bought the original building in 1839 so that he could move his store away from his house just across the street; it was taken down in 1903.

Like ice cream? If so, visit the **Benet House** (22). The original House was built by Esteban Benet, a Minorcan settler, toward the end of the Second Spanish Period in 1804.

Another reconstructed First Spanish Period dwelling, the **Ortega House**

(23) was the home of Nicolas de Ortega, an armorer at the Castillo de San Marcos. The house was extended by the British, who also added the chimneys, in the 1780s. It, too, is a gift shop.

Leave the Restored Spanish Quarter Museum area and continue down St. George Street. King Philip II of Spain decreed that all Spanish colonial towns should have a plaza with the principal streets leading from it. Construction of St. Augustine's Central Plaza began in 1598 and its layout, and that of the historic district, is little changed from the original plan. Begin this part of your tour at the Visitor Information Center at the corner of St. George and Cathedral Place.

Government House (24) is just across the street. For more than 200 years the office and home of the colonial governor stood on this site. The original wooden building was replaced in 1690 by a coquina stone structure; it burned during the siege of 1702. By 1713 the house had been restored and was once again a governor's palace. Over the years it was extensively remodeled and extended. In 1935 it was restored once more and returned to what is believed to be its appearance of 1764. Today, the upper floors house the offices of the Historic St. Augustine Preservation Board, with a museum on the first floor. *Open daily 10–4, closed major holidays. Adults $2, children $1.* ☎ *825-5033.*

Leave Government House, turn left onto Cathedral Place, walk west, and then turn left again to the **General William Wing Loring Monument** (25). The monument was erected to the memory of Confederate General Loring in 1920 by the United Daughters of the Confederacy in recognition of his service during the Seminole Indian and Civil Wars.

Continue across the Plaza to King Street. Cross King Street and turn left to the corner of King and St. George, where you'll find the **Lyon Building** (26). Built in 1886, this Moorish Revival style building was constructed with poured concrete walls more than two feet thick. Over the years it has seen service as a hotel and retail shopping center. The ground floor still contains shops and a restaurant.

Nearby stands the **Trinity Episcopal Church** (27), the first of that faith in Florida. Construction began in 1825, and the structure was enlarged in 1850, 1892, and 1902. The stained glass windows in the chapel are by Tiffany.

Cross King Street and walk to the **Plaza de la Constitucion Monument** (28) in the center of the Plaza. The 30-foot obelisk was raised in 1814 as a monument to the new liberal Spanish Government of 1812.

In the center of the Plaza is the **Civil War** Monument (29), originally erected by the Ladies Memorial Association on a site on St. George Street in 1872.

Continue east to **Potter's Wax Museum** (30) at 17 King Street. There is no particular significance to the building, but it's well worth a visit because it contains more than 170 historical wax figures made in London, England. *Open daily 9–9 from mid-June to Labor Day, 9–5 the rest of the year. Adults $5, seniors $4.25, children $2.75.* ☎ *829-9056.*

A little farther along at 9 King Street, **Seth Wakeman's House** (31) is a reconstruction of a Second Spanish Period colonial style building that stood on the site during the American Territorial period. The first floor now contains shops. **Number 1 King Street** was built in 1888 as a dry goods and clothing store. Since then it has been restored and extended into the shopping center it is today.

At this point you might want to make a side trip to the **Oldest House** in St. Augustine. The ***González-Alvarez House** (32) is at 14 St. Francis Street in the southern part of the city, and is one stop on your visit that shouldn't be missed. Walk or drive south on Avenida Menéndez to St. Francis Street. Free parking is available.

Its claim to be the oldest original house is a good one. The origins of the building date to a time immediately after the English burned the city in 1702. Ownership and appearance have changed over almost three centuries, but the original structure is still intact. The oldest section of the house is the ground floor coquina stone section. Alterations and additions made after 1763 brought the house to its present appearance, reflecting not only its Spanish origins, but British influences too. Today, the old house is the centerpiece of a museum complex that includes a Spanish-style kitchen and lovely ornamental gardens, the Museum of St. Augustine History, and the Museum of Florida's Army. There's also a gift store. *Open daily 9–5. Adults $5, seniors $4.50, students $3.* ☎ *824-2872.* ♿.

Back at the Plaza, you'll see a small open building. The **Old Market** (33) was built in 1824 on a site where there had been public markets since 1598. The bell in the cupola called the people to market where they could buy all sorts of fresh produce: vegetables, meats and fish. The original gabled roof was destroyed by fire in 1887 and rebuilt soon after.

Just to the west you'll see the **Ponce de León Statue** (34). A replica of a statue in San Juan, it was erected in 1923, a gift to St. Augustine from Dr. Andrew Anderson. Ponce de León was the Spanish Governor of Puerto Rico before his voyage of 1513 that led to the discovery of Florida.

From the statue, look to the west and you'll see the **Bridge of Lions** (35). Built in 1926, it was named for the two lions at the western end of the bridge and features Mediterranean Revival towers.

Walk north and join Avenida Menéndez, staying on the left-hand side of the street a short distance to the Catalina's Gardens Restaurant. The restaurant is in the **Carr House** (36), which stands on the original site of the home of Catalina de Porras. It was rebuilt in 1850 to its Spanish Colonial specifications.

Continue on along the Avenida Menéndez to **Treasury Street** (37) and turn left. For nearly 100 years the old guide books described this tiny thoroughfare as "The Narrowest Street in the U.S."

At the end of the block, at the corner of Treasury and Charlotte Streets, turn left and walk back to Cathedral Place. Turn right onto Cathedral place and walk east, past the **First Union Bank Building** (39) on the right. It was built in 1926 by H.E. Wolfe.

Turn left on Charlotte Street to Cathedral Place. The **Basilica-Cathedral** (38) is the last stop on your walk. Construction of the church began in 1793 and was completed in 1797. Financed by the Spanish royal treasury, with contributions of labor and materials by local citizens, it became a cathedral in 1870. The bell tower and transept were added in 1887 when the interior had to be remodeled after a fire that destroyed everything but the walls. *Tours daily at 1 and 3. Donations accepted.* ☎ *824-2806.*

Flagler College

Saint Augustine: The Flagler Buildings Tour

Henry Flagler was born in 1830 into a middle-class family in rural New York. He became one of the world's great entrepreneurs and one of the original partners with John D. Rockefeller in the Standard Oil Corporation. By the time he visited St. Augustine in 1883 he was a millionaire many time over. So impressed was he with the small coastal town that he had two new hotels built, the Ponce de León and the Alacazar. He also purchased the Casa Monica Hotel, which he renamed the Hotel Cordova. The opening of Flagler's three new hotels brought the rich and famous flocking to St. Augustine. Next, Flagler bought the local railroads which he consolidated into the Florida East Coast Railway, extending it all the way to Key West. This walking tour of Flagler's buildings includes 15 stops and takes about an hour.

GETTING THERE:

PRACTICALITIES:

FOOD AND DRINK:
See the appropriate entries on pages 221–222.

SUGGESTED TOUR:
Start the walk at **Flagler College** (40) on Cordova Street. You should be able to find parking on the next block to the north. This is one of the two original hotels built by Henry Flagler in 1888. Today, the one-time Ponce de León Hotel is acclaimed as one of the finest examples of Spanish Renaissance architecture in America. The hotel became Flagler College, a four-year liberal arts institution in 1967. *Free tours, May through August.*

Just across the street, on the corner of Cordova and King streets, the **Casa Monica** (41) is a Moorish Revival structure. It was built in 1887 by Franklin Smith, purchased by Flagler a year later, and renamed Hotel Cordova. Unfortunately, the Great Depression of the 1930s brought about its closure. Today, the building is a commercial center with shops and offices.

Back across Cordova Street, on the south side of King Street, the ***Lightner Museum** (42) occupies the old Alcazar, the second of Flagler's two hotels. Built in 1889, it was way ahead of its time. Its recreational facilities included health spas, steam baths, a gymnasium, and the world's largest indoor swimming pool. Like the Cordova, the Alcazar fell victim to the Great Depression. It was bought in 1948 by Otto Lightner, founder of *Hobbies Magazine*, and became a museum housing Lightner's considerable collection of art, antiques, and artifacts. Among the highlights is a room full of Tiffany glass, a Victorian village, and works of art nouveau. *Open daily 9–5. Adults $5, seniors $4.50, students $3.* ☎ *824-2872.*

The **Lightner Antique Mall** (43), at the rear of the museum, was once the world's largest indoor swimming pool. Today it houses an antique mall.

Continue west on King Street to Number 83, **Zorayda Castle** (44). Not so much a real castle but a scaled-down reproduction of the Alhambra Castle in Spain, it was built in 1883 as the first poured-concrete structure in town. Today it houses a museum of rare oriental art treasures and Egyptian antiquities. *Open daily 9–5. Adults $5, seniors $4, children 6–15 $1.50.* ☎ *824-3097.*

Cross to the north side of King Street and continue on to Number 102, the **Markland House** (45). This lovely Colonial Revival house of 1838 was once surrounded by an orange grove extending all the way to the San Sebastian River. It was extensively remodeled and extended in 1901, and today shelters the offices of Flagler College.

Turn north on Sevilla Street and walk on to Number 20 Valencia Street, the **Schofield House** (46). This Victorian cottage was built around 1890 as the home of Flagler's first manager of the Ponce de León Hotel. It was later purchased in 1899 by Union General John Schofield, and has since passed on to become a part of the Flagler College complex.

From Valencia Street turn right onto Sevilla and cross over to the corner, where you'll see the **Memorial Presbyterian Church** (47). Built by Henry Flagler in 1889 as a memorial to his daughter, Jenny Louise Benedict, it is a fine example of Venetian Renaissance architecture. The dome is more than 100 feet high. Flagler and his daughter are buried in the mausoleum. *Free.*

A Little farther west stands the **Presbyterian Church House** (48), built in 1890 for the Reverend John MacGonigle, its minister at that time. It was remodeled in 1925 and today serves as a center for church activities.

The **Ingram House** (49), at 32 Sevilla Street, is a Colonial Revival House built by Henry Flagler in 1894 for one of his executives. John Ingram was vice-president of the Florida East Coast Railway and mayor of St. Augustine from 1915 to 1920. It is now a part of the Presbyterian Church complex.

You should now be on the corner of Sevilla and Carrera streets looking north at the **Ancient City Baptist Church** (50). This fine old Romanesque Revival structure with its conical tower was built with Flagler's help in 1895. *Open only during the hours of worship.*

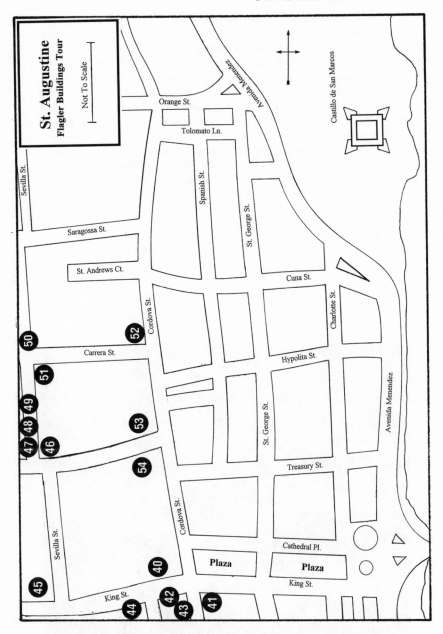

Back across the street on the east corner of Carrera and Sevilla is the **Spades House** (51), an unusual Colonial Revival structure built in 1899 as a winter home for Michael Spades of Indianapolis.

Walk east on the north side of Carrera to the corner of Carrera and Cordova where you'll see the **Grace United Methodist Church** (52). The church was built by Henry Flagler in 1887 using the same architects and builders he employed during the construction of the Ponce de León Hotel. It replaced the Olivet Methodist Church, a wooden building that was demolished to make way for Flagler's other hotel, the Alcazar.

Turn right onto Cordova Street and then right again onto Valencia Street. Number 6 is **Casa Amarylla** (53), or Wiley Hall as it's known today. The Casa was built by Henry Flagler in 1898 as a guest home for his executives. The Colonial Revival style house was sold to Albert Lewis in 1900 for use as a winter home. Later it passed to Flagler College and is now used as an administration building.

The **Artist Studios** (54), the final stop on your tour, was built by Flagler to house the artists who worked on the Ponce de León. The building has seven studios on the second floor, each with its own skylight.

Castillo de San Marcos

Saint Augustine:
*Castillo de San Marcos

The massive Spanish fortress called Castillo de San Marcos sits upon a low hill on the west bank of Matanzas Bay, along the Avenida Menéndez but separated from the highway by a grassy field.

Forever at war with England, and under constant attack by English sea rovers—Sir Francis Drake sacked St. Augustine in 1586—Spain was forced to look to the defense of the city. Construction of the great fortress began in 1672, a century after the city was founded, and completed in 1696. The walls of the massive structure were fashioned from coquina stone taken from quarries located three miles away on the other side of Matanzas Bay. The fortress never fell to force of arms. Its physical integrity remains intact, and the massive splendor of the nation's oldest masonry fort is a testament to almost 250 years of Spanish rule in northern Florida.

GETTING THERE:
See page 220.

PRACTICALITIES:
See page 221. The fortress is maintained by the National Park Service and is open daily from 8:45–4:45. Admission is $2, under 17 free but must be accompanied by an adult. ☎ 829-6506. The tour includes 20 stops and takes about an hour.

FOOD AND DRINK:
See pages 221–222.

SUGGESTED TOUR:
Parking is limited at the fort, so it's a good idea to begin at the parking area behind the Visitor Information Center just a block away to the west on Castillo Drive and walk to the **City Gate** (1). This gate, built by the Spanish in 1739, provided the only access to the north side of the city. The coquina pillars were added in 1808 when the wall was strengthened with stone.

Across the road is a section of the old **Town Wall/Cubo Line** (2) flanked by the imposing backdrop of the Castillo itself. The wall was built in the early 1700s using palm logs packed with earth. It ran from the Castillo westward to the San Sebastian River, turning into a moat, with the only access into the city through the gate you've just visited. This section of the wall is a reconstruction.

A little farther on is a grassy slope overlooking a lower area just in front of the Castillo moat. This section is the **Glacis** (3), a man-made slope that surrounds the fort. It was built with earth and protected the fort walls from cannon fire.

The area below the Glacis is the **Covered Way** (4), a walled section between the Glacis and the moat where soldiers could move about freely and still fire out across the Glacis at the enemy. In time of war it would also provide cover for civilians going to take refuge in the fort.

The **Tidal Moat** (5) completely surrounding the fort is 40 feet wide, but only one to two feet deep. In Colonial times it was kept dry, a place to graze cattle and hogs, but could be flooded if required during times of war.

Turn left and follow the covered way around the moat to the **Seawall** (6) on the east side. Once the site of the Water Battery, the seawall extends along the east side of the Castillo, and was part of the moat. The Water Battery was a section of heavy cannon, as many as six, mounted to fire over the seawall; they could be rotated through 180 degrees.

You'll soon see a small building with a large square chimney, called the **Hotshot Furnace** (7). Built in 1842 by the United States Army, it served the Water Battery with red-hot round shot. The balls were heated in the furnace, then carried to the great guns with tongs. These were fired at the wooden ships in the bay, so that any hit would be set ablaze.

Continue around the moat to the ticket booth and the **Ravelin** (8), a triangular stone structure built to protect the drawbridge and main entrance into the fortress from cannon fire. The outer drawbridge to the Ravelin was usually closed at night. The **Main Entrance Drawbridge** (9) was opened and closed by a windlass and counterweights.

The **Sallyport** (10), just beyond the main drawbridge, is the passage into the fort. Note the portcullis gate made of crossed wooden beams covered with iron. It's unusual because most European portcullis gates dropped down from above, using their own weight to hold them closed. This one opens to the side. Note also the vaulted ceiling, or Roman Arch, a design was used to accommodate the weight of the great guns above.

The **Guardroom** (11) is where the Spanish soldiers slept and cooked their meals while on guard duty. Nearby, the **Courtyard by the Well** (12) is the large open area at the center of the fort. When at peace, it was used by the soldiers for drill and inspections. In time of war, it provided refuge for the entire population of the town. Most of the rooms facing the courtyard were used for storage of food, powder, shot, and other items necessary for daily

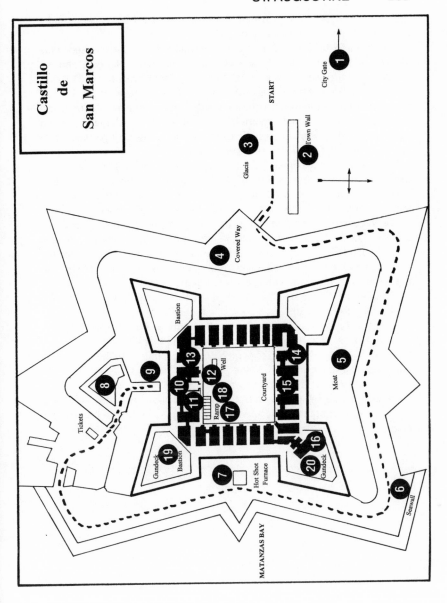

life in the fort. The well provided fresh water, which had to be carefully rationed when the fort was under attack.

Exhibits and artifacts that interpret the history of the fort are housed in the **Museum** (13). These show how it was built, attacked, defended, and expanded over a period of more than 300 years. The **British Room** (14) was reconstructed during the 20 years of British occupation beginning in 1763. It seems the soldiers quartered in the fort needed more room than their Spanish counterparts, so some of the rooms had second floors. The **Chapel** (15) was a room set aside for Roman Catholic devotions. Its walls were painted white with red trim, and the floor was made of wood.

The **Powder Magazine** (16), with its thick walls and ceiling, was where the bulk of the gunpowder used by the big guns on the ramparts was kept. Adjoining rooms were used by crews serving the great guns. The long narrow room once housed a stairway that led up to the gundeck.

La Necesaria (17) was, of course, the "necessary room," rest room to you and me. For the times, it was quite an efficient system. Human waste was passed out through a large pipe that ran under the fort and emptied into the Matanzas Bay. Flushed twice a day by seawater that entered it at high tide, the system was kept relatively clean most of the time.

The **Ramp** (18) was used to quickly move the great guns to and from the gundeck on the ramparts.

Perhaps the most interesting part of the fortress is the **Upper Gundeck** (19). The green cannon are made of bronze, the black ones of iron. Both types could fire a solid round-shot more than three miles. All the cannon on the gundeck and around the fort are original to the period.

From the top of the **Watchtower** (20) at the northeast corner of the gundeck lookouts would scan the sea and the horizon, on watch for enemy ships. If one was sighted, the spotter would ring a warning bell inside the tower.

Saint Augustine: South to Marineland

This daytrip to the St. Augustine area takes you south of the town, first to an unspoiled wilderness similar to that encountered by the first Spanish explorers in the 16th century, then to lovely gardens by the beach. The main attraction, however, is Marineland, which claims to be the world's first oceanarium and is still one of the most interesting. By being selective in your choice of attractions, this easy day out could be combined with the following one to create a circular tour of immense beauty.

GETTING THERE:

By car: from Jacksonville take Interstate 95 south for about 55 miles to Exit 92, the junction with US-1 and the location of Faver-Dykes State Park. From there follow directions in the text to Washington Oaks and Marineland.

Returning north via Routes A1A and St. Augustine allows you to add elements of the next trip into this one, or combine them into one long, possibly overnight, trip.

PRACTICALITIES:

This trip can be made on any day in good weather. Be sure to be prepared for the sun, and perhaps pack a picnic lunch.

FOOD AND DRINK:

The state parks have picnic areas, and food is of course available at Marineland. For regular restaurants, you'll do better to wait for the northbound trip along A1A. Several of these are listed on page 242.

SUGGESTED TOUR:

Faver-Dykes (1) makes a good first stop on this daytrip because its wild environment presents an illusion of remoteness, reminiscent of the landscape as it must have been when the Spanish explorers first landed on Florida's shores in the late 1560s.

The park incorporates more than 750 acres of pine and hardwood forests, hammocks, pinelands, bayheads, swamps, and marshes. Plant communities provide habitats for many species of wildlife, including wading birds, waterfowl, alligators, and otters. In the uplands, close to Pellicer Creek, deer, turkeys, hawks, owls, squirrels, bobcats, foxes, and opossums make their homes and are often seen along the creek itself.

If you like wildlife, you should try one of the two loop hiking trails. Both are easy, pleasant walks. One begins near the picnic area and winds through the pinelands. The other starts at the camping area and leads through a mature hardwood hammock. The picnic area overlooking the creek is great place to take time out for a cold drink. *Faver-Dykes State Park, 1000 Faver-Dykes Road.* ☎ *794-0997. Daily 8–sunset. $3.50 per vehicle.* ♿.

From Faver-Dykes, return to I-95 and continue south to its junction with St. Jude Road. Turn east and drive two miles to the intersection of Route A1A. Turn left onto A1A and drive north for five miles to **Washington Oaks State Gardens** (2).

The sometimes wild Atlantic Ocean to the east, and the scenic Matanzas River to the west, form the natural boundaries of the 389-acre Washington Oaks State Gardens. At low tide the coquina rock shoreline, tranquil tidal pools, and boulder-strewn beaches provide a vast feeding ground for a multitude of sea and shore birds. Across the road, bordering the Matanzas River, are scenic tidal marshes and hammocks where raccoons, gray squirrels, pileated woodpeckers, and a variety of wading birds can be seen. The land is part of Belle Vista Plantation, the one-time home of General Joseph Hernandez who commanded this part of Florida during the Second Seminole War. Today, it's a place where you can enjoy a quiet picnic on a sunny afternoon, or a stroll through the ornamental gardens and groves, along the beach or the river bank. For those who carry a fishing pole, this is a wonderful place to go bobbing for speckled trout, bluefish, redfish, and flounder. *Washington Oak State Gardens, 6400 North Ocean Blvd., Palm Coast, FL 32137.* ☎ *445-3161. Daily 8–sunset. $3.50 per vehicle (max. eight people).* ♿.

Rejoin Route A1A and drive two miles north to *****Marineland** (3). Constructed in 1938, it claims to be the world's original oceanarium. More than 1,000 marine animals and fish are on display, including Nelly; at 40 she's the oldest known living dolphin. You can watch specialists working with injured animals and birds and, if you arrive at the right time, you can enjoy the performing penguins, sea lions, and dolphins, and watch divers hand-feeding the sharks. There's also a 3-D movie running throughout the day that's well worth viewing. *9507 Ocean Shore Boulevard (A1A),* ☎ *471-1111 or 800-824-4218. Daily 9–5:30. Adults $14.95, seniors $11.96, youths 13-18 $9.95, children 3-12 $7.95.* ♿.

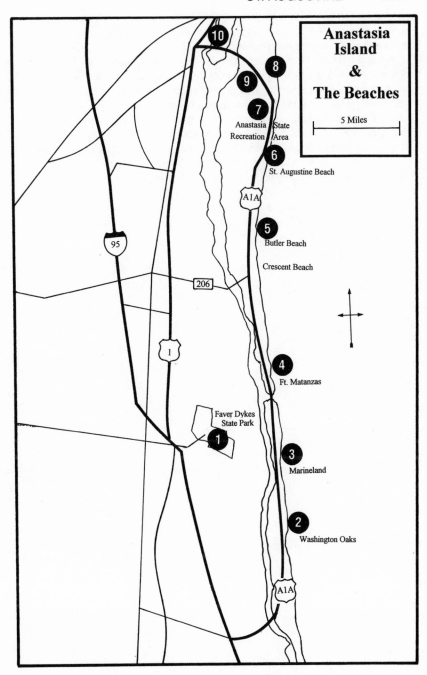

Anastasia
Island
&
The Beaches

5 Miles

Rejoin Highway A1A and drive north for three miles to **Fort Matanzas** (4). Completed in 1742, it was intended to convey, in no small way, the Spanish colonial government's determination to hold its possessions on the American mainland against all hazards. The fort lies on west bank of the Matanzas River, immediately north of an inlet from the Atlantic, and its purpose was to defend the inlet and river against enemy ships. The mighty seacoast guns mounted on the ramparts could fire a round-shot more than three miles and easily threaten any ship on the waterway. Fort Matanzas takes its name from a nearby site where, in 1565, Pedro Menendez captured and then executed more than 300 Frenchmen after their unsuccessful action against the new Spanish colony at St. Augustine. The first building on the site was no more than a wooden watchtower. Following a failed English invasion in 1740, however, the Spanish decided o a more durable stronghold. The new fortress was constructed from the same coquina stone as the massive Castillo de San Marcos. *8635 A1A,* ☎ *471-0116. Open daily 9–5; ferry service 9–4:30. Guided tours by Park Service Rangers. Free.*

Saint Augustine: Anastasia Island and the Beaches

Not far from Saint Augustine's historic Plaza, just across the Bridge of Lions, is Florida's first seaside playground. Miles of spectacular sun-drenched shores and beaches, a seaside recreation area, the nation's first alligator farm, and a working lighthouse are featured on this relaxing daytrip to one of Florida's most enticing barrier islands.

The beaches are often remote, a world where seabirds wheel in the ocean spray, sabel palms and sea oats grow wild on 20-foot-high sand dunes, and where you can spend endless hours combing the shores for sand dollars, moon snails, and angel wings. Farther out, snow-white sails dot the horizon as sailboats and fishing charters carry deep-sea anglers out in search of the "big one."

This trip combines easily with the previous one to Marineland, either by staying overnight or by cutting out some of the attractions. No additional mileage is involved.

GETTING THERE:

By car: From Jacksonville, take Interstate 95 south for about 45 miles to Exit 93, then FL-206 east to Crescent Beach. Turn north on Route A1A to Butler Beach and the other attractions.

Those continuing on from the previous daytrip should head north on A1A to Butler Beach.

PRACTICALITIES:

This trip can be made on any day in fine weather. Be sure to use an adequate sunscreen lotion, wear sunglasses, and be prepared for the beaches.

The **Area Code** for all sites is 904. For further information contact **St. Augustine Tourism**, 1 Riberia St., St. Augustine, FL 32084, ☎ 829-5681 or 800-653-2489.

FOOD AND DRINK:

>**The Oasis**, 4000 A1A, is a great place to stop for lunch. As you head north toward St. Augustine from Butler Beach, be on the lookout for Dondanville Road. From there it's just a short drive to the restaurant. They do great burgers, sandwiches, soups, chowders, and fresh oysters. ☎ 471-3424. $.

>**Aruanno's**, 647 A1A Beach Boulevard, specializes in Italian dishes, steaks, and fresh seafood. Non-smoking. Tuesday through Thursday and Sunday 5–9, Friday and Saturday until 9:30. ☎ 471-9373. $$.

>**Beachcomber**, 2 A Street (on the ocean on Anastasia Island), serves great seafood, steaks, and fresh oysters. Open daily for breakfast, lunch, and dinner. ☎ 471-3744. $.

SUGGESTED TOUR:

See map on page 239.

Butler Beach (5) is just north of Crescent Beach on Highway A1A. The beach and park are named for Frank Butler, a leading African-American businessman in St. Johns County during the early years of the 20th century. Butler ran a market on Washington Street in Lincolnville, a segregated section of St. Augustine settled by former slaves after the Civil War. At that time they were excluded from both the white areas of town and the beaches. Frank Butler became president of a realty company and owned a large tract of land with oceanfront some seven miles south of town, which he opened to St. Augustine's black residents. Later, he donated the beach to the state. *Butler Beach, A1A. Open daily 8–sunset. $3.50 per vehicle (max. eight people).*

Drive north from Butler Beach on Highway A1A for five miles. The next stop, **St. Augustine Beach** (6), is on Anastasia Island where the beaches run for miles. This is the perfect spot to sunbathe, fish, swim, windsurf, or go shopping. The water's warm, the fishing is great, and the shops are full of interesting gifts and collectibles. And, when you're hungry, there's no better place to eat than on Anastasia Island. More than 150 restaurants, cafés, gourmet bistros, shrimp shacks, and other eateries serve seafood fresh from the docks.

Anastasia State Recreation Area (7) is just a little farther north. This is the barrier island where Juan Ponce de León is supposed to have landed in 1513. He was so taken with the abundance of plant life and wildflowers that he called it Florida, and claimed the land for Spain.

The Spanish first settled St. Augustine 1565. To build the new colony they needed materials, which they found here on Anastasia Island. They called the stone from the quarries "coquina"; this was a soft, porous limestone containing shell and coral fragments, easily cut and shaped. Coquina hardens with exposure to the elements, making it ideal for their purposes. Later, the coquina rock was used to build the nearby Castillo de San Marcos, the nation's oldest masonry fortress. The soft material could take the impact of a large cannon ball, smother it, and show little damage for having been hit.

Today, more than 450 years after Ponce de León first stepped ashore, this section of the island remains still quite special. Aside from its beautiful beaches, tidal lagoons and marshes, hammocks and moss-draped live oaks, it's noted for its richly varied and abundant wildlife. Shore birds such as gulls, terns, sandpipers, pelicans, egrets, and herons inhabit the park. During the spring and fall all sorts of migratory birds visit the marshes and wooded areas on their journeys to and from their natural habitats in the north.

The quarries on Anastasia that supplied most of the building materials for the new Spanish colony are still an important part of the St. Augustine experience. The 2,000-seat amphitheater that occupies the site of the one-time Spanish royal quarries is the setting for Florida's state play, *Cross and Sword*. This historical drama by Paul Green was first presented here on June 27, 1965, and depicts the events of 1565 as well as the interaction between the Spanish settlers and Native Americans. Performances are held most evenings except Sunday throughout the summer. *Anastasia State Recreation Area, 1340-C A1A South, St. Augustine, FL 32084. ☎ 461-2033. Open daily 8–sunset. $3.50 per vehicle (max. eight people). &. Performances late June through August, Tues.–Sun., at 8:30 p.m. Tickets: Adults $12, seniors $11, under 13 $6. ☎ 471-1965 for info.*

From Anastasia State Park, stay on A1A and go north. The **St. Augustine Alligator Farm** (8) is about a mile from the Bridge of Lions. This is one of the oldest continuously-operated attractions in Florida. It was created specifically to entertain visitors, not to supply materials to handbag factories, sometime in the early 1890s at about the time when St. Augustine was making its transition into a tourist destination. People have always had a morbid fascination for Florida's most famous resident. Maybe it's the stories of mighty beasts nonchalantly chewing up struggling human food. Whatever; the attraction was a success from the beginning, still thriving and prospering today. More than 1,700 alligators and crocodiles live in the facility; the most famous of which is Gomek, a 17.5-foot giant saltwater crocodile from New Guinea. *St. Augustine Alligator Farm, State Road, A1A, 32085. ☎ 824-3337. Shows every hour. Open daily 10–5. Adults $10.95, children 3–10 $6.95.*

The next stop is the **St. Augustine Lighthouse** (9), which can be seen from the Alligator Farm, three blocks north of Highway A1A. One of St. Augustine's most familiar landmarks, the lighthouse was constructed on the northern tip of Anastasia Island in 1874 as one of a series along the Atlantic coastline. An earlier watchtower, built by the Spanish during the first period, then razed by the British in 1763, collapsed into the sea in 1880. The Keeper's Quarters, a lovely old two-story brick house set in a shady grove of trees, and the lighthouse itself are open to the public. Those with plenty of stamina can go all the way to the top for a spectacular view. *St. Augustine Lighthouse & Museum, 81 Lighthouse Avenue.* ☎ *829-0745. Adults $4, seniors $3, children $2.*

The final stop is the **Fountain of Youth Park** (10). From the Lighthouse, return to Highway A1A and cross the Bridge of Lions. Turn right on San Marco and drive north until you see the sign for the park. This is the very spot where Juan Ponce de León is supposed to have first set foot on the American mainland on April 3, 1513. It's also the probable landing site of Pedro Menéndez de Avilés and his colonists in 1565. Credible archaeological evidence suggests that this is so, and that it's probably the site of the original settlement. Today, it's a very pleasant spot, with a spring reputed to be the Fountain of Youth and several exhibits. Why not sit for a moment or two and let your imagination take you back in time? Try to imagine those far-off days, and the Spaniards wading ashore from their longboats, their great galleons at anchor just off-shore. Sends shivers down your spine, doesn't it? *Fountain of Youth, 155 Magnolia Avenue.* ☎ *829-3168. Open daily 9–5. Adults $4.75, seniors $3.75, children 6–12 $1.75.*

Downtown Tallahassee

Florida's capital city represents the other side of the state, not geographically but culturally. Tallahassee is more akin to the old south—cities like Savannah, Charleston, and New Orleans—than it is to the resort communities farther south. It owes its existence as much to the great plantations that surround it as it does to politics. For more than eight centuries Tallahassee has been the center of power in Florida, first as a Native American ceremonial place, then as the hub of government.

Despite its distance from both navigable waters and other great cities, and its reputation as a "sleepy town," Tallahassee has managed to hang on to its capital status. Its deep-rooted Southern heritage is reflected in the capitol buildings, ante-bellum homes, oak-lined streets, sprawling plantations, Civil War battlefields, and historic churches.

More than 12,000 years ago, Paleolithic Indians and giant mastodons roamed the area of which Tallahassee is now the center. Its modern history, however, begins over 450 years ago in 1539 when Hernando de Soto—hardly a daytripper—set up a winter encampment here and celebrated the first Christmas on American soil. Later, during the early 17th century, the Spanish established their presence among the Apalachee Indians, created missions such as San Luis de Talimali, and brought Christianity to the area. But this was not to last. Wars between European colonists virtually wiped the Apalachees from northern Florida, and by 1704 most of the Spanish missions were destroyed. By the end of the 18th century, Creek and Seminole Indians repopulated what once belonged to the Apalachee; they too eventually were forced out by white settlers.

In 1832, William Pope DuVal, the new territory's first civilian governor, established a meeting place at Tallahassee and declared it Florida's capital. The first government buildings consisted of three long cabins that served until a two-story stone capitol building was completed in 1826. This was replaced by the Old Capitol in 1845. By the outbreak of the Civil War, Tallahassee led the state in population and wealth. At war's end, Tallahassee was the only Confederate capital east of the Mississippi not to fall to Union force of arms. The Battle of Natural Bridge in March, 1865, was a glorious victory for Confederate forces at Tallahassee.

The New Capitol was completed in 1977, and the old one restored to its 1902 appearance complete with red and white candy-striped awnings and dome adorned with stained glass.

Tallahassee is a city full of opportunities. It's an intimate, Old-World sort of place, nestled in the foothills of the Appalachian Mountains where the rolling terrain is dotted with plantations, towering pines, cypress, dogwoods, and magnolia trees. The area is surrounded by hundreds of shimmering lakes, springs, rivers, and swamps. It's a town where the present meets the past in the downtown districts, along the canopied roads and avenues where live oaks draped with Spanish moss line the walkways and parks. Here historic buildings that have lived through centuries of national development co-exist side-by-side with the modern structures of state government. This is Florida's Plantation Country: more than 70 of them are scattered among the fields and forests between Tallahassee and Thomasville, Georgia. It's a land of springs and rivers where America's most famous "Tarzan," Johnny Weissmuller, and "Jane," Maureen O'Sullivan filmed many of the water scenes in the movies. Tallahassee lists 122 properties in the National Register of Historic Places.

Ideally, you should combine this tour of downtown Tallahassee with the following one of the Park Avenue Historic District, and possibly with the one to the Tallahassee state parks. Doing so will require an overnight stay.

GETTING THERE:
By Car: From Jacksonville, take Interstate 10 and head west. It's a straight run of 165 miles and, at the speed limit, shouldn't take more than two and a half hours.

By Air: You can also fly in and rent a car. Tallahassee Regional Airport is 10 minutes from downtown and serviced by Delta, US Air, Air South, US Air Express, ASA-Comair, and Continental.

By Train: You can do the trip by Amtrak, but it's somewhat inconvenient and you'll have to stay overnight. The Amtrak terminal is five minutes from downtown on Gaines and Railroad Drive. ☎ 800-872-7245.

By Bus: Tallahassee is reachable by Greyhound/Trailways, but it's a long trip and you'll have to stay overnight to make it worthwhile. ☎ 800-231-2222.

GETTING AROUND:
Most of your daytrip inside the city limits can be accomplished on foot, but you might use your car to get from place to place. Parking is not a problem.

The Old Town Trolley provides free transportation—a nice touch—through the downtown area, Monday through Friday from 7 a.m. until 6 p.m. Trolley route maps are available at the Visitor Information Center in the New Capitol Building, ☎ 800-628-2866.

Taltran city buses provide access in and around Tallahassee, and to more outlying areas, with more than 30 scheduled routes. ☎ 891-5200.

If all else fails, grab a taxi.

PRACTICALITIES:

The **Area Code** for Tallahassee is 904.

Tallahassee's climate, much like Jacksonville's, is one of mild winters, cool in spring and fall, and warm summers with lots of sunshine, and is ideal for indoor and outdoor activities. True, it can be wet at times, especially in spring and fall, so be sure to check the forecast before you leave. This trip involves quite a bit of walking.

Most of Tallahassee's attractions and sights are open daily. On Sunday, however, one or two are closed, and still others open late and close early, so it's best if you make the trip on Mondays through Saturdays.

FOOD AND DRINK:

If you like good food, this trip is a must. While Tallahassee boasts of the finest and freshest seafood available—the Gulf of Mexico only is only 30 minutes to the south, and Panacea (blue crab capital of the world) and Apalachicola (where the best oysters in the world come from) not much farther away—its cuisine covers a range of specialties from southern-style cooking to gourmet menus. Be sure to try a platter of fresh mullet, known as the "trash" fish in most regions; it simply melts in the mouth.

Andrew's Café, 228 South Adams Street, is just the place to stop off on either the Downtown or Park Avenue walking tours. It's a cafeteria-style New York deli with inside or outside dining right on historic Adams Street Commons. In the evening you might want catch Andrew's Second Act for elegant dining and a menu that includes fresh seafood dishes and one of the finest wine lists in the Tallahassee area. ☎ 222-3444. Lunch $; dinner $$.

Georgio's, 104 Washington Street, is a classy restaurant with a great atmosphere and a continental menu that features fresh seafood, beef, chicken, veal, lamb, and pastas. This is a popular spot, so reserve. ☎ 893-4161. $$.

Chez Pierre, 115 North Adams Street, is also a great lunch or dinner stop. The bistro serves exceptional French country cuisine that includes the likes of escargot, salmon Napoleon, beef Wellington, coquilles St. Jacques, coq au vin, and French pastries. Very popular; reservations recommended. ☎ 222-0936. $$$.

Barnacle Bill's, 1830 North Monroe Street, is all that the name implies—a somewhat rowdy, down-home atmosphere where the service is often harassed but good, and the food is exceptional. Famous for its seafood, the restaurant serves more than 3,000 pounds of fresh oysters each and every week. ☎ 385-8734. Lunch $; Dinner $$.

Nicholson's Farmhouse, in Havana, 15 miles north of Tallahassee on Route 12, is a bit out of the way, but if you're looking for something different, something special, this is it. The old farmhouse is famous for its aged, hand-cut steaks, seafood, chops, and chicken, all served in a historic and charming setting. Open for dinner only, Tuesday through Saturday, it's a very popular restaurant. Call ahead. ☎ 539-5931. $$.

TOURIST INFORMATION:
Tallahassee Area Visitor Information Center, New Capitol Building, West Plaza Level, PO Box 1369, Tallahassee, FL 32302. ☎ 800-628-2866 or 413-9200.

SUGGESTED TOUR:
There are a couple of walking tours in Tallahassee, as well as some added attractions that will take you to outlying areas of the city. This first tour is a fairly extended walk around the downtown area. The second one (page 252) goes to the scenic boundaries of William DuVal's original city where you can walk, sit or simply relax in one of the most beautiful parkland areas in the state.

Did William DuVal, first governor of the Florida Territory, plan this quarter-mile city grid of streets and public squares with daytrippers in mind? Probably not, but Downtown Tallahassee was definitely laid out with some vision. True, it has been allowed decline somewhat but now, after a period of restoration and revitalization, you can stroll William DuVal's capital and enjoy the fine architecture, restaurants, and shops that are the result of his dream.

Begin your tour at the Visitor Information Center in the New Capitol Building. You can park just across West St. Augustine Street, between South Bronough and South Duval.

The New Capitol (1), enter at the West Plaza Level, was designed by New York architect Edward Durrell Stone, and dedicated in 1978. The 307-foot-high structure is an example of the "New Classical" movement of the mid-20th century. Be sure to visit the observation room on the 22nd floor where you can enjoy a commanding, panoramic view of Tallahassee. During the legislative session, you can watch the proceedings in the House and Senate from the public galleries on the fifth floor. Visitors can wander around on their own, or take a guided tour. Open *Mon.–Fri. 9–5, Sat.–Sun. 8:30–4:30.* ☎ *413-9200. Free.* ♿.

The Old Capitol (2) is adjacent to the New Capitol on the corner of Monroe Street and Apalachee Parkway. This is Tallahassee's most dominant historic landmark. Designed by Cary Butt of Mobile, Alabama, it's a simple, yet elegant Greek Revival building circa 1845. It served the people of Florida for more than 130 years before yielding to the new building in 1978. Following the exodus of the legislature it was suggested that the old structure be demolished, but the very thought of this aroused such an outcry that building restored instead. Today, you can tour the long-abandoned legisla-

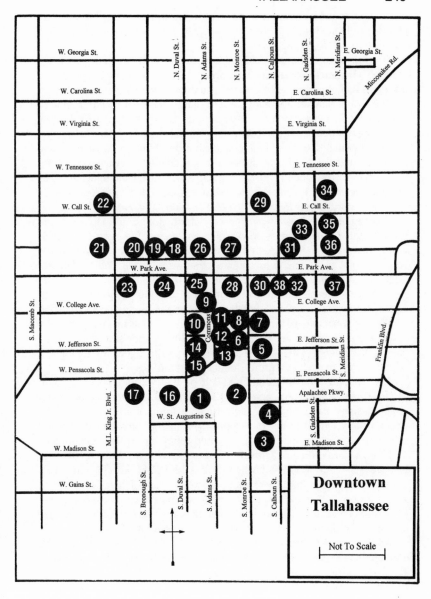

Downtown

Tallahassee

Not To Scale

tive chambers and explore a number of interesting exhibits that interpret Florida's political history. *Open Mon.–Fri. 9–4:30, Sat. 10–4:30, and Sun. noon–4:30.* ☎ *487-1902. Free.* ♿.

From the east exit of the Old Capitol, across Monroe Street, you'll see Florida's **Vietnam Era Veterans' Memorial** (3). The black marble memorial is inscribed with the names of Florida's casualties of the Vietnam conflict.

The Union Bank Building (4) lies east of the memorial on the southwest corner of Apalachee Parkway and Calhoun Street. It is one of the few remaining examples of Federal-style commercial architecture in Florida, and one of the state's earliest financial institutions built to serve the local planters. After the Civil War, it became the Freedman's Saving Bank for former slaves. Threatened with demolition, it was saved and relocated to its present site in 1971. Today it houses a museum dedicated to Florida's banking history. *Open Tues.–Fri. 10–1, Sat.–Sun. 1–4. Free.* ♿.

Cross Apalachee Parkway and proceed north along South Monroe to the **Leon County Courthouse** (5) on Washington Square. The curved entrance-way is very much in the style of the Old Capitol and City Hall. Washington Square is one of the five public squares that were part of William DuVal's original plan of Tallahassee. *Open Mon.–Fri. 8:30–5. Free.*

Across the street is the **Tin Front Store** (6), a 10½-foot- wide building with a second-story bay window. Something of an anomaly, it was constructed in an alley between two existing buildings in 1890. With its tin and glass front, it was once described as "the most artistic little parlor store in Florida." During its existence, it has served as a millinery store, a jewelry store, and a clothing store, as well as a professional office building.

The Exchange Banking Building (7) is on the next block at 201 South Monroe. Its elaborate, terra cotta and cast stone trim and Neo-Egyptian and Greek designs make this 1927 high-rise something of a treasure. The Exchange Bank failed during the Depression and its president committed suicide so that his insurance policy would repay the bank's stockholders.

Lively's Corner (8), just across Monroe to the west, was built in 1875 and first saw service as Matthew Lively's drug store. But its most exciting times were certainly those from 1892 until just after the turn of the century during which it operated as the Leon Bar, and more than lived up to its name— Lively—as one of the most popular watering holes in town. A city ordinance banning the sale of alcohol brought about its demise in 1904.

Adams Street Commons (9)—a section of Adams Street between Call and Jefferson streets—was completed in 1978. Very much in keeping with Tallahassee's rich history, the buildings—restaurants, shops, and offices— are small-scale and exude a certain Southern charm.

From the corner of College and Adams, on the east side of the street, look west and you'll see the **Masonic Hall** (10). Originally built in 1926 to house the Masons and the Independent Order of Oddfellows, the hall is a fine example of Neo-Classical architecture. It now houses the Governor's Club, a private institution of which the Governor of Florida is an honorary member.

As you turn the corner onto Adams Street there are a series of alleys that run behind the downtown buildings, providing access to the rear entrances. Today, one of them, **Gallie's Alley,** (11) is the setting for special events, exhibitions, and fairs.

Langston's Fish Market (12), 217 South Adams Street, was for much of this century a meat and seafood market. Built in 1890 in the Renaissance Revival style, it now houses offices.

Walk north to the corner of Adams and Jefferson streets where you'll find **Gallie's Hall** (13). Originally built in 1873 by grocer Alexander Gallie, for many years the two-story building with its distinctive iron gallery was the cultural and social center of Tallahassee. Performances included concerts, lectures, minstrel shows, and church socials. As one resident noted, there was "no place to go but the church and Gallie's theater." The old building was converted into offices in 1980.

Tallahassee's City Hall (14) is at 300 South Adams Street. The building is distinctive in that it was designed to provide a transition between the old and the new: the white buildings of state government and the historic brick buildings of the downtown area. Go inside and up to the second floor; there the city showcases local and national artists. *Open Mon.–Fri. 8:30–5. Free.*

To the south of City Hall the **Olympic Courtyard** (15), dedicated in 1993, honors the British Olympic Team, which selected Tallahassee as its official training site for the 1996 Summer Games in Atlanta.

Look southwest across Duval and Pensacola streets and you'll see the **Supreme Court Building** (16), a typical court building of Neo-Classical architecture complete with Doric columns. Designed by James Gamble Rogers II and completed in 1948, its most significant feature is the magnificent rotunda. *Open Mon.–Fri. 8–5. Free.*

The final stop on the downtown tour is the **Museum of Florida History** (17) at 500 South Bronough Street, west of the Supreme Court Building. Doing the museum properly will take some time, but you'll find it well worthwhile. Exhibits include prehistoric artifacts: the bones of a nine-foot-high mastodon, treasure recovered from sunken Spanish Galleons, Civil War memorabilia, and a reconstructed steamboat, to name a few. The building also houses the State Archives and State Library. ☎ *488-1484. Open Mon.– Fri. 9–4:30, Sat. 10–4:30, Sun. noon–4:30. Free.*

Tallahassee Park Avenue Historic District

The focus of this second daytrip in Tallahassee is on the historic homes, churches, civic buildings, and the seven beautiful parks that form the center of the Park Avenue Historic District. This area was once the northern boundary of the city as William DuVal saw it. It began with a 200-foot-wide open space cleared in the 1820s as a part of the city's defenses against Indian attack. In the late 1880s, work was started to landscape the clearing and turn it into a linear series of parks. Today, Park Avenue is a pleasant blend of old and new, listed in the National Register of Historic Places. It's a place to stroll in the sunshine and listen to the birds singing in the trees. Your walk here should be a pleasant experience; one you're sure to remember.

Additionally, this trip describes two other attractions that can be added to either this or the previous daytrip. By rushing a bit, both daytrips might be combined in a single day, or you might opt to stay overnight and include a visit to the nearby state parks, outlined on page 258.

GETTING THERE:

GETTING AROUND:

PRACTICALITIES:

FOOD AND DRINK:

TOURIST INFORMATION:
    See pages 246–248 for all of the above.

SUGGESTED TOUR:
See map on page 249.
Begin at **The Columns** (18), one of Florida's finest remaining examples of Greek Revival architecture. The impressive structure, with its two-story entrance portico, was built by William Williams in 1830. Williams—his nickname was "Money"—was an extremely wealthy banker, but despite the rumors, he did not bake a nickel into every brick used in the construction of the building. Like most of Tallahassee's old structures, the Columns was nearly lost to the wrecking ball in 1971, but was saved by the Tallahassee Chamber of Commerce who bought, relocated, renovated, and occupied it. *100 North Duval Street.* ☎ *224-8116. Open Mon.–Thurs. 8–5:30, Fri. 8–5.*

From the Columns, walk west to the **LeRoy C. Collins/ Leon County Public Library** (19). Named for a former governor and leader in Florida's Civil Rights movement, the library contains a display that highlights his career. *200 West Park Avenue. Open Mon.–Thurs. 10–9, Fri. 10–6, Sun. 1–6.*

Continue west and cross the corner of Bronough and Park Avenue to the **St. James C.M.E. Church** (20). Once known as St. James Colored Methodist Episcopal Church—Colored was later changed to Christian—and constructed in 1899, the building underwent extensive remodeling in 1948. The pointed lancet windows are typical of Gothic Revival architecture. Today, the old church houses offices.

The next stop is the **Old City Cemetery** (21) on the west side of Martin Luther King Jr. Blvd. Established just outside the then city limits in 1829 by Florida's Territorial Legislature, the burial ground is a graphic tableau of Tallahassee's history. The permanent residents include governors, slaves, yellow fever epidemic victims, and Civil War dead. A true reflection of the times, the cemetery was segregated. Blacks, including Union dead from the Battle of Natural Bridge, were buried in the western half; whites in the eastern section. A self-guided tour brochure is available at the entrance kiosk. *Open daily sunrise to sunset.*

Across Call Street to the north is **St. John's Episcopal Cemetery** (22). The church bought this land in 1840 to be the final resting place for members of its congregation. Several notables are interred there, including two governors and Prince and Princess Murat. Murat, the Prince of Naples and nephew of Napoleon Bonaparte, owned a large plantation nearby and was well known for his extravagant lifestyle. His wife, the Princess, was Catherine Dangerfield, a great grand-niece of George Washington.

From the Old City Cemetery, walk east along the path through the following three parks: The first, **Cherokee Park** (23) is just across M.L. King Blvd. on the south side of Park Avenue. Named for a variety of roses found in the central planting bed, this is the first of the seven parks along the Avenue, and one of five planted by the Tallahassee Improvement Association around the turn of the century.

Lovely live oak trees adorn **E. Peck Green Park** (24), as they do many others in Tallahassee. E. Peck Green was dedicated to the beautification of the city, and the park named for him was established in the 1890s.

MaCarty Park (25) is especially beautiful from December through February when the camellias bloom in showy profusion.

Cross to the north corner of Park Avenue and Adams Street and the **First Presbyterian Church** (26). This is Tallahassee's oldest house of worship, built during the years 1835 to 1838. Construction was financed by its congregation who purchased pews. Worship at the Greek Revival church was segregated, as were all things during those days. Slaves were placed in the north gallery away from the rest of the members. It seems the old church has quite a history. Early settlers, so the story goes, barricaded themselves inside the church during the Seminole War for protection. Another legend maintains that the steeple bell was offered to the Confederacy to aid the war effort; the offer was declined.

On the next block, still on the north side of Park Avenue, the **U.S. Courthouse** (27) is another example of the strong Neo- Classical influence on Tallahassee's architecture. Built by the Works Progress Administration (*WPA*) during the Great Depression of the 1930s to house the U.S. Post Office and Courthouse, it features mighty columns and an impressive cupola. Inside are many fine WPA murals. *Mon.–Fri. 9–4:30, Sat. 10–4:30, and Sun. noon–4:30. Free.* &.

Back on the south side of Park Avenue, opposite the U.S. Courthouse, **Ponce de León Park** (28) was established by the owners of the León, a large and elaborate Victorian hotel that once stood on the site of the courthouse. It was the first of the seven parks incorporated here on Park Avenue during the 1880s. Today, it's a place to relax under the canopy of live oaks, or sit by the fountain and enjoy a quiet moment or two.

Turn left and walk north on Monroe Street to the corner of Monroe and Call and cross to the east side of the street and **St. John's Episcopal Church** (29). Often called the "Gentlemen's path to Heaven," this is where the moneyed people of Tallahassee made their devotions. Built in 1880 after a fire totally destroyed the original structure, it contains a 12-bell carillon, one of the few in the country that is still rung by hand.

Back on Park Avenue, **Bloxham Park** (30), the fifth in the series, was named for William D. Bloxham, governor of Florida in the late 19th century. Here, you'll see one of the most magnificent displays of live oak trees outside of a natural area in Florida.

B.C. Lewis, a one-time pharmacist-cum-banker and founder of what was to become the State Bank that also bears his name, built the **Lewis House** (31) around 1845 on the north side of the street as his private residence. The house has been refurbished and converted to offices.

Opposite the Lewis House, on the south side of Park Avenue, is **Lewis Park** (32), number six in the series and the second to be established in 1885.

A memorial was dedicated to the great man by his son, William Cheever Lewis.

Walk north on the west side of Gadsden Street to the **Perkins House** (33). Built in 1903 in true Colonial Revival style with Palladian windows and roof balustrades, this is one of Tallahassee's most architecturally significant buildings. The verandah and the porte-cochere are later additions that reflect the Prairie style of architecture. George Bretton Perkins was a prominent lawyer and real estate developer.

Continue north to the corner of Call and Gadsden and the **Whitehouse** (34). This was the home of William R. Wilson of Wilson's Department Store of Tallahassee. The heavy brackets at the roofline are an original feature. The building was converted to apartments in 1940 and named the Whitehouse.

Turn south to the other corner of Call and Gadsden and the **Munroe House** (35). This is yet another of Tallahassee's magnificent old homes that's been turned into apartments. Built in 1903 as the family home of Maria Therese Meginniss Munroe, most of the original Queen Anne and Colonial Revival detailing has, unfortunately, long since disappeared.

A little farther south is the **Meginniss-Munroe House** (36). Originally built in 1854 by a wealthy businessman as a wedding present to his bride, this lovely old home has quite a history. It served as a hospital for wounded soldiers after the Civil War Battle of Olustee near Lake City. Then, in 1903, it was uprooted from its site where the other Munroe House now stands, and rolled on logs to its present location. Today it is the home of the LeMoyne Art Foundation. *125 North Gadsden Street. Open Tues.–Sat. 10–5, Sun. 2–5.*

Genevieve Randolph Park (37) is last in the series of seven parks, and honors the woman who lead the Tallahassee Improvement Authority in establishing and planting the chain of parks.

The final stop on your tour is the **Knott House Museum** (38) at Park Avenue and Calhoun Street. At the end of the Civil War, the old house, also known as the "House of Rhymes," was occupied by Union General Edward McCook and his troops. It was from the front steps here that the erstwhile general read the Emancipation Proclamation on May 20, 1865, thus freeing the slaves of north Florida. To this day, May 20th is still celebrated as Emancipation Day. The house was built in 1843, but it wasn't until 1928 that the family from which it takes its name moved in. William Knott was a successful politician, his wife, Luella, an accomplished poet, musician and leader of the Temperance Movement. Together, the Knotts added the Colonial Revival portico, but it was Luella who decorated and furnished the house. She wrote poems and tied them to many pieces of furniture, thus the house's nickname. *301 East Park Avenue.* ☎ *922-2459. Open Wed.–Fri. 1–4, Sat. 10–4. Adults $3, Children 5–16 $1.50.*

ADDITIONAL ATTRACTIONS:

There two interesting places in Tallahassee that don't quite fit in with this or the previous tour. Both are worth a visit, and are close to the city. *See map on opposite page for locations.*

Lake Jackson Mounds State Archaeological Site:

Take Interstate 10 to its junction with Highway 27, then turn north and drive two miles to the site.

Lake Jackson is located north of the city. It's an area once inhabited by a tribe of Indians that, according to the evidence, indulged in a socio-religious complex cult. It seems the community was a thriving one, reaching the peak of its prosperity sometime around A.D. 1200.

The complex itself consists of a series of seven mounds; six of which are thought to be temple mounds, the other a burial mound. Only a part of the original settlement and two of the mounds are located within the state site. The largest mound is some 36 feet high with a base that covers an area of over 86,000 square feet—a massive construction project considering the tools available at the time. There's an interpretive center and a number of exhibits containing artifacts—pottery, burial objects and jewelry—and Park Service guides offer tours on request. *Lake Jackson Mounds State Archaeological Site, 1313 Crowder Road, Tallahassee, FL 32301.* ☎ *922-6007. Open daily 8 until sunset. Free.*

Maclay State Gardens:

Take Interstate 10 to its junction with Highway 61/319 and drive north for a half-mile.

Alfred B. Maclay was a man with a dream. In 1923, while on a visit to Tallahassee, Maclay and his wife, Louise, bought this piece of real estate with the idea of creating an ornamental garden for the public to enjoy. Alas, Maclay died before his dream could be fulfilled, but Louise took it up and in 1953 donated the land to the State of Florida.

The lovely park is open all year round, but the high blooming season is from January 1 until April 10. To catch the most spectacular colors you should plan your visit for late March. This is also a great place to enjoy a picnic lunch. *Maclay State Gardens, 3540 Thomasville Road, Tallahassee, FL 32308.* ☎ *487-4556. Open daily 8 until sunset. $3.25 per vehicle (up to eight people and children).* ♿.

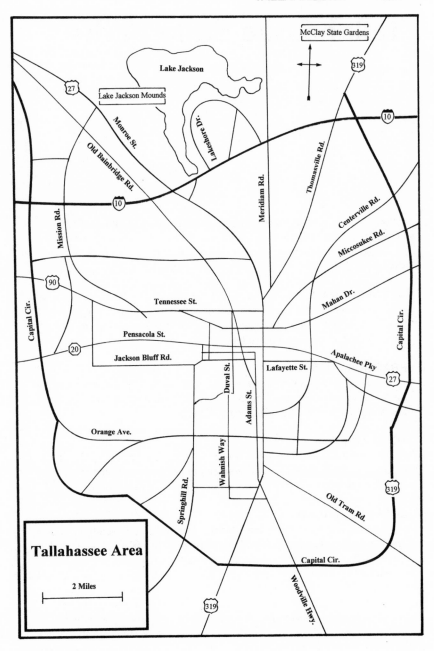

McClay State Gardens

Lake Jackson

Lake Jackson Mounds

27

Monroe St.

Old Bainbridge Rd.

Lakeshore Dr.

Meridiam Rd.

Thomasville Rd.

319

10

10

Mission Rd.

Centerville Rd.

Miccosukee Rd.

90

Mahan Dr.

Capital Cir.

Tennessee St.

Capital Cir.

Pensacola St.

20

Jackson Bluff Rd.

Duval St.

Adams St.

Lafayette St.

Apalachee Pky

27

Orange Ave.

Wahnish Way

Springhill Rd.

319

Old Tram Rd.

Tallahassee Area

2 Miles

Capital Cir.

Woodville Hwy.

319

Tallahassee State Parks

There are three very special state parks in the area to the south of Tallahassee between the city and the Gulf of Mexico. One is an area of great natural beauty, one a Civil War battlefield, and the last a site of special historical significance. All three can be visited in one day.

GETTING THERE:

From Jacksonville, take Interstate 10 to Tallahassee (see page 246) and the junction with Florida Highway 61. From there, the total round trip through the parks is about 60 miles.

PRACTICALITIES:

Florida's state parks are open daily from 8 until sundown. Some of the historic sites and museums, however, are closed on Tuesdays, Wednesdays, and some major holidays. The **Area Code** is 904.

FOOD AND DRINK:

The best place for lunch is in the restaurant at Wakulla Springs State Park; it's the first stop on the tour and you should get there around noon. Other than that, there's not much available once you leave Tallahassee.

SUGGESTED TOUR:

From the junction of Interstate 10 and Highway 61, turn south on 61 and drive 16 miles to **Edward Ball Wakulla Springs State Park** (1). You'll need to spend at least an hour here, more if you stop for lunch.

Named for financier Edward Ball, the Wakulla Springs complex is one of the premier locations of the Florida State Park System. The highlight of the 2,860-acre park is one of the world's largest and deepest fresh water springs. Seven underground rivers are the source of the great spring, and they push more than 400,000 gallons of water per minute up into the lake above. On April 11, 1973, scientists measured a record peak flow of 14,325 gallons of

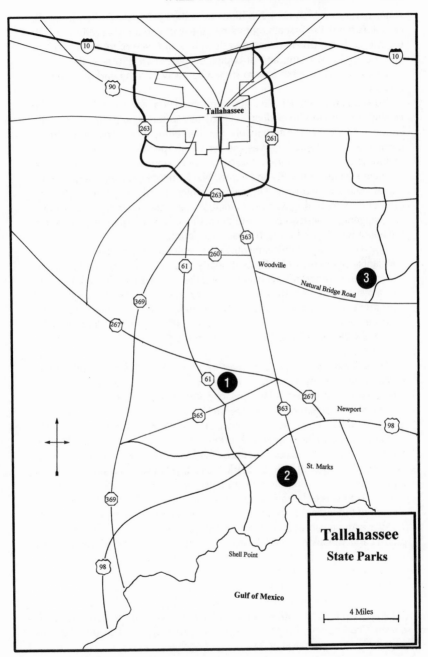

water per second, some 1.2 billions of gallons per day. Earlier, in 1958, explorers made the first attempt to map the ever-widening caverns beneath the spring. Later, divers penetrated them to a distance of more than 6,000 feet. Beyond that point, and at depths of more than 250 feet, their lights revealed the walls of the cavern stretching away into the darkness and the unknown.

You can cruise the lake in a glass-bottomed boat and gaze down into the crystal clear waters to a depth of 120 feet where you'll clearly see the entrance to a cavern. Alternatively, you can enjoy a boat trip downstream through ancient cypress groves and see many species of Florida's wildlife, including alligators, white tail deer, raccoon, opossum, wild turkey, nine different species of herons and egrets, black vultures, turkey vultures, bald eagles, kites, and osprey. During the winter months the park is host to thousands of migrating water fowl including the hooded merganzer, American widgeon, American coot, and the lesser scaup. The park is included in the nationwide Audubon Christmas Bird Count.

If you like, you can take time out and go swimming; the water maintains a constant temperature of 70°F. Additionally, you might join one of the ranger-led snorkeling programs available during the summer months. Walkers can take a hike; a six-mile trail along the park service roads provides another rare opportunity to view the local plant and wildlife. *Wakulla Springs State Park, 1 Spring Drive, Wakulla Springs, FL 32305.* ☎ *922-3632. Open daily 8–sunset. $3.25 per vehicle (up to eight people).* ♿.

From Wakulla Springs, drive east on Highway 267 for five miles to its junction with Highway 363. Turn south on 363 and continue on for five more miles to **San Marcos De Apalache State Historic Site** (2).

The history of San Marcos dates back to 1528 when Panfilo de Narvaez arrived in the area bringing with him a force of 300 men. He was followed in by Hernando de Soto, along with 600 men, in 1539. It wasn't until 1679, however, that a fort was constructed by the Spanish governor of Florida at the junction of the Wakulla and St. Marks River. It was a wooden structure, soon replaced by a more durable one, and then, in 1739, by a stone stronghold. The third fort was only half complete when it was delivered to the English as a result of the war with Spain. Unfortunately, that fort is long gone.

War came again to San Marco in 1861 when Confederate forces occupied it and renamed it Fort Ward. For almost four years a Union naval squadron blockaded the mouth of the St. Marks River. Today, a museum occupies the site where the fort once stood. Inside, there are displays of pottery, tools, and artifacts unearthed in and around the area.

San Marcos de Apalache State Historic Site, 1022 DeSoto Park Drive, Tallahassee, FL 32301. ☎ *922-6007. Open Thurs.–Mon., 8–noon and 1–5, closed Thanksgiving, Christmas, and New Year's Day. Admission $3.25 per vehicle (up to eight people).* ♿.

From San Marcos, drive north on Highway 363 to its junction with Highway 98/30. Turn east and drive two miles to Newport, where you'll turn north again on the Newport/Natural Bridge Road and drive six miles to the **Natural Bridge Battlefield State Historic Site** (3).

Tallahassee was the only Confederate state capital east of the Mississippi River never to suffer the ignominy of falling to Union forces. Good luck, good intelligence, and plenty of courage made this possible.

During the final weeks of the war, in March 1865, a large force of Union troops arrived by sea hoping to take the defenders at Tallahassee by surprise. They landed on the shores of the Apalachee Bay and began working their way northward toward the city. Confederate observers sent warning of the approach. A call for volunteers to reinforce the meager garrison was made and, almost within hours, the numbers of Confederate defenders began to swell. It was a somewhat ragtag force of regulars, old men, and boys that faced the Union Army at the natural bridge on the St. Marks River. Unpromising they might have been, but they were more than a match for the Union forces. Three times the Federals hurled themselves against the Confederate line of battle, and three times they were repulsed.

Today, Natural Bridge is a peaceful place to spend a quiet moment or two, to let your imagination wander back in time and ponder the great deeds and horrors of war that took place here. If you visit during the summer months, you can watch living history and military re-enactments laid on by Park Service employees and local volunteers. *Natural Bridge Battlefield State Historic Site, 1022 DeSoto Park Drive, Tallahassee, FL 32301.* ☎ *922-6007. Open daily 8–sunset. $3.25 per vehicle (up to eight people).* ♿.

From Natural Bridge, take the Woodville road east to Highway 363. Turn north on 363 and drive back to Interstate 10, then turn east again and head on back to Jacksonville.

Trip 44

The Buccaneer Trail Scenic Drive

Finally, there's one last driving tour you might like to try while you're in the Jacksonville area. Some sections of it have already been covered in other daytrips, some have not. Still, the Buccaneer Trail—so named because it was once used by pirates—is a fully fledged daytrip in its own right, and a fine way to combine the best of many into one glorious day of scenic driving and sightseeing. It's a drive that will take you for miles, either north or south depending where you decide to start, along one of the most attractive highways in Florida. From Amelia Island all the way to St. Augustine and beyond, it's the road less traveled, a picturesque drive with any number of optional stopping-off points along the way.

GETTING THERE:

The Buccaneer Trail itself—a section of Highway A1A between Amelia and Marineland—is easy to find; deciding where to begin your tour, though, is an interesting question. Just head east out of Jacksonville on either of highways 10 or 90 to Highway A1A and you're on your way; more about that later.

PRACTICALITIES:

As this is a driving tour and there are plenty of indoor stops along the way, good weather is not as important as it is for a walking tour. But grand scenery is always best viewed in sunshine, so pick a time when the weather is good. If you do it on a Sunday you might find one or two places open late and close early.

FOOD AND DRINK:

There are any number of good restaurants on the Buccaneer Trail, and plenty of places to enjoy a picnic lunch. The following are just a few of the highlights:

> **The Palace Saloon** on Centre Street in Fernandina Beach on Amelia is a must. No visit to the island would be complete without a visit to the old watering hole, and to eat lunch there is a real treat. Specialties include fresh seafood, sandwiches and soups. Open 11–2 a.m. 117 Centre Street. ☎ 261-6320. $$.

Aw Shucks, 950 Sawgrass Village Drive in Ponte Vedra, is another neat place, either for lunch or dinner. It's light and airy with outdoor decks overlooking a small lake. They serve a variety of fresh seafood or well-prepared steak. Open 11:30 a.m. to 11 p.m. ☎ 285- 3017. $–$$.

Matanzas Bay Café in St. Augustine, 12 Avenida Menendez (just across from the Castillo), is open for lunch and dinner. The dining room is on the second floor and provides a view of the fort; it's a great place to stop for lunch. The menu features fresh seafood, steaks, chicken, and pasta. Reservations accepted. ☎ 829-8141. $$.

TOURIST INFORMATION:

Amelia Island Chamber of Commerce, The Depot, Centre Street, Fernandina Beach, FL 32035. ☎ 1-800-2-AMELIA.

St. Augustine Visitor Information Center, 10 Castillo Drive, St. Augustine, FL 32084. ☎ 825-1000

SUGGESTED TOUR:

You can take your pick for a jumping-off point, but for the sake of continuity we'll start at the northern end of the Trail and travel south. From Jacksonville, take Highway 10 east to Highway A1A, turn north and drive all the way to **Fort Clinch State Park** (1) at the northernmost point of Amelia Island.

The 1847 Civil War fort has been carefully preserved and remains much as it was in the dark days between 1861 and 1865. You'll enjoy watching the Park Service Rangers, dressed in period uniforms, carrying out the daily chores of a Civil War garrison. *Fort Clinch State Park, 2601 Atlantic Avenue, Fernandina Beach, FL 32034.* ☎ *261-4212. Open daily 8–sunset. $3.25 per vehicle (up to eight people).* ♿.

From Fort Clinch, take A1A into Fernandina Beach and stop in at the **Amelia Island Museum** (2) for a quick look at the Island's history and a guided walking tour of the historic district; the little Victorian seaport has quite a past. If you like, you can get a bite to eat at the Palace Saloon. *The Museum is open daily 10-5; closed Sunday. 233 South 3rd Street.* ☎ *261-7378. Admission is free. Guided tours of the museum are given twice daily at 11 and 2, and cost $2.50 per person. Guided walking tours of the Historic district begin at $5 per person.*

Continue south on A1A, across the Nassau River to **Talbot Island State Park** (3). This is a wild land of rich and diverse habitats; an excellent spot for bird watching, picnics, and taking pictures.

Return to the Buccaneer Trail and drive south through Little Talbot Island and more than five miles of sandy beaches, perhaps taking time out for a swim.

The Palace Saloon in Fernandina Beach

As you make your way down A1A, crossing the Fort George River, you'll come to the entrance to the Fort George Island Cultural Site. This area is known as the Timucuan Ecological and Historic Preserve. **The Preserve** (4) and the **Kingsley Plantation** (5) are described in detail on page 206.

Leaving the Timucuan Preserve, you'll see the Napoleon Bonaparte Broward Residence on your right, and a weathered sign that marks the spot where Jean Ribatl and band of French colonists landed on Fort George Island in 1562.

From Timucuan, the Buccaneer Trail takes you to the **St. Johns River Ferry Boat Landing** (6) where you'll board the brand new *Jean Ribault* ferry boat for a short but spectacular ride across the river to the commercial fishing village of Mayport on the south bank of the St. Johns. Mayport is home to northeast Florida's deep sea fishing fleet and the *LaCruise Fun Ship*, a floating casino that sails daily for international waters where gambling is legal.

As the Buccaneer Trail continues southward you might want to make a short side trip to **Kathryn Abbey Hanna Park** (7), once a part of the 375-acre estate of Elizabeth Stark, the woman who established the Girl Scouts. Turn left on Wonderwood Drive. The park is open daily, admission is free, and you can hike through the woods to the beach for a picnic lunch.

As you continue south on A1A, you'll pass through **Atlantic Beach**, **Neptune Beach**, and **Jacksonville Beach**. These seaside communities all

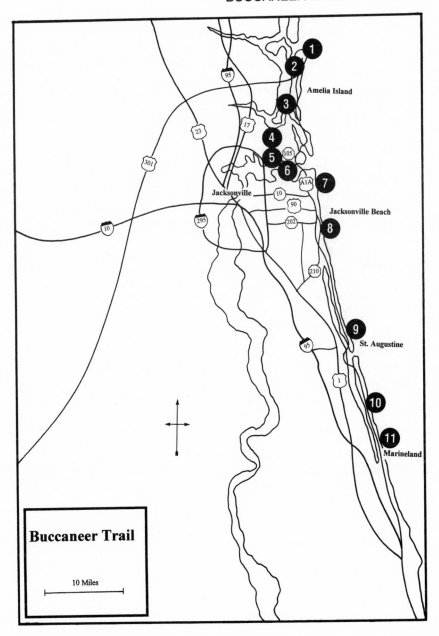

Buccaneer Trail

10 Miles

offer outstanding opportunities for shopping, dining, and family oriented experiences, including several spectacular stretches of beach.

Entering St. Johns County, A1A meanders past a number of very expensive homes in Ponte Vedra Beach, the home of golf's Tournament Players Club (TPC), the PGA Tour National Headquarters, and **Sawgrass**, one of the most famous and magnificent golf courses in Florida. If that's not enough, you can explore **Guana River State Park** (8), which is where many historians believe Juan Ponce de Léon first stepped ashore way back in 1513. Guana River is a wild and desolate place, a 2,400-acre region of coastal river channels, salt water creeks, and marshes. It's also home to a vast range of plant life, seabirds, and mammals. Huge sand dunes, some more than 40 feet high, rise above the shoreline to act as a natural barrier against the sometimes furious action of the ocean. If you're a nature lover, you really should take the time to visit. *Open daily 8–sunset. 2690 South Ponte Vedra Blvd., Ponte Vedra Beach, FL 32082.* ☎ *825-5071.* ♿. *$3.50 per vehicle up to eight people.*

The next stop on your tour southward along the Buccaneer Trail is **St. Augustine** (9), the oldest city in the United States. This section of the trip is covered extensively in another part of this book, beginning on page 220. Not-to-be-missed highlights are the **Spanish Quarter** where you'll find the oldest house, school, and store in the United States, and the Castillo de San Marcos. St. Augustine is also a great place to stop for lunch.

From America's oldest city, the Buccaneer Trail continues southward to the **Fort Matanzas National Monument** (10). Built in 1740 as a part of the Spanish defensive line, it was the scene of very violent times and, in 1565, the massacre of more than 300 French soldiers and sailors by the Spanish conquistador, Don Pedro Menendez. *8635 A1A,* ☎ *471-0116. Open daily 9–5; ferry service 9–4:30. Guided tours by Park Service Rangers. Free.*

The Buccaneer Trail, as far as we are concerned, ends a few miles farther south at ***Marineland of Florida** (11). Here you can take a peek at what lives beneath the surface of the Atlantic, chat with Nelly—she's the oldest known living dolphin—and watch animal specialists working with injured animals and birds. You can also watch the performing penguins, sea lions and dolphins, and the divers hand-feeding sharks. *9507 Ocean Shore Boulevard (A1A),* ☎ *471-1111 or 800-824-4218. Daily 9–5:30. Adults $14.95, seniors $11.96, youths 13–18 $9.95, children 3-12 $7.95.* ♿.

From here you can return to Jacksonville by way of the Buccaneer Trail, or you can take the quickest route and drive north to Highway 206, turn left and go to the junction with Interstate 95, turning north for a straight run into Jacksonville.

Trip 45

Gainesville

Gainesville was originally a Timucuan Indian village. It became part of the settler's world in December 1817 when the land upon which it stood was part of a land grant given to Don Fernando de la Meza Arredondo by the Spanish king. Alachua County was created seven years later after Florida was ceded to the United States, but it was Henry Flagler's Fernandina-to-Cedar-Key Railroad that brought it into the modern world, and gave it its status as the county seat. The name was selected by popular vote in honor of General Edmund P. Gaines, captor of Aaron Burr and the local military commander during the Second Seminole War.

During the Civil War, Gainesville was staunchly Confederate. Two battles were fought here: the first on February 16, 1864, was no more than a skirmish, but the second on August 17 the same year was a full-blown, knock-down, drag-out battle during which Captain John Dickinson and Company H, Second Florida Cavalry routed the Federals, killing or capturing almost all of them.

Gainesville, with a population of about 85,000, lies in the heart of northern Florida some 85 miles southwest of Jacksonville. Today, its main claim to fame is its university, the oldest in Florida. This vast, sprawling campus is where more than 40,000 students and a faculty of 4,000 live, work, and study in an atmosphere more akin to a tropical resort than a center of higher learning. Gainesville is the cultural center of Alachua County, so you'll find lots to see and do. There are at least 20 major attractions worth mentioning, including the Fred Bear Museum, Kanapaha Botanical Gardens, Harn Museum of Art, and the Historic Thomas Center. Beyond the city limits, Alachua county presents even more opportunities for the dedicated daytripper. Micanopy, small community some 10 miles south of Gainesville, is Florida's second-oldest city. There are more than a half-dozen other towns inside the county limits, all worthy of a visit. Then there are the major state parks, historic sites, and natural areas. You can't see it all in a single day, so pick and choose from the diverse selection described on both this trip and the following one.

GETTING THERE:

Gainesville is about 70 miles southwest of Jacksonville. Head west on Interstate 10. When you reach the junction with Highway 301, turn south and drive to Waldo and its junction with Highway 24, which will take you all the way in.

GETTING AROUND:

In Gainesville most of your sightseeing will be done by car. It's a fairly large city, and the attractions are widespread. Parking is not a problem. If you decide to stop off in any of the other featured towns, you can walk.

PRACTICALITIES:

The **Area Code** is 352.

Some of Gainesville's attractions are closed during the early part of the week, especially on Mondays. One or two are also closed on Sundays, so you'll want to take note of opening times and adjust your daytrip accordingly.

FOOD AND DRINK:

There are lots of nice places to eat in Gainesville, and the fare is as diverse as are the restaurants. Seafood is, as always in Florida, a staple, but there are enough ethnic eateries to suit almost every taste. Micanopy, for a town as small as it is, has more than its fair share of good restaurants and cafés, and there are one or two great spots in High Point, Alachua, and towns and villages east and west. In short, if you like good food you're in for a treat. Some choices are:

Gainesville:

Cody's Steakhouse (5220 SW 13th Street) is open for lunch and dinner and specializes in steak and prime rib. Reservations accepted. ☎ 377-4885. $$.

Sovereign (12 SE 2nd Avenue) is a rather elegant restaurant set in a restored carriage house circa 1878. The cuisine is continental. Open for dinner only; closed Sunday. Reservations accepted. ☎ 378-6307. $$$.

Morrison's Cafeteria in the Gainesville Mall on 13th Street is a great place for. The choice is wide: roast beef, chicken, fish, etc., and the food is usually hot and well prepared. Open daily for lunch and dinner. ☎ 378-7422. $.

Micanopy:

Shady Oaks Ice Cream Parlor (203 Cholokko Boulevard) is a must stop-off on your driving tour. Gourmet ice cream, sundaes, shakes, soda, and homemade fudge. ☎ 466-0725. $.

Silver Spur (22822 North Highway 441) is a great place to eat dinner. They specialize in alligator, frog legs, and seafood. Reservations accepted. ☎ 591-4915. $$$.

Wildflowers Café (201 North Highway 441) is the place to eat lunch. Closed Mondays. ☎ 466-4330. $–$$.

TOURIST INFORMATION:
Alachua County Visitors and Convention Bureau, 30 East University Avenue, Gainesville, FL 32601. ☎ 374-5260, FAX 338-3213.

SUGGESTED TOUR:
There are 13 stops on this tour. If you take your time and do it properly, you probably won't be able to get them all in, so pick and choose according to your interests. A good place to start is the **Devil's Millhopper State Geological Site** (1). It's two miles northwest of Gainesville, off Highway 232. You'll be coming into Gainesville on Highway 24; when you come to the intersection with 232, turn right and head west until it joins Highway 441/20/232. Turn right and follow the signs for 232, after a short distance it turns west again and you can follow it all the way to the Millhopper, on your right.

The Devil's Millhopper is a natural geological formation that has fascinated people from as far back as the early 1880s— a huge sink hole created by the collapse of a large underground cavern. Water from tiny streams tumbles 120 feet down the steep sides of the great basin to disappear through the cracks and crevices into the unknown. During the 1800s, farmers used to grind their grain in grist mills, on top of which was a funnel-shaped container called a "hopper" that fed the grain into the machine. Because fossilized bones, teeth and other bits of ancient life have been found at the bottom of the sink, local legends have it that this is the hopper that once fed bodies to the devil; hence, Devil's Millhopper.

Much of Florida sits on a limestone plate, a very hard rock that is easily dissolved in weak acid. Rainwater forms such an acid from contact with carbon dioxide in the air. As it passes downward through decomposing plant material on the earth's surface it becomes even stronger, and when it reaches the limestone plate small cavities appear as acidic action dissolves the rock. These expand and eventually become caverns.

The walls and ceilings continue to dissolve to a point where they can no longer support the great weight from above; the ceiling collapses and a sink is formed. The Millhopper is not unique. There are hundreds of them scattered across northern Florida. This one, however, does provide a clear view of the state's geological past. Each layer of sediment can clearly be seen, and each contains a record of the events and life in the area: extinct marine life, bones and teeth of land animals, etc. The sink is 120 feet deep and 500 across. A one-half-mile trail follows its rim, and there's a 221-step stairway to the bottom. Down there, you can enjoy a spectacular view of the water, the plants, and other wildlife. A word of warning: the walk up and down is an experience you'll never forget, but be sure you're in good shape as the return journey to the surface is strenuous.

Beyond the sink, the 62-acre park contains three distinct natural communities: the sandhill, hammock, and swamp. Lofty pines grow in the dry soil of the sandhill, broadleaf thrives in the moist and fertile soil of the hammock, while gums and willows inhabit the swamp. All provide homes for a variety of small animals and birds. Those visiting on a Saturday can take advantage of ranger-guided walks to see the park at its best. *Open daily from 8–sundown. Devil's Millhopper Geological Site, 4732 Millhopper Road, Gainesville, FL 32606.* ☎ *336-2008.* &. *Admission, $3.25 per vehicle.*

From the Devil's Millhopper, turn right onto Highway 232 and dive west for two miles to the **San Felasco Hammock State Preserve** (2). Within the bounds of its 6,500 acres, San Felasco incorporates "one of the finest examples of the climax mesic hammocks remaining in Florida." The park is home to many species of wild birds and animals, but it's the plant life that makes San Felasco so unusual. Extreme changes in elevation and the geological structure, along with sandhills, hammocks, and swamps, offer ideal conditions for a diverse cross-section of plant life. Sinkholes, creeks, ponds, and marshes also provide homes for a wide range of wildlife, rare plants, birds, and animals.

If you like to hike or walk, you'll enjoy a visit to this preserve. San Felasco rangers offer a program of guided hikes and nature walks—a great way to see all the interesting features—or you can go off on your own. It's also a great place to eat a picnic. *Open daily 8–sundown. San Felasco Hammock State Preserve, C/O Devil's Millhopper State Geological Site, 4732 Millhopper Road, Gainesville, FL 32601.* ☎ *336-2008.* &. *Admission, $3.25 per vehicle.*

From San Felasco, drive west Interstate 75. Take the on-ramp leading south and drive to Exit 75, then take Archer Road south to 63rd Boulevard, turning right to the **Kanapaha Botanical Gardens** (3).

If you love flowers, this is the place for you. The gardens are named for the nearby Lake Kanapaha. The word, pronounced kuh-nap-uh-hah, is derived from two Timucuan Indian words that mean "palmetto leaves" and "house," and refers to the thatched dwellings that were their homes. The entrance road to the park was once an Indian trail, and was the route taken by the English naturalist William Bartram, whose extensive journals describe the area during the American Revolution.

The gardens are an extensive tract of magnificent natural landscape incorporating many rare and unusual plants imported from around the world. These include giant snake arums, bamboos, rare vines, lotuses, and exotic carnivorous plants; all integrated into the meadows and forests on the shores of Lake Kanapaha where spring color begins as early as February.

There are eight major gardens within the Kanapaha complex. The **Butterfly Garden** is set with masses of color especially designed to attract these exquisite winged creatures. The **Vinery** is a walk through ornamental lattice archways festooned with exotic flowering vines from the farthest reaches of

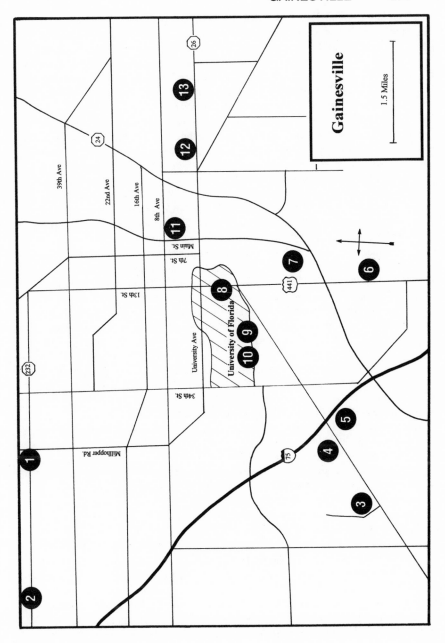

Gainesville

1.5 Miles

the planet. Kanapaha's **Herb Garden** is the largest in the southeastern United States and includes such Old-World remedials as witch hazel, toothache tree, licorice, comfrey, sweet mace, and many more. In the **Bamboo Garden** you'll see Florida's largest collection of dwarf bamboo, giant timber bamboo, sweetshoot bamboo, Chinese goddess, fernleaf, and the beautiful black bamboo. The **Hummingbird Garden** is an unusual treat. Here the floral collection, plants, and trees attract large numbers of exotic birds. You can sit in the central gazebo and watch the small-scale aerobatics show put on by the tiny multi-colored birds. In the **Rock Garden**, the desert comes to Kanapaha as colorful plants and a flowering rock garden where multicolored sprawlers clamber over huge boulders. The **Bog Garden** has a central lily pond where you'll see the world's largest water lily, the Brazilian Victoria. This must be the high point of a summer visit to Kanapaha; try to make it in August or September. Finally, the **Sunken Garden**, developed in the largest of several sinkholes, is a walk along an extensive system of boardwalks that provides an unrestricted view of the many rare and unusual plants in the garden: ferns, ginger, palms, and the endangered Florida Torreya. These eight major gardens are the focal points of Kanapaha, but there's much more: the **Palm Hammock**, **Water Gardens**, **Fern Cobble**, **Woodland Wildflower Garden**, and the **Carnivorous Garden**, all provide novel experiences. And if that's not enough, beyond and around Kanapaha is a huge wildlife sanctuary that provides homes to all sorts of birds and animals, including the bald eagle and Florida's most famous resident, the alligator. A full tour of the gardens shouldn't take more than 1½ hours, but you could easily spend a full afternoon wandering around. *Open Mon., Tues., and Fri. 9–5; Wed., Sat., and Sun. 9–dusk; closed Thurs. 4625 Southwest 63rd Boulevard.* ☎ *372-4981.* ♿. *Adults $3, children 6–13 $2, under 6 free.*

Return to 63rd Boulevard and drive north on Archer to SW 41st Place and **Kanapaha Park** (4). More than a park and more than the war memorial it's meant to be, it's dedicated to the men and women of Alachua County and the University of Florida who laid down their lives in the cause of freedom during a half-dozen wars. It's "a unique lesson in history," a graphic display of time on a linear scale laid down in granite, brick, and tile for a 219-foot walk where one foot equals one year. It represents 10 conflicts from the Revolutionary War through Desert Storm and will include even more as the years go by. *Open 24 hours a day, seven days a week. Tower Road & SW 41st Place, Gainesville.* ♿. *Free.*

From Kanapaha Park, take Archer back to Interstate 75 where you'll find the **Fred Bear Museum** (5). If you've ever picked up a modern bow and arrow, the chances are it was one Fred's, made at Bear Archery. Fred was, for many years, a world-class archer and bow hunter who traveled the world promoting proper wildlife management, the sport of bow hunting in general, and the quality of his own products in particular. The museum is unique. Its collections include trophy animals such as elephant, caribou, moose, lion, tiger, bear, wolves, and many other species of small and big game. These share space on the walls with authentic African, Eskimo, and Native American spears, weapons, and artwork. Lighted showcases contain artifacts— ancient tools and weapons—that date back through the ages to arrow points used by Persian warriors killed at the Battle of Marathon in 490 B.C., as well as ivory and relics from the Stone Age that predate recorded history. For something really different, you won't want to miss this one. *Open Wed.– Sun. 10–6. Fred Bear Drive at Archer Road, Gainesville, FL 32601.* ☎ *376-2411.* ♿. *Adults $3.50, seniors $3, children 6–12 $2. Families (two adults and their minor children under 12) $8.50.*

Take Interstate 75 south to the next exit. From there, take Highway 331 north to Highway 23 and turn south. Go to Highway 441 and follow the signs for **Paynes Prairie State Preserve** (6). Paynes Prairie is a 19,000-acre preserve in one of the most important and historically significant areas in Florida. It is part of a basin formed when the limestone bedrock dissolved and the terrain settled and became covered by marsh, wetland, and large areas of open water. Since its formation millions of years ago, the basin has probably changed very little. The area that lies within the preserve has been home to man for more than 12,000 years. During the late 1600s it was the site of the largest cattle ranch in Spanish Florida. During the 1700s, it was the home of the Seminoles, and the prairie is thought to have been named for one of their chiefs, King Payne. They were still there when William Bartram, the English naturalist, visited the area in 1774; he described the basin as the "great Alachua Savannah." Most of the wildlife Bartram found still make their home in the preserve where some twenty distinct biological communities exist.

Although Paynes Prairie is just one stop on your tour, you could easily spend an entire day here, especially if you like fishing, cycling, or hiking on trails through the hammocks and marshes. A visitor center contains a variety of exhibits, along with an audiovisual program that interprets the preserve and its natural history. Park service rangers conduct weekend guided hikes during the winter months—a great way to see the park if you have the time. Open daily 8 until sundown. *Visitor center open 9–5. Paynes Prairie State Preserve, Route 2, Box 41, Micanopy, FL 32667.* ☎ *466-3397.* ♿. *Admission, $3.25 per vehicle.*

Drive north on Highway 441 until it intersects with South Main Street, where you'll find **Bivens Arm Nature Park** (7). Bivens is a small park compared to some, just 57 acres of oak hammock and marshland traversed by a 1,200-foot promenade. There's also a wildlife sanctuary and nature center, lots of room and tables for a picnic, and a covered pavilion. *Open daily 8:30–5:30. 3650 South Main Street.* ☎ *334-2056. Free.*

The University of Florida (8) is next on the list. From Bivens, return to Highway 441 and drive north to its junction with Museum Road, turning west onto the campus.

The University of Florida in Gainesville, the oldest university in Florida, began life as the private Kingsbury Academy, which was combined with the East Florida Seminary when it moved from Ocala. It became a part of the University in 1905 when the Buckman Act merged many of Florida's state schools. By the turn of the 20th century major changes were already under way. New Gothic-style buildings were constructed and Buckman Hall and Thomas Hall completed in 1906. Today, it's regarded as one of the nation's premier universities and, with a faculty of more than 4,000 and student body in access of 39,500, it's one of the ten largest.

There are a couple of stops to make on campus. You should already be on Museum Road; the **Florida Museum of Natural History** (9) is at its junction with Newell Drive. Ranked among the top natural history museums in the country, this is the shining star in Florida University's firmament. It contains a collection of exhibits that varies from paleontology and animal life to cultural diversity and computers. It's a leading research facility where, from archaeological digs to studies of fossils and living plants and animals, the museum faculty and staff spend much of their time delving into our planet's past. The collections here contain more than ten million specimens of modern and fossil plants, reptiles, birds, and mammals. And it's a teaching institute where, not only students at the University extend their knowledge of all living things, past and present, but children, too, can build a volcano, learn about plants, fish, and animals from ants to sharks, and so develop a better understanding of the world around them. Visitors can explore a cave or Maya palace, trek through a temperate forest, and examine, hands-on, all sorts of artifacts and specimens. *Open 10-5 Mon.–Sat.; Sun. and holidays from 1–5; closed Christmas Day. Museum Road, University of Florida, Gainesville, FL 32611.* ☎ *392-1721.* ⅄. *Free.*

Also located on the University of Florida campus is the **Samuel P. Harn Museum of Art** (10). The best way to get there is to follow Museum Road all the way to Southwest 34th and turn left. From there it's just a short distance to the Harn, a must-visit for art lovers. Housed in an imposing modern building of brick and glass, the museum is Florida's newest and largest facility of its kind, and offers an ever-changing variety of exhibits. New as it is, and even though it's light and airy, the Harn has a heavy, Old-World atmosphere you can almost reach out and touch. Its permanent exhibits feature American paintings, African and pre-Columbian collections, as well as many contemporary works of art. *Open 11–5, Tues.–Fri.; 10–5 Sat.; 1–5 Sun.; closed Mon. and State holidays. Hull Road and Southwest 34th Street, Gainesville, FL 32611.* ☎ *392-9826.* ⅄. *Free.*

To visit the **Thomas Center** (11) from Hull Road, go north on Southwest 34th to University Avenue, turn east and drive to Main Street. Turn north there and go to 6th Avenue NW. Gainesville's Cultural Center is housed in a lovingly restored Mediterranean Revival-style hotel which, since its beginnings in 1906, has seen many changes. The old structure will welcome you, as it has done many thousands of visitors through the years. Once inside, get a map of the building and embark upon a self-guided tour through ten rooms and galleries, all decorated in 1920s style with works of art and period hangings and draperies. From there, it's outside for a walk through some of the loveliest landscaped gardens you're ever likely to see. *Open 8–5, Mon.– Fri.; 1–4, Sat.–Sun. 306 Northeast 6th Avenue, Gainesville, FL 32601. ☎ 334-2197. ♿. Free.*

Return to Main Street, going to University Avenue where you'll turn east once more and drive to number 513 and the **Matheson Historical Center** (12). This is a wonderful place to visit. As much an archive as it is a museum, its collections of paper artifacts include more than 18,000 Florida post cards, 1,200 Stereo-View cards, 400 Florida prints, 50 historical Alachua County and Florida maps, and some 2,500 volumes of local and state history. *Open 9–1, Tues.–Fri.; 1–5, Sun.; closed Mon. and Sat. 513 East University Avenue, Gainesville, FL 32611. ☎ 378-2280. Nominal admission.*

The **Morningside Nature Center** (13) is the final stop on this tour of Gainesville and it, too, is on University Avenue at number 3540; just turn east as you leave the Matheson. As much a petting zoo as nature center, Morningside is a 278-acre living history farm that depicts the life and times of a North Florida farmer of 100 years ago. The farm features an 1840 cabin, a turn-of-the-century kitchen, an heirloom garden, and an old barn, as well a good number of barnyard animals kept in the style of the early 19th century. But it's much more than that. The nature center also offers more than seven miles of boardwalks and trails through sandhill, long-lead pine forest, and cypress habitats where you can see, up close, more than 130 species of birds and 225 more of wildflowers. Other features include live animal exhibits, educational programs, and a wildlife observation blind that's ideal for nature photographers. *Open daily 9–5. 3540 East University Avenue, Gainesville. ☎ 334-2170. Free.*

Small Towns of Alachua County Scenic Drive

Although Gainesville is its major population center, Alachua County also has a half-dozen smaller communities that are unique in their own way and well worth a visit. Like the moons of Saturn, they completely encircle the great university town and make for a great day of sightseeing. This scenic drive takes in not only each of the county's tiny townships, but also a number of interesting state and local parks along the way.

GETTING THERE:
Just follow the directions for the Gainesville daytrip (page 268) to Waldo where Highways 301 and 21 meet, but instead of heading into town on Highway 21, take time out to visit.

PRACTICALITIES:
Most of the attractions you'll visit are open daily. However, many of the shops in the small communities, except for Micanopy, are closed on Sunday. The only consideration you have is the weather, as this is a sightseeing trip with perhaps a stroll or picnic along the way.

FOOD AND DRINK:
Each community has at least one nice little café; Micanopy is blessed with a number of delightful restaurants and ice cream shops (see page 268). If you feel the need for something more, you can always drive into Gainesville for lunch or dinner. Alternatively, there are several agreeable picnic spots along the way.

TOURIST INFORMATION:
Alachua County Visitors and Convention Bureau, 30 East University Avenue, Gainesville, FL 32601. ☎ 374-5260, FAX 338- 3213.

SUGGESTED TOUR:

The tour includes seven towns and six of Florida's great natural wonders and preserves. **Waldo** (1) is the first stop. As you drive in from Jacksonville on Highway 301 you'll find it little more than a main street and a number of old, well-preserved buildings that date from the late 19th century, very much a picture of small-town rural Florida. Waldo is a product of the railroad and its period of state-wide expansion. Today, it's is still in the railroad business with the only Amtrak station in Alachua County. Railroad Days, an annual festival that celebrates Waldo's heritage, is held each year in the last week of April.

From Waldo, take Highway 24 into Gainesville, about 17 miles. Once there, take Highway 441 northwest for 12 miles to **Alachua** (2). Alachua is a relatively new town compared to Florida's long history. Incorporated in 1903, and surrounded by rolling hills and farmland, it is an important commercial and agricultural center in the county. The recently redeveloped, spacious downtown area is lined with historic commercial buildings and lovely old homes, a combination that makes for a charming thoroughfare and a great place to stroll and window shop. Alachua is one of those neat little towns with a facade that symbolizes the essence of what we've come to regard as the "good life" of America. And the residents there must feel that way, too, as they celebrate the *Good Life Jubilee* in October of each year.

From Alachua, continue northwest on Highway 441 for seven miles to **High Springs** (3). This little town is quite special. Prior to 1884 when the town was established, it had been home to Indians, Spaniards, and pioneering American settlers. When the Savannah, Florida and Western Railroad was extended from Live Oak to Gainesville, someone thought this seemed a likely spot for a stop along the way. Just a whim, perhaps? Or did that someone know something? High Springs soon became an important railroad center, the more so when in 1896, the Plant System built engine shops, a roundhouse, a hospital, and section offices on a large tract of land west of the town center. New jobs were created, and hundreds of railroad workers flocked into the town, which in turn expanded by adding new stores, churches, and schools.

Industries, namely phosphate mining and agriculture, also added to the High Springs' growing economy in the early years of 20th century, but always it was the great steam trains and the shops that kept them running that were the backbone of the community's prosperity.

The streets and avenues of High Springs are aligned with the railroad tracks that gave the city its life. They offer an eye-opening panorama of architectural styles and variations that run the gamut from old-world Victorian elegance to modern ranch. Most of the original wooden buildings did not survive the great hurricane of 1896 and a series of fires that devastated the business district, but several of the brick buildings pre-date the 20th century.

From High Springs, take Highway 441 north for six miles to **O'Leno State**

Park (4). Set on the banks of the scenic Santa Fe River, like many of the great outdoor parks in northern Florida, O'Leno is a land of hardwood hammocks, sink holes, river swamps, and sandhill communities. Developed in the early 1930s by the Civilian Conservation Corps, it was one of the first state parks in Florida. The Corps' suspension bridge, one of the park's features, still spans the river, a tributary of the Suwannee which enters the park only to disappear into one of the several sinkholes and flow underground for several miles before reappearing again.

If you like to walk, you can park the car and enjoy one or both of two scenic nature trails: the Santa Fe trail which meanders along the river bank to the sinkhole where the river disappears underground; and the Limestone trail, a much shorter but extremely scenic walk. Nature lovers should be on the lookout for alligators and turtles. O'Leno is also a great place for a picnic lunch as tables and grills are provided. *Open daily 8–sunset. O'Leno State Park, Route 2, Box 1010, High Springs, FL 32643. ☎ 454-1853. ⅙. $3.50 per vehicle up to eight people.*

You may find **Ichetucknee Springs State Park** (5) is a bit out of your way (about 15 miles) but, if you have the time, it's well worth a visit. From O'Leno, take 441 back to High Springs, and then Highway 27 east to Fort White. Turn right onto Highway 47, drive to the junction with Highway 238, turn left and drive three miles to the park.

Here, some 233 million gallons of sparkling water flow each day from a series of springs to form the headwaters of Ichetucknee River which, after a journey of some six miles or so through hammock and swamp, flows into the Santa Fe River. Like O'Leno, the park's natural environment is one of hammock, swampland and forest. The river's head spring was declared a National Natural Landmark by the U.S. Department of the Interior in 1972.

Snorkeling in the crystal waters of the spring is a popular pastime, as is tubing on the fast-flowing waters of the river. There's a free in-park shuttle service to the put-in point. Additionally, you'll find an attractive nice picnic area and several walking trails through the wetlands and hammocks. *Open daily 8–sunset. Ichetucknee Springs State Park, Route 2, Box 108, Fort White, FL 32038. ☎ 497-2511. ⅙. $3.50 per vehicle.*

Return once more to High Springs. This time take Highway 47 across the Santa Fe River to Highway 236 and turn east. From here the route takes you by three more delightful stops along the way. With nine spectacular natural springs, including the incredible Devil's Eye, **Ginnie Springs** is a mecca for serious scuba divers. Next is **Blue Springs**, another delightful spot on the river. **Poe Springs**, only four miles from High Springs, is the third diversion, with more than 200 acres of parkland set along the river banks.

Take Highway 41 south for 12 miles to the little town of **Newberry** (6). Although very small, just 1,600 population, it's a pretty place, very much a part of rural Florida that few tourists ever get to see. This is mainly because the fast routes, such as Interstate 75 just a few miles to the east, speed them

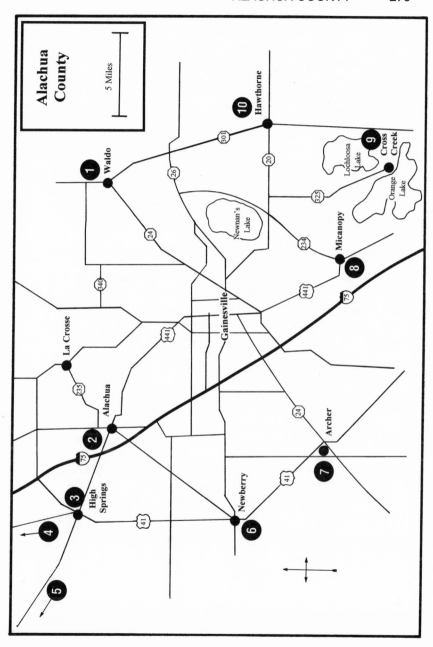

ever southward to the great seaside resorts. Newberry also came into being as a result of the railroad and phosphate industries. Today it's a community where agriculture is the mainstay of the economy and the watermelon is king. If you visit in June, you'll be able to attend the *Watermelon Festival*.

Archer (7) is another sleepy little town just a few miles farther south on Highway 41. Located in the southwest portion of Alachua County it, too, was laid out in 1853 by Henry Flagler's Florida Railroad when they built the link between the eastern seaport of Fernandina and Cedar Key on the Gulf of Mexico. In 1880, Quakers from Indiana and Ohio came to Archer and planted vast orange groves, which were destroyed during the terrible winters of 1894 and 95.

From Archer, take Highway 346 to its junction with Highway 121 and turn south two miles to the junction with Highway 320. Turning east, go three miles to the junction with Highway 324 and bear left to ***Micanopy** (8). This little town just south of Gainesville and west of Orange Lake is one stop that's really a must. Not only is it the oldest inland town in Florida, it's also one of the most interesting, and high on the list of every serious antique collector.

Too small to show up on many maps, Micanopy is one of those places with a great big heart. The people are friendly and willing to do their best to please. The shops are neat and tidy, full of interesting knick-knacks, memorabilia, antiques, arts and crafts, holiday clothing, and all kinds of gift items. The cafés and restaurants are bright and breezy and offer a variety of good things to eat, not to mention the best ice cream in northern Florida. The scenery borders on spectacular, and the town itself is an odd, though delightful, collection of historic buildings and homes. If you go to the movies, you've probably already seen it, for it was the setting for *Doc Hollywood*, starring Michael J. Fox. Try to visit in November when the town puts on its best front during the annual Fall Festival.

Before leaving Micanopy, be sure to visit the ***Historical Society Museum** (Cholokko Boulevard and Bay Street). You can't miss it, it's located in the old Thrasher Warehouse, which has a wooden shingled roof and a large, antique Coca-Cola sign. The museum is filled with all sorts of bits and pieces of local history and memorabilia, artifacts and exhibits that interpret Micanopy's history from the earliest times. *Open Fri.–Sun. 1–5. Nominal admission.*

The next stop is three miles out of the way, but worth the effort. Take Highway 346 east to its junction with Highway 325. Turn right (south) there and drive on to the **Marjorie Kinnan Rawlings Historic Site** (9) in Cross Creek. This cracker-style home is where the great lady wrote her Pulitzer Prize winning novel, *The Yearling*, and *Cross Creek*, the chronicle of life at the Creek. Cross Creek is no more than a bend in a country road, four miles from the tiny community of Island Grove, and set on the shores between Orange and Lochloosa Lakes. In 1928, when she arrived with her husband, it was wild country, backwoods in every sense of the word, but she immediately felt an affinity for the place. And so Marjorie Kinnan Rawlings sat on her verandah among the orange groves writing the books that would become American classics and capturing the Old-World atmosphere and the beauty of the countryside. Today, her home is one of Florida's most popular attractions. The old house has been preserved in much the same condition as it was when she lived in it. The Florida Park Service conducts tours of the home but, as it is small, groups are limited to ten people at a time. *Open 10–11.30 a.m., and 1–4.30 p.m., Thurs.–Mon. Closed Tues. and Wed., Thanksgiving, Christmas, and New Year's Day. Route 3, Box 92, Hawthorne, FL 32640.* ☎ *466-3672.* ♿. *Adults $2, children 6–12 $1, 5 and under free.*

The final stop on your scenic dive is **Hawthorne** (10). From Cross Creek, take Highway 325 southeast to its junction with Highway 301 and turn north; from there it's a drive of about nine miles. This is sporting country. Set amid more than a hundred lakes, almost as many small rivers and creeks, and several hundred square miles of wetlands and wildlife preserve, the little town is a major inland fishing center. The lakes, especially Lochloosa and Orange, both of which are close by, offer some of the finest bass fishing in the state—smallmouth, largemouth, sunshine, and striped—and all are well stocked with crappie, shell-cracker, and bream, as well as catfish. As with most tiny rural towns in Florida, apart from the scenery that surrounds it, there's not that much to see once you get inside the city limits. It's a typical little farming community, quiet and clean, and the main street makes for a pleasant walk in the sunshine.

From Hawthorne, you're on the way back to Jacksonville. Take Highway 301 north through Waldo and on to its junction with Interstate 10. Turn east, and it's a straight run in.

Section VI

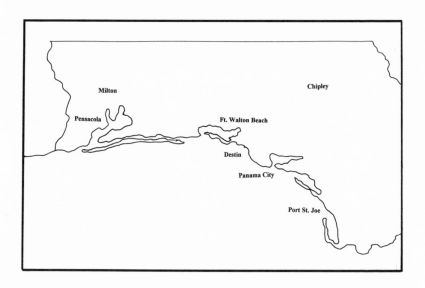

Milton   Chipley

Pensacola

Ft. Walton Beach

Destin

Panama City

Port St. Joe

THE NORTHWEST

Pensacola represents your westernmost base of operations. In today's busy, unnatural world of fumes, worry, and no time at all for simple enjoyment, the old city still means fresh air, sunshine, and pure good fun. It's a waterfront community famous for its miles of sugar-white sand that also offers a wealth of attractions ranging from a world-renowned aviation museum to a nationally accredited zoo. It's a city steeped in the history of more than 400 years, during which the flags of five nations have flown over it, and it changed hands more than a dozen times. Many would claim the community is even older than St. Augustine.

It was in 1559 that Spanish conquistador Don Tristan De Luna landed on the shores of Pensacola Bay with 1,400 men. Even in those early days, Pensacola's first visitor saw it as something special. De Luna immediately set up a colony of more than 1,000 people. Alas, it failed, and was abandoned two years after its founding in 1561. St. Augustine wasn't established until 1565, four years later. It would be another 139 years before the area was settled for a second time.

In 1689, Don Abdrés de Ariola with 350 men stepped ashore at Gulf Breeze and established the first permanent settlement in the area. The don built his fort on the site of the present-day Naval Air Station. Once again, the royal standard of Spain fluttered over Pensacola. Then, in 1719, the Spaniards built a second fort on Santa Rosa Island, close to the spot where Fort Pickens now stands. It was taken by the French soon afterwards, and Pensacola itself fell to them in 1722, but not for long.

After Spain regained control of the area, they built a new settlement on Santa Rosa Island. The idea was that a village there could be better defended. Unfortunately, the conquistadors failed to remember the one enemy against which there could be no defense: the hurricane. The new settlement was destroyed, and further attempts to colonize Santa Rosa were abandoned. Today, a small stockade, erected in 1752 near Historic Pensacola Village, is all that remains; a testament to those far-off, turbulent times.

In 1763, as part of the Treaty of Paris, Florida was ceded to England. Now the Union Jack flew over Pensacola. The English stayed for only a short time—18 years—during which they set about establishing some sort of order to the one-time Spanish colony. They laid out the streets of what is now the Historic District, set out gardens and dug public wells to provide fresh water. The Spanish returned in 1781; the United States took possession of the city in 1821.

Civil War came to Pensacola in 1861 and the Confederate Stars and Bars flew bravely over the city. During those early days of the conflict things were fairly even between the armies of North and South: Federal forces held Fort Pickens, while the Confederates hung on to Fort McRee. Finally, in 1862, the Confederates were forced to evacuate the city, and most of the residents fled, leaving Pensacola in Union hands.

Tourism began in 1886. Not because it had suddenly become famous as a resort, but because the great Apache war chief, Geronimo, and some of his warriors were being held at Fort Pickens. Hundreds of sightseers cruised the waters near the fort, hoping to catch a glimpse of a legend.

Today, Florida's Northwest—Pensacola in particular—is very much overlooked by the vacationing public. True it's slowly but surely being discovered, but there's still a long way to go, which is unfortunate because the area encompasses some of the state's best beaches, attractions, and parks. Happily, almost all of them remain unspoiled. Some areas are quite remote, windswept, and isolated; some are more accessible, very much a part of the modern metropolitan experience. From Pensacola in the west, all the way to Panama City on the Upper Gulf Coast, there's so much to see and do. It's a land of crystal rivers, rolling hills, snow-white beaches and sea-coasts, moss-draped trees, and fine old homes on avenues lined with tropical trees and shrubs. It's the remote barrier islands where only the soft sounds of the surf and the lonely call of a wheeling seagull disturb the silence, and it's a dozen or more state parks dedicated to the preservation of all that Florida once was: its endangered wildlife, plants, and environment.

This is not a land of glitz and high times. True you can find some of that if you look hard enough for it, but it's a place to spend quiet hours on the beach, hiking beautiful nature trails, bird watching, and fishing. It's a place to get away from the noise and brass of the resorts to the south.

If you're a fisherman, you'll find no better place to do it than in Pensacola. Each year, the city sponsors a number of nationally and internationally known tournaments, including the International Billfish event in July. Charter boats are available the year round.

For 150 miles to the east and west of Pensacola the northwest coast has been set aside as the **Gulf Islands National Seashore**, a long chain of barrier islands and beaches that stretches from South Mississippi to West Florida. The islands protect and preserve the beaches, wide-open spaces, and historic sites from the natural elements: wind and surf. At the heart of the National Seashore, Pensacola is flanked by a pair of those barrier islands: **Perdido Key** to the west and **Santa Rosa Island**, better known as Pensacola Beach, to the east. These two islands offer miles of pristine sand, emerald green ocean, magnificent vistas and, best of all, plenty of peace and quiet.

Historic Pensacola

The marks of the Spanish, French, English, and Confederate occupations still remain a part of the Old City. You can stroll oak- and magnolia-shaded avenues first mapped out and named by the English, then renamed by the Spanish: Cervantes, Palafox, Intendencia, Tarragona, etc. Visit the old neighborhoods, two of which are listed on the National Register of Historic Places, while another has been deemed a historic district by the city. Many of the residences and shops within Pensacola's historic districts are living examples of architectural periods spanning the centuries from Colonial times through the Great Depression. The section of the city we are concerned with here, the Seville District, includes Historic Pensacola Village with side trips out and around to other significant attractions.

The Seville District has enjoyed a long and eventful history, most of it dating from the late 18th century when traders, trappers, and Indians peddled their goods here. The settlers who built homes on the waterfront and in Seville Square were a mixed lot: English, Spanish, French, and Scottish, along with great numbers of slaves and free blacks. The economy was driven by the sea and the harbor, with myriad ancillary industries: fishing, shipping, warehousing, lumber, brickyards, the military and, later, railroads. Today, most of what you'll see dates from early to late 19th century: Folk Victorian, Creole, etc. Most of the stops are within walking distance of one another, so you can park your car and enjoy a morning or afternoon in the sunshine among some of the most appealing surroundings in Northwest Florida.

GETTING THERE:
By Air: Pensacola is served by American Airlines, Continental, Delta, Northwest Airlink, and US Air Lines, as well as a number of small commuter airlines.
By Road:
Southbound into Pensacola on I-65: take the Flomation exit (Exit 69) onto Highway 113 and follow it south through Flomation, Alabama, to Highway 29. Follow 29 south through Century, Florida, and on into the city where it accesses Interstate 10 east and west.
East/Westbound on Interstate 10: Go to Exit 4, the junction with Inter-

state 110, and turn south; 110 will take you right into downtown Pensacola, and will connect with Highways 98 East, 98 West, and Business 98.

By Train: Pensacola is served by Amtrak, ☎ 1-800-USA-RAIL.

By Bus: Greyhound/Trailways, ☎ 904-476-4800 or 800-231-2222.

GETTING AROUND:

If you have a car, getting around is not a problem. If you're arriving by air, it would be a good idea to rent one. Otherwise you'll have to rely on the Escambia County Transit System which can, at times, be more than a little inconvenient. The other alternative is to take a cab. You can also sign up for any one of a number of tours offered by local companies (contact the Convention & Visitors Bureau for a list); convenient, but restrictive. It's best to do it on your own if you can.

ACCOMMODATIONS:

As in most major cities in Florida, acquiring decent lodgings is not a problem. Prices depend very much on location: if you don't mind staying in one of the outlying areas you can do it for $40 or $50 per night; stay downtown, or close to the beaches, and you'll pay upwards of $120 per night. Reservations? Again, if you don't mind a room on the outer fringes of the city, you can drop in whenever you like unless, of course, there's some special event going on, such as the Annual Billfish Tournament. Downtown or on the beaches you'll need to make reservations ahead of your visit.

PRACTICALITIES:

The **Area Code** for Pensacola and most of northwest Florida is 904.

Weather: Northwest Florida is mild in winter, cool in spring and fall, and warm in the summertime, which means lots of sunshine. The average winter temperatures range from an evening low of about 45°F—although it can often get down below freezing in January and February—to a daytime high of around 65°; in spring and fall the range is 60° to 75°; in summer 73° to 88°; and in the fall 61° to 78°. As to rainfall, Northwest Florida gets its fair share of the wet stuff, especially in spring and fall. It can also get a little blustery, with at least a couple of tropical storms and one hurricane per year. The weather, however, unless you become involved in a major storm, should not be a problem. The nasty stuff never lasts for long, and there's always something to see and do even on the wettest of days.

FOOD AND DRINK:

Situated on the Gulf of Mexico and regarded as one of the deep-water fishing capitals of the world, Pensacola is famous for its seafood. While you can find almost any cuisine to suit your fancy, you won't want to miss the oysters, shrimp and, especially, the fresh-from-the-ocean amberjack—a real treat if you like fish.

Some choice restaurants are:

Mesquite Charlie's (5901 North "W" Street) is an Old-World saloon-style restaurant with high ceilings, lots of stone and timber decor, and an atmosphere to suit. The specialty is, of course, steak cooked over mesquite charcoal. Open for dinner only from 5 p.m. Reservations accepted. ☎ 434-0498. $$.

Skopelos (670 Scenic Highway), overlooking Pensacola Bay, is a light and airy restaurant with colorful table decorations and lots of glass and mirrors. The specialty is Greek cuisine, along with traditional seafood and steaks. Open for dinner from 5 p.m. It's often busy, so make a reservation. ☎ 432-6565. $$.

Barnhill's Country Buffet (two locations: one at Warrington & Entrance Road, the other at North Davis & Olive Road) offers something really different. Service is, as the name suggests, all buffet, but you can eat everything from seafood to red meat to chicken, along with a variety of country desserts. Great food at reasonable prices. Open for lunch and dinner. Warrington Road, ☎ 456-2760; North Davis, ☎ 477-5465. $.

Boy On A Dolphin (400 Pensacola Beach Boulevard) is on the water's edge, has lots of atmosphere and a seafood menu with a real difference. Open for dinner only from 4 p.m. Reservations are a must if you want to dine on Saturday. ☎ 932-7954. $$$.

McGuire's Irish Pub and Brewery (600 East Gregory Street) is reminiscent of the type of restaurants and pubs more likely found in Philadelphia, Boston, and Chicago than in the deep south. The food is great (be sure to try the Irish stew), the atmosphere authentic, and the ales, brewed on the premises, are as good as you're likely to find outside of Ireland. Open for lunch and dinner from 11 a.m. ☎ 433-6789. $$.

Yamato (131 New Warrington Road) claims to be the "best tasting show in town," as so it might be. Typical of the eat-as-it's-cooked, Japanese-style restaurants, the chefs are talented, and rarely make a mistake as they slice, dice, and season. Open for lunch and dinner. ☎ 453-3461. $$.

TOURIST INFORMATION:

Pensacola Convention and Visitors Information Center, 1401 E. Gregory Street (at the foot of Pensacola Bay Bridge), Pensacola, FL 32501. ☎ 800-874-1234 or 434-1234, FAX 432-8211.

Satellite Information Centers are located in the T.T. Wentworth Museum and Century City Hall.

Pensacola Chamber of Commerce, 117 W. Garden Street, PO Box 550, Pensacola, FL 32593. ☎ 438-4081, FAX 438-6396.

SUGGESTED TOURS AND LOCAL ATTRACTIONS:

Seville Square (1), bounded by Adams, Alcaniz, Zaragoza, and Government Streets, is where the survivors of an early attempt to settle Santa Rosa Island established a permanent settlement after a hurricane destroyed their village in 1752. Here they built a fortified outpost called San Miguel. After the French and Indian War of 1763, the English took West Florida and erected a stockade. It was during the English period of occupation that the street system was mapped. When the Spanish re-captured the area in 1781, they retained the original English layout of the streets, changing only the English place and street names to Spanish; the modern street map details the English layout and Spanish names just as they were more than 200 years ago.

Historic Pensacola Village (2) is a grouping of museums devoted to West Florida history. More than that, many of the museums are housed in old homes, and the village itself is a quaint area that imparts a deep feeling, a sense of momentous times and the early struggles for survival. *Historic Pensacola Village is open daily 10–4, closed holidays.* ☎ *444-8905.* ᕙ. *Adults $5.50, seniors $4.50, children 4–16 $2.25.* The museums within the Village are:

Charles Lavallé House (3), at 205 East Church Street, is one of the finest examples of French Creole architecture in Pensacola. Built is 1805 by Charles Lavallé (pronounced La-val-LAY) in partnership with Marianna Bonifay, a French woman from the Caribbean, the old house has a high-pitched roofline and a wide overhanging porch. Originally intended for use as a duplex rental property, it has been carefully restored to reveal, not only its simple quadrant floor plan, but its brick nogging and graceful lines as well. Even the colors used for both interior and exterior decorations are in line with those known to have been used in early 19th-century Pensacola, faithfully re-created from ochre and red clays found locally.

Dorr House (4), 311 South Adams Street, was the home of Clara Barkley and Eban Dorr following their marriage in 1849. The marriage united two of Pensacola's leading merchant families, both of English ancestry. The old, two-story house with its Victorian-era trim and simple Gulf Coast features— brick piers and "jib" windows—is a classic example of its time.

Julee Cottage (5), 210 East Zaragoza Street, is an example of what became known as a "to the sidewalk" residence. It was bought in 1805 by Julee (pronounced Jew-lee) Panton, a "free woman of color," and was later owned by a succession of free black women. This is not where it was first built, and it lost much of its original framing in the move. Its pegged framework and beaded ceilings, however, were saved and restored during its reconstruction as a Black History Museum.

Museum of Commerce (6) is in the Transportation Building at the corner of Zaragoza and Tarragona Streets. An old-time Pensacola street scene has been reconstructed within the old warehouse and contains representations of many businesses common to the Victorian era, including a fully-equipped

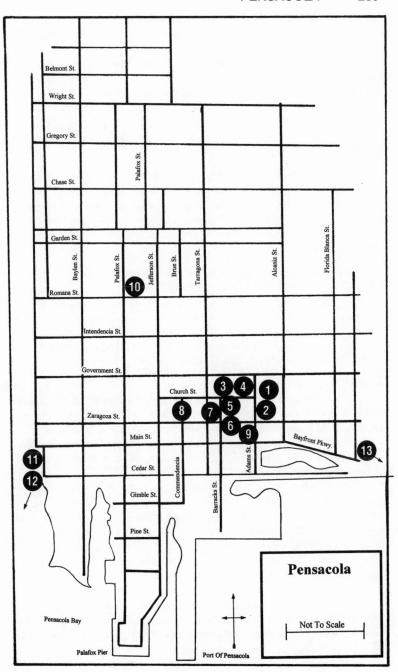

print shop, pharmacy, toy shop, and a hardware store; some are open for business. There's also a number of horse-drawn carriages and an early 20th-century gas station.

Museum of Industry (8), 200 East Zaragoza Street, is housed in the Hispanic Building, a late 19th-century warehouse. Exhibits interpret the industries prevalent in Pensacola during the early 1800s, of which lumber had the most influence on the city's development. Others show that Pensacola was an early naval stores supplier, selling tar, pitch, and durable woods for maritime use. The shipping and railroad industries are also represented.

T.T. Wentworth Florida State Museum (9), at 330 South Jefferson Street in the restored City Hall—a wonderful example of Mediterranean Revival architecture—houses exhibits that interpret the history (actual and natural) of West Florida. There's also a children's museum, lots of Coca-Cola memorabilia from the Hygeia Bottling Company, and a vast array of archeological finds and fossils.

Pensacola Historical Museum (10), 405 South Adams Street, is in the Old Christ Church, which had a long and sometimes turbulent history. Since its construction in 1832 it served as a Federal Civil War barracks, prison, hospital, and chapel. Today it houses an eclectic collection of historical artifacts and memorabilia, including Indian pottery, glass, utensils, and weapons, as well as old clothing, silver, coinage, bottles, etc. *Open 9–4:30 Mon.–Sat.* ☎ *433-1559. Adults $2, children 4–16 $1.*

ADDITIONAL ATTRACTIONS:

Civil War Soldiers Museum (11), at 108 South Palafox Street, houses one of the finest collections of Civil War artifacts you're ever likely to see. Exhibits include weapons of all types and sizes, letters, maps, uniforms, and a number of life-size dioramas that depict the life and times of the Civil War soldier in the field. *Open 10–4:30 Mon.–Sat.* ☎ *469-1900. Adults $4, children 6–12 $2.*

*****National Museum of Naval Aviation** (12), at the Pensacola Naval Air Station at the end of Navy Boulevard, is one of the largest air and space museums in the world. Inside the great, hangar-like exhibition areas you can see more than 100 aircraft representing Navy, Marine Corps, and Coast Guard aviation from the earliest times; from the first flight in a wood-and-fabric biplane to space travel in the a Skylab Command Module. Kids of all ages—you too, dad—can strap themselves into the cockpit for a pretend flight, and try their hand at defending a ship from the gun batteries. The museum also tells the story of the human side of Naval Aviation and features memorabilia from each significant era, including personal mementos from historic battles, flight logs, instruments, and flight gear. *Open 9–5 daily.* ☎ *452-3604.* ♿. *Free.*

In the National Museum of Naval Aviation

Fort Barrancas (13) is also inside the Naval Air Station. This is one of several forts built by the Spanish along the western Florida coastline in the late 1500s. Surrounded as it is by a wide dry moat, access is possible only by way of a drawbridge. There's not much else to see other than the view, but it's a great place to sit for a while and take it easy. *Open Apr.–Oct., 9:30–5 daily; rest of year Wed.–Sun. 10:30–4. Tours at 2 and 11 through June and July; Sat. and Sun. at 2 the rest of the year.* ☎ *455-5167. Free.*

Veterans Memorial Park (14), at the corner of Bayfront Parkway and Romana Street, contains a half-size replica of the Vietnam Veterans Memorial in Washington D.C. There's also a "Huey" helicopter and a World War I veterans memorial. *Open 24 hours daily.* ☎ *433-8200.* ♿. *Free.*

Gulf Islands National Seashore and the Beaches

Miles of white sands and rolling dunes covered with oats and seagrass, an emerald green ocean that stretches southward to meet an endless sky, and here and there a few humans walk or fish or play or sit on the beach watching the weather and feeling the worries of the world drift away on the rolling surf. Sounds like some far-away Caribbean island, but it's not. It's a typical day, summer or winter, on the beaches at Pensacola. True, if it's company you crave, you can find crowded sands, but you can easily avoid the long lines and enjoy the Gulf Islands National Seashore by yourself. The Seashore and Big Lagoon State Park offer huge swaths of untrampled, easily accessible beaches open to the public.

The waves come in all sizes. While the Gulf may, in places, send surf crashing ashore, more sheltered bodies of water on both Pensacola Beach and Perdido Key provide wonderful wading areas for the kids.

GETTING THERE:
Santa Rosa Island (Pensacola Beach): From the Historic District, take Gregory Street and the Bay Bridge (Highway 399) to Gulf Breeze and the Beaches beyond.

Perdido Key: From downtown Pensacola, take Highway 292.

GETTING AROUND:
The only way is to take your car. There's plenty of parking available.

PRACTICALITIES:
The **Area Code** is 904.

The beaches and attractions listed below are all open daily, so you can take the trip whenever you please.

The weather is always the big concern when heading out for a day at the beach. Here it's often changeable, going quickly from blue skies to sudden showers. Watch the forecasts and you shouldn't have any problems.

The sun in summer is hot, so be sure to use sunscreen with a factor of at least 15.

TOURIST INFORMATION:

Gulf Islands National Seashore, 1801 Gulf Breeze Parkway, Gulf Breeze, FL 32561. ☎ 934-2600.

Gulf Breeze Chamber of Commerce, 1170 Gulf Breeze Parkway, Gulf Breeze, FL 32562. ☎ 932-7888.

FOOD AND DRINK:

This is packed lunch country. True, you'll find a concession stand or two, some fast food joints, and even an occasional restaurant, but it's best that you provide for yourself. There are plenty of picnic areas, some with tables and grills.

LOCAL ATTRACTIONS:

Your first choice will be which way to go: Perdido Key or Santa Rosa Island (Pensacola Beach). On the one hand, you'll find miles of unspoiled sand, remote and windswept, just the place for time out away from the crowds, to be alone with a special friend, or to be by yourself to think. On the other, you'll find more miles of unspoiled sand, but you'll also find some company, not much, but company just the same. Let's begin by taking the Bay Bridge and going south to Gulf Breeze and then Pensacola Beach.

Gulf Breeze is a tiny resort town just across the water from Pensacola, a place of bays, lagoons, rivers, and neat little shopping centers. The town offers all sorts of recreational opportunities, including boating, water skiing, sailing, fishing, diving, tennis, and golf. It's also home to the:

*Gulf Breeze Zoo (1), a unique zoological garden that houses and maintains more than 700 animals. It's small zoo compared to some, but well worth a visit. The animal's areas are spacious and closely resemble the natural habitats of their native lands. Other highlights include a wonderful Japanese garden, a children's petting zoo where the kids can get know all sorts of small domestic animals, and an outdoor amphitheater where you can see a live elephant show or animal demonstration. Top off your visit with a train ride through a 30-acre wildlife park where the animals roam free. *Open 9–4 daily with extended hours during the summer.* ☎ 932-2229. furth. *Adults $9.25, seniors $8.25, children 3–11 $5.25.*

From Gulf Breeze it's on across the water via Highway 399 to **Pensacola Beach** (2). First discovered by Spanish explorers, the beach, part of the Gulf Islands National Seashore, offers miles and miles of unspoiled sand, crystal-clear water, and a strong flavor of history—all with a minimum of fuss or traffic.

At the west end of the island is **Fort Pickens** (3), one of a chain of forts constructed during the early part of the 19th century to protect Pensacola Harbor. It was used to great advantage during the Civil War and later became the prison for the Apache Indian War Chief, Geronimo. You can take a guided tour of the fort, or wander around on your own. *Open 9–5 daily. Guided tours Monday through Friday at 2; Saturday and Sunday at 11 and 2.* ☎ *934-2635. Admission $4 per vehicle.*

As for the **Beaches** (4), well, you're on your own. There are a number of different stretches to choose from. Any one of them will provide a daytrip to remember: surf fishing, parasailing, windsurfing, body surfing, swimming and, of course, sunbathing.

If you decide to go west and drive south on Highway 292 to **Perdido Key** (6) you'll find that, in places, and even though it's only 15 miles from downtown Pensacola, it can be a very remote island. Discovered by the Spanish in 1693, it has long been one of those special getaway places for beach connoisseurs. More than 70% of the key is protected parkland offering a user-friendly setting for everything from nature walks to beaches that were rated number 12 in the nation by Dr. Stephen Leatherman at the University of Maryland's Laboratory for Coastal Research.

The **Perdido Key State Recreation Area** (7) is a 247-acre park on a barrier island that protects the mainland from the great storms of the hurricane seasons, and provides natural habitats for the sea birds and other marine life. It also offers an unspoiled stretch of wide sandy beach, rolling dunes covered with seagrass and oats, and one of the last really romantic spots in northwest Florida. For now, at least, Perdido Key remains a quiet little backwater where you can sit or swim in the sunshine and forget, for a moment or two, life in the fast lane. *Open 8–sunset daily.* ☎ *492-1595. Admission $3.25 per vehicle.*

Big Lagoon State Recreation Area (8), complete with observation tower, is a bird watcher's paradise. The park provides habitats for many species of land and water birds: nuthatches, cardinals, the great blue heron, and others. It's an area where wide, pristine beaches and great salt marshes meld with the Gulf Islands National Seashore and the Intracoastal Waterway. If you like to fish, this is the place. Brought along a picnic lunch? Settle down and enjoy it here; you won't find a better place. Here you can spend hours in the sunshine, swimming, shelling, strolling, or just plain loafing. If you're a photographer, the wildlife, the seascapes, and the observation tower offer opportunities you won't want to miss. *Open 8–sunset daily.* ☎ *492-1592. Admission $3.25 per vehicle.*

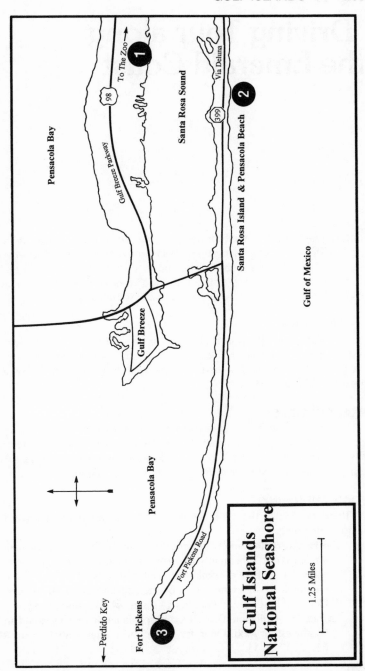

Gulf Islands
National Seashore

1.25 Miles

Trip 49

*Driving Tour along the Emerald Coast

The Emerald Coast, named for the sparkling green waters of the Gulf of Mexico, stretches eastward from Pensacola through the tiny seaside towns of Navarre, Fort Walton Beach, Destin, and then on to Panama City Beach where you'll find the pace of life closer to that of Florida's more famous resorts. All are neat little towns, each with a personality all its own.

GETTING THERE:

This is a trip you must make either in a car, van, or RV. No public transport system offers a convenient link along the coast. Take Highway 98 south across the Bay Bridge to Gulf Breeze and follow it east, hugging the shore, all the way to Panama City.

PRACTICALITIES:

Many of the attractions are open seven days a week, some open and close at odd times and on unlikely days of the week. This should not present any problems as there's plenty to see and do any day you choose to make the trip. Just check the listings in the text before making side trips.

FOOD AND DRINK:

There are lots of nice little seaside cafés and restaurants for you to sample, including:

The Hog's Breath Saloon (on Santa Rosa Island at Fort Walton Beach) is an Old-World fisherman's bar-turned-seafood-restaurant. The atmosphere is authentic—dark and cool with lots of nets and other memorabilia—and the oysters on the half-shell are fresh and juicy. Open for lunch and dinner from 11 a.m. ☎ 243-4646. $–$$.

La Paz (950 Gulfshore Drive, Destin) specializes in fresh seafood and Southwestern food. Open for lunch and dinner from 11 a.m. ☎ 837-2247. $–$$.

Sweet Basil's (11208 Front Beach Road, Panama City Beach) is an Italian restaurant and, as such, specializes in all things pasta. Open for lunch and dinner from 11 a.m. ☎ 234-2855. $–$$.

Aside from the many restaurants and cafés you'll find along the way, you'll also be visiting a number of attractions and seaside parks with picnic areas. Some are just too good to pass by. If you like to eat a picnic lunch, this is one trip that will provide plenty of opportunities to do so, and in style.

TOURIST INFORMATION:

Apalachicola Chamber of Commerce, 57 Market Street, Apalachicola, FL 32320. ☎ 653-9419.

Destin Chamber of Commerce, 1-21 US 98E, Destin, FL 32540. ☎ 837-6241.

Greater Fort Walton Beach Chamber of Commerce, 34 Miracle Strip Parkway, Fort Walton Beach, FL 32549. ☎ 244-8191.

Panama City Convention & Visitors Bureau, PO Box 9473, Panama City Beach, FL 233-6503. ☎ 800-722-3224.

SUGGESTED TOUR:

This is a long trip, scenic and enjoyable, and highly recommended. It may be that you won't be able to complete it in a single day. If not you have a couple of options: you can quit when you've seen enough and return to Pensacola, or you can find a room for the night and continue on the next day. The drive to and from Pensacola is too long to consider making the journey twice on consecutive days.

So, from Pensacola, take Highway 98 east across Pensacola Bay to Gulf Breeze and then drive east for 32 miles into **Fort Walton Beach** (1).

Fort Walton Beach, and Destin just a few miles to the east, represent the heart of the Emerald Coast. The area's beaches, more than 24 miles of them, are consistently rated among the best in the world. Surrounded by the Gulf of Mexico, Choctawhatchee Bay, Santa Rosa Sound, innumerable lakes and bayous, and scattered throughout with hundreds of docks and harbors set among the seaoats, sand pines, and blossoming magnolias, this stretch of the Panhandle coast comes as close to paradise as you can imagine. With an average of 343 sunny days per year, you're practically guaranteed the best of weather in which to enjoy it.

More than 100 area restaurants serve the "freshest seafood in Florida." These range from casual beach and bay-side seafood shacks to gracious ante-bellum estates and elegant cafés. The local operators claim there's always at least 20 types of fish available to eat during any single season.

Fort Walton Beach is a typical little seaside town with all the usual attractions: beaches, walks, aquarium, fairgrounds, gift shops, watersports, and restaurants. The walk along Fort Walton's Miracle Strip is a quiet stroll most of the time, passing lots of specialty shops and stores where you can always find that little gift with a difference. Drive on across the bridge to Santa Rosa Island and there are more gift shops, along with several cafés and restaurants (including the Hog's Breath Saloon) that rate among the best in Florida. From Santa Rosa, the road heads eastward along the coast past mile after mile of amusements and attractions to Destin and beyond.

Destin (2), known as the "World's Luckiest Fishing Village," is the deep-sea fishing capital of northern Florida. This area of the Gulf yields more billfish each year than any other, and the little town boasts of five saltwater world records. Down on the waterfront, dozens of experienced charter captains are available to take you offshore to try your hand in search of "the big one." But Destin is more than that. For more than nine miles the sand from the beaches that parallel Highway 98 and its sister road, Highway 2378, spill out onto the blacktop. These beaches, with their rolling dunes and waving seagrass, are consistently rated among the best in the nation. Most of the year they are quiet, with lots of room to play, picnic, and just laze the day away. Be sure to stop along the way—you can do so almost anywhere that takes your fancy—and enjoy a wade in the cool, clear waters of the Gulf.

Just east of Destin, on Highway 98, **Henderson Beach** (3) is one of those special spots the locals know well, but tourists don't often hear about. Here you can wander for hours along snow-white sands that stretch, so it seems, on forever. Stroll among the scrub oaks, southern magnolias, dune rosemary, and wade in the deep-green waters of the Gulf of Mexico. All of this provides a natural habitat for a variety of marine wildlife that includes friendly gulls, black skimmers, sanderlings, brown pelicans, and sea turtles. It's also a place where you'll find some of the finest surf fishing, safest swimming, and the best picnic areas. Access is provided by a system of wooden boardwalks that protect the dunes and the fragile plant life. *Open daily from 8–sunset.* &. *Admission $3.25 per vehicle.*

*Grayton Beach State Recreation Area (4) lies 18 miles east of Destin off Highway 98. Drive to the junction with Highway 283, turn right and head straight in.

Grayton Beach is one of the oldest cities on Florida's Gulf Coast, and its 356-acre recreation area offers plenty to see and do. The beaches are white and soft, and the sea is deep-green, clear and refreshing. It's a wonderful area, an absolutely must-visit stop. There are public restrooms, a boat ramp, several swimming areas, a nature trail, and a picnic area. *Open daily 8–sunset.* &. *Admission $3.25 per vehicle.*

From Grayton Beach, head eastward again on Highway 98 to **Panama City Beach** (5). It's a drive of about 25 miles, during which you'll pass through the little seaside communities of Hollywood Beach and Laguna Beach. Both are worth a visit.

Panama City Beach is the Panhandle's premier resort area. For more than 27 miles the beaches unroll in a breathtaking display of great natural beauty.

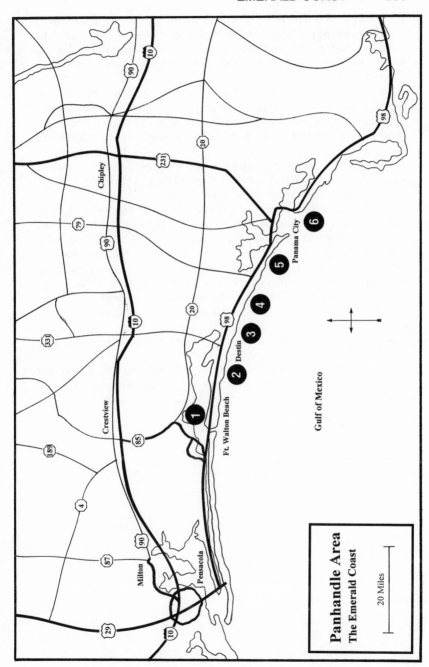

Panhandle Area
The Emerald Coast

20 Miles

This, along with a waterfront strip of more than ten miles of amusements, attractions, theme parks, zoo, amusement parks, museums, and night clubs make for a daytrip all its own. You are now some 90 miles out of Pensacola, and this, except for one more stop just a couple of miles or so down the road, is the end of the line.

Like so many other coastal resorts, Panama City claims to be the "Seafood Capital of the World." Is the claim a good one? You'll have to judge for yourself. What you will find is a diversity of fine and colorful restaurants serving everything from fresh amberjack to oysters, and from lobster to shark.

Take Highway 98 out of Panama City Beach and head east to its junction with Highway 3031. Turn right there and follow the signs to the St. Andrews State Recreation Area; it's just three miles from the city.

*St. Andrews State Recreation Area (6) is the final stop on this daytrip. With its beach rated *Number One in America* for 1995 by Dr. Stephen Leatherman, this park offers something very special, yet it remains virtually undiscovered by the vacationing public. For miles in either direction, the shoreline stretches away into the distance. With its white sand, dazzling under the hot Florida sun, deep emerald waters of the Gulf of Mexico, St. Andrews is one of those places you see only in suntan commercials: a place for families to come together, for children, for naturalists, and for lovers to walk barefoot on a warm summer evening along a deserted sandy shoreline beneath a big Florida moon. You just can't miss this one. *Open daily from 8 a.m.* &. *Admission $3.25 per vehicle.*

From St. Andrews, it's back to Pensacola, a drive of about 95 miles. It will take at least two hours, if you don't stop, so you can plan your departure accordingly. Just get back onto Highway 98 and return the way you came.

State Parks to the Northeast

There are more than 120 state parks, recreation areas, and historic sites in Florida. The northwest portion of the state is particularly well blessed with such preserves. Rarely will you find yourself far from one or another. Each is unique, an oasis offering all sorts of recreational opportunities from swimming to golf, or diving to tennis. Many are wildlife reserves, vast tracts of land set aside to preserve a portion of the local environment from future development. Some are of historical significance, places where events that shaped Florida's early development took place: battlefields, plantations, Indian grounds, archaeological sites, etc. The five listed here are significant for different reasons and, unfortunately, while each is well worth a visit, you won't have time to see them all in a single day. So read them through and pick out the ones that appeal most to you.

GETTING THERE:

All five state parks and recreation areas listed can be reached fairly easily by traveling east on I-10. Torreya State Park is a little out of the way, but not enough to make a visit prohibitive.

PRACTICALITIES:

The **Area Code** is 904.

Once you arrive, you'll do almost all of your sightseeing on foot. Be sure to wear comfortable shoes and clothing.

All five parks are open daily the year round, so you can go whenever you like. Saturdays and Sundays can be crowded at some places. On weekdays you may have the parks almost to yourself.

FOOD AND DRINK:

Of course, there are fast-food outlets at many of the Interstate exits along the way, so you'll never be very far from one of those. You're also sure to find one or two "mom 'n pop" restaurants and cafés in the small towns you'll pass through. As this is an outdoor daytrip, however, you might like to consider taking along a picnic. Your hotel will be pleased to provide a packed lunch, or you can do it yourself in style, with steaks, burgers, and other such goodies cooked on a grill provided in the state park of your choice. Check the text for availability.

TOURIST INFORMATION:

Department of Natural Resources Park Information, 300 Commonwealth Boulevard, FL 32399-3000. ☎ 488-9872.

SUGGESTED TOUR:

From Pensacola, take I-10 and head east for 15 miles to its junction with Highway 87. Turn north there and drive one mile to the intersection of Highway 90 and turn east again. Drive on for five miles to Harold, turn north and follow the signs; **Blackwater River State Park** (1) is about three miles from the town.

Blackwater River, still in a natural state for most of its length, is considered to be one of the finest and purest sand- bottom rivers in the world. It's a haven for nature lovers and water sports enthusiasts alike. The river itself offers some of the finest canoeing to be found anywhere, and the naturalist will delight in the diversity and abundance of the wildlife to be found. Still something of a backwater, Blackwater River State Park is quiet, rarely crowded, and offers a relaxing sojourn into the great outdoors seemingly far away from the hustle and bustle of the nearby seaport city. If you're an angler, the river offers plenty of good sport. Hikers will enjoy the nature trails along the riverbank, and the more active among you can take to the waters and swim. If you've brought a canoe, you can paddle upriver for miles. Public restrooms are available and there's a nice picnic area with tables and grills. *Open 8–sunset daily.* ☎ *623-2363.* ♿. *Admission $3.25 per vehicle.*

Ponce de León Springs State Recreation Area (2) is 70 miles east of Pensacola, just north of the Highway 81 exit of I-10. It is said that Ponce de León's legendary "Fountain of Youth" was probably one of Florida's beautiful natural springs. And of all of them, it is certainly true that the natural springs at Ponce de León State Park would qualify among the best. The main spring consists of two flows from a natural limestone cavity, one into the Choctawatchee River, and the other into the Gulf of Mexico. Between them, they produce more than 14 million gallons of the purest water each day. The temperature of the water remains constant at a refreshing 68°F, and provides a cooling refuge from the heat of the summer sunshine. Activities you can enjoy include swimming in the waters of the spring, hiking the nature trails, sunbathing, and picnicking. *Open 8–sunset daily.* ☎ *836-4281.* ♿. *Admission $3.25 per vehicle.*

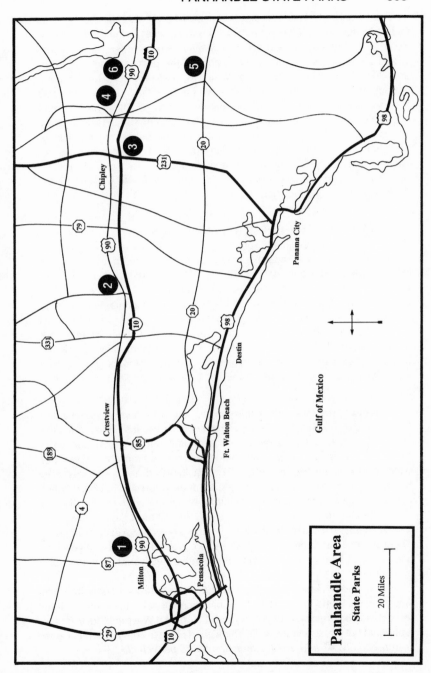

Panhandle Area
State Parks

20 Miles

From Ponce de León, continue east on I-10 for 23 miles to Chipley. **Falling Waters State Recreation Area** (3) is three miles to the south off State Route 77A. You might describe Falling Waters as being interesting, but that would be inadequate as the main feature of the park is something of an anomaly. The 67-foot waterfall from which the area takes its name is natural enough, but the Falling Waters Sink is something different. More than 100 foot deep and 20 foot wide, it's a great cylindrical pit into which a small stream flows and then simply disappears. It's quite a mystery. Aside from the spectacular scenery, you can spend time swimming, hiking, and picnicking. For photographers, Falling Waters offers opportunities not to be missed. Facilities include public restrooms, a swimming area at the Sink, several nature trails, and a picnic area. *Open 8–sunset daily.* ☎ *638- 6130.* ♿. *Admission $3.25 per vehicle.*

Florida Caverns State Park (3) is just north of Marianna, 15 miles east of Chipley. This state park offers something more than the usual recreational facilities. It includes a natural series of interconnecting caves containing hundreds of limestone formations such as stalactites, stalagmites, columns, rimstone, flowstones, and draperies. All are composed of calcite, which is dissolved from the limestone when the surface water containing carbolic acid percolates through the rock and into the cave. Guided tours of the caves are a fascinating experience. They are run daily by knowledgeable park service guides. Beyond the caves, the park offers opportunities for fishing, boating, hiking, and picnicking. There are public restrooms and a picnic area. *Open 8–sunset daily.* ☎ *482-9598.* ♿. *Admission $3.25 per vehicle.*

*Torreya State Park (4) lies thirty miles east of Marianna, via I-10 and Highway 270. This is the final refuge of the rare Torreya tree, from which the park gets its name. The extraordinary high bluffs along the Apalachicola River, and the deep ravines carved into the rocks by thousands of years of water erosion, make the area around Torreya State Park a very special place. Sometimes rising to more than 150 feet, the densely forested bluffs provide a natural refuge for many rare and beautiful species of wildlife. The Torreya tree, once plentiful throughout the area was, for the most part destroyed by disease. It is now found only on the high bluffs along the Apalachicola River. There are other rare trees and plants here too, including the Florida yew tree and the U.S. Champion winged elm, along with a great variety of wild shrubs and flowers.

Hikers and backpackers will enjoy the seven-mile-long Loop Trail, the Apalachicola Bluffs Trail, and the National Recreational Trail. If you're a little less actively inclined, you might try a stroll along the Weeping Ridge Trail— a pleasant but less strenuous walk. This a good place to enjoy a picnic. *Open 8–sunset daily.* ☎ *643-2674. Admission $3.25 per vehicle.*

From Torreya, continue east of I-10 to Sneads. **The Rivers State Recreation Area** (5) is on State Route 271 two miles north of the city. The tri-state location of Three Rivers, the hardwood and pine forests, the hilly terrain, Lake Seminole, the Flint, Apalachicola, and Chattahoochee Rivers, all contribute to a setting of unparalleled natural beauty for one of Florida's premier recreation areas. It is also home to a variety of wildlife, making it a mecca for nature lovers. White-tailed deer and gray foxes roam the woodlands, while squirrels and birds inhabit the treetops. It's a place to retreat from the rigors of daily life in the city, a place to dream and become one with the wonders of nature. The fishing, both on the lake and on the rivers, is excellent. Lake Seminole is one of the Bass capitals of the nation. Largemouth and smallmouth bass, catfish, bluegill, speckled perch, and bream are only a few of the species anglers can expect to find here. From water skiing to canoeing, from hiking to picnicking, there's something to do for just about everyone. There's a swimming area, several nature trails, a boat ramp, and a picnic area. *Open 8–sunset daily.* ☎ *482-9006.* ♿. *Admission $3.25 per vehicle.*

PHOTO CREDITS

Pages 9, 195, 264	Courtesy of the Amelia Island Tourist Development Council.
Pages 17, 24, 29, 41	Courtesy of the Greater Miami Convention and Visitors Bureau.
Page 69	Courtesy of the Greater Fort Lauderdale Convention and Visitors Bureau.
Pages 78, 97, 101	Courtesy of the Walt Disney Company.
Page 83	Courtesy of the Orlando/Orange County Convention and Visitors Bureau.
Page 105	Courtesy of Sea World of Florida.
Page 109	Courtesy of Universal Studios Florida.
Pages 136, 137	Courtesy of the Kissimmee-St. Cloud Convention and Visitors Bureau.
Pages 139, 168, 169	Courtesy of the Sarasota Convention and Visitors Bureau.
Page 143	Photo by John Jezak.
Page 149	Courtesy of Busch Gardens Tampa.
Page 157	Courtesy of the St. Petersburg/Clearwater Area Convention and Visitors Bureau.
Page 199	Courtesy of the Jacksonville Convention and Visitors Bureau.
Page 291	Courtesy of the Pensacola Convention and Visitors Bureau.

Index

Special interest attractions are also listed under their category headings.

Daytrips™

● OTHER AMERICAN TITLES ●

DAYTRIPS NEW ENGLAND

Discover the 50 most delightful excursions within a day's drive of Boston or Central New England, from Maine to Connecticut. Includes Boston walking tours. 336 pages, 60 maps, 48 photos.

DAYTRIPS WASHINGTON, DC

50 one-day adventures in the Nation's Capital, and to nearby Virginia, Maryland, Delaware, and Pennsylvania. Both walking and driving tours are featured. 352 pages, 60 maps, 48 photos.

DAYTRIPS NEW YORK

107 easy excursions by car throughout southern New York State, New Jersey, eastern Pennsylvania, Connecticut, and southern Massachusetts. 7th edition, 336 pages, 44 maps, 46 photos.

● IN PRODUCTION ●

DAYTRIPS PHILADELPHIA AND THE PENNSYLVANIA DUTCH COUNTRY

Thoroughly explores the City of Brotherly Love, then goes on to probe southeastern Pennsylvania, southern New Jersey, and Delaware before moving west to Lancaster, the "Dutch" country, and Gettysburg.

HASTINGS HOUSE
Book Publishers
50 Washington St., Norwalk CT 06854
Phone (203) 838-4083, FAX (203) 838-4084
Internet: http://upub.com

•EUROPEAN TITLES•

DAYTRIPS LONDON
Explores the metropolis on 10 one-day walking tours, then describes 40 daytrips to destinations throughout southern England—all by either rail or car. 5th edition, 336 pages, 57 maps, 94 photos.

DAYTRIPS FRANCE
Describes 45 daytrips—including 5 walking tours of Paris, 23 excursions from the city, 5 in Provence, and 12 along the Riviera. 4th edition, 336 pages, 55 maps, 89 photos.

DAYTRIPS GERMANY
55 of Germany's most enticing destinations can be savored on daytrips from Munich, Frankfurt, Hamburg, and Berlin. Walking tours of the big cities are included. 4th edition, 336 pages, 62 maps, 94 photos.

DAYTRIPS HOLLAND, BELGIUM AND LUXEMBOURG
Many unusual places are covered on these 40 daytrips, along with all the favorites plus the 3 major cities. 2nd edition, 288 pages, 45 maps, 69 photos.

DAYTRIPS ITALY
Features 40 one-day adventures in and around Rome, Florence, Milan, Venice, and Naples. 3rd edition, 304 pages, 45 maps, 69 photos.

DAYTRIPS ISRAEL
25 one-day adventures by bus or car to the Holy Land's most interesting sites. Includes Jerusalem walking tours. 2nd edition, 206 pages, 40 maps, 40 photos.

•IN PRODUCTION•

DAYTRIPS IRELAND
By Patricia Tunison Preston, author of several highly respected guidebooks to the Emerald Isle.

DAYTRIPS SPAIN AND PORTUGAL
By Norman P.T. Renouf. 50 One Day adventures in and from convenient bases including Madrid, Barcelona, Seville, Lisbon, and Oporto—with daytrips to many exciting destinations. Gibraltar and Morocco are also included.

ABOUT THE AUTHOR:

BLAIR HOWARD was bitten by the travel bug more than 30 years ago when, during a stint in the Royal Air Force, he spent a year in paradise on a tiny island in the middle of the Indian Ocean. From there, his travels have taken him to the Far East, North Africa, across most of Europe, to the islands of the West Indies, the Bahamas, Bermuda, and to almost every state in the Union. With camera in hand, or slung nonchalantly around his neck, he hopped from one location to another, finally settling down in a small rural town in Tennessee, or so he thought. But the travel bug had bitten deep, and he soon found that there's no cure for wanderlust. So, using Tennessee as his base, he set out once again, this time to write about the wonderful places he visits. Today, after several million miles in the air and on the road, and more than 260 articles and nine books, he's still at it, visiting and revisiting exotic locations around the world.